IGNITE THE Entrepreneur

Other internationally best-selling compilation
books by IGNITE for you to enjoy

————————

Ignite Your Life for Women

Ignite Your Female Leadership

Ignite Your Parenting

Ignite Your Life for Men

Ignite Your Life for Conscious Leaders

Ignite Your Adventurous Spirit

Ignite Your Health and Wellness

Ignite Female Change Makers

Ignite the Modern Goddess

Ignite Love

Ignite Happiness

Ignite Your Inner Spirit

IGNITE THE Entrepreneur

WHY ENTREPRENEURS LOVE WHAT THEY DO AND HOW THEY FOUND THEIR SUCCE$$

FOREWORD BY **Brandon Dawson**
CEO and Co-Founder of Cardone Ventures

INTRODUCTION BY **Didi Wong**
International Award-Winning Keynote Speaker, & TV Producer

PREFACE AND
FEATURE CHAPTER BY **JB Owen**
Founder of Ignite and JBO Global Inc.

PRESENTED BY

ALLISON LEWIS • ANA-MARIA TURDEAN • ANAY PATEL • ANNABEL WILSON
ASHLEY BAXTER • BEN BEARD • BRENDA NEUBAUER • BRYCE MCKINLEY
CHARLES HAI NGUYEN • CHRISTOPHER DE GREER, DC, MS • CLINTON E. DAY, MBA
COSTINEL PASAT • CYNTHIA CAUGHIE • ELLERY SEARS • JASON BAUCH • JB OWEN
JOSE LUIS CAMACHO • JONATHAN DOMSKY • JUDY (J.) WINSLOW • KAREN RUDOLF
KATHLEEN SINCLAIR • KULBIR MUTI • LAURIE H DAVIS • DR. MARTA DAVIDOVICH OCKULY
MEGHAN HUTHSTEINER • MIKE LEDOUX • MIKKO JARRAH • NADIA LA RUSSA
PARNELL JAMES QUINN • PAUL BATTAGLIA • RAVI MUTI • SALANA WHITEHEAD • STEVE NEALE
TANJA JADE POWELL • TARA LEHMAN • THERESA ALFARO DAYTNER • YAMILCA RODRIGUEZ

PUBLISHED BY IGNITE AND PRINTED BY JBO GLOBAL INC.

Ignite The Entrepreneur Copyright © 2021 JBO Global Inc.

Publisher's Note: We are delighted to offer the thirteenth compilation book in the IGNITE series. Our mission is to produce inspiring, motivational, and authentic real-life stories that will Ignite your life. Each book contains unique stories told by exceptional authors. They are of the highest caliber to offer engaging, profound, and life-changing examples that will impact the reader. Our mandate is to build a conscious, positive, and supportive community through our books, speaking events, writing workshops, Ignite experiences, podcasts, immersions, a TV show, and our product marketplace. We always welcome new book ideas and new authors onto our platform. Should you desire to be published and featured in an Ignite book, please apply at www.igniteyou.life/apply or reach out to us by email at support@igniteyou.life.

All rights reserved. No part of this publication may be reproduced, distributed, or transmitted in any form or by any means, including photocopying, recording, other other electronic or mechanical methods, without the prior written permission of the publisher, except in the case of brief quotations embodied in critical articles or reviews, and certain other noncommercial uses permitted by copyright law. For permission requests, write to the publisher, addressed "Attention: Permissions Coordinator" at the address below.

Limitation of Liability: Under no circumstances shall IGNITE, JBO Global Inc., or its affiliates, or authors be liable of any indirect, incidental, consequential, special, or exemplary damages arising out of or in connection with your use of any exercises or information contained in this book. Please be advised that if you choose to follow any of the suggestions offered by the authors, you do so of your own accord. It is up to you to seek professional advice before you implement any lifestyle changes. The views, thoughts, and opinions expressed in this text belong solely to the individual authors and not necessarily to the publisher, editorial team, nor the experts the authors may reference.

Published and printed by JBO Global Inc.
5569-47th Street Red Deer, AB
Canada, T4N1S1 1-877-677-6115

Cover design by JB Owen
Book design by Dania Zafar

Designed in Canada, Printed in China
ISBN 978-1-7923-4174-8
First edition: May 2021

Ordering Information: Quantity sales. Special discounts are available on quantity purchases by corporations, associations, and others. For details, contact the publisher at the above address. Programs, products, or services provided by the authors are found by contacting them directly. Resources named in the book are found in the resources pages at the back of the book.

Amazon™ is a registered trademark of Amazon.com, Inc.

Barbie™ is a registered trademark of Mattel, Inc.

BEGrowthDriven.com is a registered trademark of author Jose Luis Camacho

BMW™ is a trademark of Bayerische Motoren Werke Aktiengesellschaft.

Cadillac™, Corvette™, and Pontiac™ are registered trademarks of General Motors LLC.

Crock-Pot is a registered trademark of Sunbeam Products, Inc.

Dale Carnegie™ is a registered trademark of DALE CARNEGIE & ASSOCIATES, INC.

Facebook™ is a registered trademark of Facebook, Inc.

Ferrari™ is a registered trademark of Ferrari S.p.A.

Fluzzletube™ is a registered trademark of author Salana Whitehead

Ford Motor Company™, Ford F150™, and Mustang™ are registered trademarks of Ford Motor Corporation.

Forbes™is a registered trademark of Forbes Media LLC

Google™ search and YouTube™ are registered trademarks of Google, LLC.

Instagram™ is a registered trademark of Instagram, LLC.

Kmart™ is a registered trademark of Kmart Properties, Inc.

Lamborghini™ is a registered trademark of AUTOMOBILI LAMBORGHINI S.P.A.

LEGO™ is a registered trademark of LEGO

LEXUS™ is a trademark of TOYOTA JIDOSHA KABU-SHIKI KAISHA.

Lincoln Logs™ is a registered trademark of HASBRO, INC.

Mary Kay Cosmetics™ is a registered trademark of Mary Kay Inc.

McDonald's™ is a trademark of McDonald's.

MERCEDES-BENZ™ is a trademark of DAIMLER AG.

METALLICA™ is a registered trademark of Metallica

Mindvalley™ is a registered trademark of Mindvalley.

Netflix™ is a registered trademark of Netflix, Inc.

NFL is a registered trademark of the National Football League

Perspex® is a registered trademark of Perspex International Ltd.

Planet Sub™ is a registered trademark of Wikimedia Foundation, Inc.,

Procter & Gamble™ is a registered trademark of The Procter & Gamble Company

ROLLS-ROYCE™ is a trademark of Rolls-Royce Motor Cars Limited.

Scholastic Book Fair™ is a trademark of Scholastic Inc.

Street Fighter II™ is a registered trademark of CAPCOM U.S.A., INC.

Subway™ is a registered trademark of SUBWAY IP LLC

TED X™ is a registered trademark of Ted Conferences, LLC

Trans Ams™ is a registered trademark of Sports Car Club of American, Incorporated.

Tyco™ Corporation is a registered trademark of Tyco International.

U-Haul™ is a registered trademark of U-Haul International, Inc.

United States Postal Service® is a registered trademark of the United States Postal Service.

Visa™ is a registered trademark of Visa International Services Association.

Wells Fargo™ is a registered trademark of Wells Fargo & Company.

Wonder Woman® is a registered copyright of DC Comics

Zoom™ is a registered trademark of Zoom Video Communications, Inc.

Dedication

This book is for all the entrepreneurs all over the world who are believing in themselves and making their dreams become a reality. Entrepreneurs lead by working, guiding, coaching, providing, teaching, organizing, administering, directing, and supporting both themselves and those around them. Entrepreneurs dream big and go all out in pursuit of their dreams, regardless of the circumstances. As the world is changing, more than ever, entrepreneurs have to step up and stand out in their industries and markets so that the changes being made are for the good of all.

We dedicate this book to every entrepreneur who has held on to the mission that drives them, the hope that inspires them, and the genius within them that makes them amazing at what they do.

TESTIMONIALS FROM AUTHORS

"Ignite is the easiest and most professional platform to help you become an author that I have found. They really take great care of us from beginning to end and do everything to help us get the best version and author out of us."

— Mikko Jarrah

"The experience of writing with Ignite was more enjoyable and transformative than I had imagined. It became more than writing my story, it included developing myself and my viewpoint as well as developing my confidence, self-trust, and the opportunity to learn from all involved. From the team and editors to the other authors in the community, there is a palpable sense of family, positivity, and professionalism that continues to fuel my progress. Thanks to all for your contributions!"

— Judy (J.) Winslow

"I was thrilled for the opportunity to write my story for *Ignite the Entrepreneur* as it brought clarity and vision for what I want to do next. Because I had recently failed at a business, I was hesitant to start over. However, this book has motivated me and opened up many new ways I can be successful. Plus, I met new partners I can look to for advice and encouragement."

— Kathleen Sinclair

"Being part of *Ignite the Entrepreneur* has been an amazing experience. I really enjoyed practicing writing in Writer's Nest, checking the drafts with the editors, gaining business skills, and meeting amazing individuals during weekly meetings. The Ignite team has been very helpful and friendly. Writing my chapter was also a wonderful opportunity to relieve life events and share them with the readers. Definitely recommend participating in Ignite projects."

— Ana-Maria Turdean

"JB's energy is infectious and the Ignite book process is amazing. It is easy and seamless. The editors are great at pulling the story out of you. I enjoyed the journey and I feel that it has changed my mindset and motivated me to help others and get my story out there."

— Allison Lewis

"My experience of writing my story with the Ignite team has been nothing short of amazing. Allowing them to dive in and take them with me on my journey of writing it down—brought out things that I would have never imagined that I would share. I highly recommend the experience!"

— Brenda Neubauer

"The editing process was great! I completely rewrote my story three times and the editors were very patient with me. They offered guidance on structure and context, which really helped mold the final outcome I was happy with. Overall, this was an introspective lesson and allowed me to redefine the 'why' behind future endeavors."

— Christopher De Geer, DC, MS

"I thoroughly enjoyed the Ignite process and my time with the editors. I like that the editors asked high-quality questions, allowing me to find my own words. Thank you to JB and Peter for creating this opportunity for the Ignite authors!"

— Paul Battaglia

"I have learned so much since joining the Ignite community. First and foremost was the editing experience and what is involved, which will support me so much for writing future books. Ignite is a firm believer in the saying, 'Teamwork makes the dream work.' The support and education are also over the top. Thank you everyone for helping to make my dream as a writer come true."

— Laurie H Davis

"The experience of writing this book has been out of this world. I don't consider myself a writer, but the team wanted to make sure they keep my tone of voice, they added details I did not think of, and they added a sophisticated flavor to the words. I loved writing this chapter so much that I'm considering writing my own book. JB has a magical team as well as a magical and masterful knowledge. She has changed my life and I can't wait to have a bigger impact in the world."

— Yamilca Rodriguez

"The experience opened me up to what's possible when you take control of your own narrative."

— Ashley Baxter

"Writing with Ignite has been awesome so far. The editors were very positive and encouraging in their feedback. The deadline has helped me move forward on my goal instead of taking a long time to get it done."

— Ben Beard

"If you have put off writing your book — Ignite is the perfect platform to move you from unpublished to best-selling author! The added benefits are uncountable! Just trust and leap... you will be blessed beyond imagining!"

— Dr. Marta D. Ockuly

Contents

PREFACE
Message from the Publisher

It goes without saying that 2020 was the hardest year in the last decade for entrepreneurs and business owners. When we began this book in the fall of 2019, our goal was to complete it and hold the book launch in the spring of 2020. Little did we know that this would not happen. As the pandemic began to hit the world that winter and into the spring, life changed for many; including each and every entrepreneur in this book.

I remember attending our weekly Zoom™ meetings and facing worried faces and perplexed business owners not sure how to react. Shutdowns, restrictions, and shelter-in-place orders hit the business world hard and brick-and-mortar institutions were decimated with closures. Each week, as we plowed through our story writing process, someone would report a new crushing hit. We were aghast at what was happening; unsure, unclear, and flailing in the lockdowns and horrifying news reports.

Some of the authors had to leave the project. Businesses were drowning, funds were bleeding out, and family had to come first. Some authors tried to stay on track but, over time, lost the zest for their entrepreneurial ambitions as they were being pummeled into closure and wiped out of all they'd built. Many of the calls included tears of worry, stress, and strain. Some fell ill and we even had a few losses of lives among us. Many, if not all of us, had to shift where we had been to forge forward and create something new.

I want to give an admirable salute to all the authors who rose from the ashes like phoenixes to preserve and complete their stories. I also want to share my love and blessings to those who are here in spirit only and offer them my supportive grace for letting go. I want to honor those new authors who joined the project after we gathered our strength and gave it one more go. This book has taken 19 months to complete; not the four to five months of the other books we've done. It has been filled with ups and downs; highs and lows. Like the entrepreneurial journey itself, we have had to shift and pivot along the way. We had to reinvent the project and rally the authors over and over again.

It is likely not a coincidence that this happened while writing this book. In the center of all the outward chaos, the authors dove into their inward transformation. They became inventive and developed new strengths. Many had great ideas around their companies and were even inspired to start new divisions and offer aid where it was needed most. In fact, some really wonderful businesses were born during this time and some phenomenal business owners were birthed out of passion and necessity.

That is the beauty of becoming an entrepreneur. You have to be tough. Ingenious. You have to see how you can solve problems for those in need. You have to give more and go for it full-out. That is the essence of being an entrepreneur: rolling with the punches and being fast to react and execute well. The entire creation of this book was a lesson in Self and perseverance, and we all learned it, whether we wanted to or not.

Now, in the spring of 2021, we have finally reached the finish line. Most of us are back on track in our businesses and all of us are better people for it. Our book journey has paralleled our life journeys, which is the case in business also. We *are* our businesses. Entrepreneurs are the life force of the companies they create. They are what drives everything forward; and when they prevail, the world benefits.

With new and beautiful opportunities on the horizon, I look forward to all that will come of this time we've had together. I want to thank each of the authors and project leaders who have been here from day one and all of the authors who are here today. You all have brought a specialness to this project; even those whose stories didn't make it in the book. For those who will be at the book launch with us, I want to say "Bravo!" and "Hallelujah, we did it!" It wasn't easy, but it was worth it! My heart goes out to you and the whirlwind you've been through, yet my face smiles with joy for the achievements you have made. I saw you all conquer the mountain and make it here. I gloriously stand in awe of all that you have done.

With tremendous love and blessings…
XOXOX,

JB Owen

P.S. I am truly honored for all the people who took part in this book, not just the authors themselves but also my team who took pay cuts to make it through the hard times and then rallied through the anguish that showed up in the editing sessions while people processed all that was happening to their lives and businesses. Graphics had to be more positive, IT had to create more connections, videos needed to be compelling as HR and Happiness kept us going in our hearts. It is no doubt that through the unknowns, the odd hours, and the 'figuring it out,' we became like family. We bonded and built something unprecedented and magical. I have to put it in writing how blessed I am to have every one of these indualtals on my team and in my life. They are the never-ending spark that Ignites a flame in me to do more, be more, and become the unrelenting entrepreneur I know I was born to be.

You know who you are, and I love you with all my heart!

IGNITE TEAM

JB OWEN
Founder and CEO

PETER GIESIN
CTO

CATHERINE MALLI-DAWSON
HR and Operations Manager

CAROLINA GOLD
Administrative Coordinator

KATIE SMETHERMAN
Brand Manager and Web Design

ANDREA DRAJEWICZ
Head of Editing

ALEX BLAKE
Senior Editor

CHLOE HOLEWINSKI
Editor and Project Manager

MICHIKO COUCHMAN
Editor

MEG HUTHSTEINER
Happiness Strategist

TREVOR GOLD
IT & Tech Specialist

DANIA ZAFAR
Manager of Ignite Press

LIANA KHABIBULLINA
Graphic Designer

WHAT IS AN IGNITE BOOK?

BY JB OWEN

Inside the pages of this book, you will find a part of you. Your story, your thoughts, your worries, wishes, ideas, and dreams will be reflected in a story shared here by one of our authors. We know this because Ignite stories represent the human emotions in all of us. They are Universal and common. They reflect what all of us feel and touch upon the very essence that makes us human; in our human experience.

The very word *ignite* signifies the goal of our books and describes the intention behind the stories that are shared inside. We see our books as gifts to the world. Every one we publish is done so with the idea of inspiring, uplifting, and igniting the reader in the process. We believe we are a bridge for all human connection, and that each story is a beacon for what is possible for every person on our earth.

As you begin reading the upcoming pages, you will find that every story starts with a *Power Quote*. It is a self-affirming, self-empowering, self-inspiring statement designed to awaken you. It is designed to uplift you, push you forward, and encourage you to break outside your comfort zone. Power quotes are phrases that you can use when you need encouragement or a dose of hope. They are meaningful statements intended to provoke thought, Ignite ideas, spark action, and evoke change. Every power quote written in Ignite is that which is already within you so that you can be all that you desire to be.

Below the power quote, you will find each author's personal *Intention*. These are the personal insights and genuine wishes the author wants to share with you. They are the reasons they have written their story, filled with both purpose and meaning. Each author has the desire to IGNITE something special in you and they share that eloquently in their intention. They want you to know right from the beginning what they feel their story will do for you.

After the intention you dive right into the Ignite *Story*. It is a genuine account of how the author went through their life to emerge a greater expression of themself. Through their unique experiences and circumstances, the authors explain how their Ignite moments transformed them, awakened them, and set them on a new trajectory in life. They reveal their honest feelings and share their personal discoveries. They give you an insightful account into the moment that resulted in magnificent change and elevated their consciousness.

We all have *Ignite* moments that change us, define us, and set us forth on a wonderful new journey of inner exploration. These stories are derived from those very moments and told in the most endearing and heartfelt way. They show that *life-altering* situations are designed to impact us in a way that ultimately inspires us to love ourselves more and appreciate those around us more completely.

Once you have completed the story, you will find a list of *Ignite Action Steps*. Each author shares a powerful, doable action that you can take to move toward greater fulfillment and adopt new habits that will benefit you. Each action step is an effective idea, unique process, and powerful practice that has been successful in their lives. The hope is for you to implement them in your life and then use them daily to manifest positive change. Each Ignite Action Step is different and unique, just like you are, and each has proven to have amazing results when done diligently and consistently.

As you sit down to read this book, know that it is not required to read it in the traditional way, by starting at the beginning and reading through to the end. Many readers flip to a page at random and read from there, trusting that the page they landed on holds the exact story they need to read. Others glance over the table of contents, searching for the title that resonates with them. Some readers will go directly to a story recommended by a friend. However you decide to read this book, we trust it will be right for you. We know that you may read it from cover to cover in one single sitting or pick it up and put it down a dozen times over a long period of time. The way you read an Ignite book is as personal as every story in it, and we give you complete permission to devour it in whatever way fits you.

What we do ask is, if a story touches you or in some way inspires you, that you reach out and tell the author. Your words would mean the world to them. Since our book is all about Igniting humanity, we want to foster more of that among all of us. Feel free to share your sentiments with the authors by using their contact information at the end of each chapter. There isn't an Ignite author who wouldn't love to hear from you and know how their story impacted your life.

We know that the phrase 'Ignite moments' will now become a part of your vocabulary. You'll begin to think about your own impactful moments and the times in your life that Ignited you in a new way. If sharing your story feels important or writing your Ignite moment is percolating to the surface, please reach out to us. We believe every person has a story and everyone deserves to be seen, heard, and acknowledged for that story. If your words are longing to come forth, we want to support you in making it happen. Our desire is to Ignite a billion lives through a billion words, and we can only do that by sharing the stories from people like you!

As you turn the page, we want to welcome you to the Ignite family. We are excited for what is about to happen; because we know the stories in this book are about to Ignite you. As you dive into the upcoming pages, a million different emotions will fill your heart and a kindred spirit will be established. We know that this will be a book that both awakens and blesses you. May you be honored, loved, and supported from this page forward and all your Ignite moments be one of exceptional change.

IGNITE THE ENTREPRENEUR

BRANDON DAWSON

FOREWORD BY BRANDON DAWSON

Early in my career, I learned the importance of mentorship — drafting behind someone who is ahead of you and has accomplished the goals you are trying to accomplish. I recognized the significance of gaining experience from entrepreneurs who have "made it" and of utilizing their skills to better my own. That is why it is both a pleasure and an honor, even if just for a moment, to be able to be a mentor to you. Mentorship is a key component of success and that is why I am happy that you have chosen this book to provide mentoring inspiration in your journey. I hope that within these pages you will find stories, words, and ideas to propel you forward in *your* unique entrepreneurial adventure.

Finding the courage to become an entrepreneur is no small endeavor. Many people take the leap, but only a few of them make it. Statistics show about 20 percent of businesses will fail within their first year, and about 50 percent of small businesses fail by their fifth year. Many try and even more fail to take that leap and to persevere until you reach the dream. Success in your business comes down to how successful you are in working on yourself. Your leadership skills and willingness to grow within *you* will determine how well you grow your business, the team you assemble, and the customers you serve. It is a dedication and willingness that requires every fiber of you—when you can master that, you will become the master of your success.

I'll admit, I didn't always have this self-improving mindset. I wasn't what people would label a born success, nor did I have on paper what others deemed as the skills to achieve it. I graduated high school with a 2.4 GPA and struggled throughout school. I grew up in a small Oregon town with a lot of farmland nearby, but not a lot of business mentors.

As a teenager, I lived with my dad, my stepmom, and her three boys. Although my parents weren't rich, they wanted us to have a good education. Every year, they found a way to save $5,500 so that the three of us kids could attend a private Christian school. Finding creative ways to source and to save these funds became a devoted family activity. One of the main ways we did this was by harvesting and selling walnuts from our orchard. It was an arduous task and very time-consuming. I didn't always enjoy it, but I knew it had to be done to help make ends meet. By the time I was a junior in high school, I was helping to bear the burden of my tuition by working in the walnut orchard during the day as well as working evenings in a restaurant as a busboy.

Despite my busy workload, I found time to have fun and be a 17-year-old boy, staying out late with my girlfriend and pushing the boundaries of my freedom. That particular summer, I stayed out past my curfew three nights in a row and found myself in the doghouse with my parents. My punishment just so coincidentally happened at the same time that my parents were leaving for a short out-of-town trip. Even though I was in trouble, I was somewhat comforted knowing that I wouldn't lose my car as a penalty (because I still needed to drive to my job). Despite orders to abide by their restriction, I figured that if I left early for work, I could sneak some moments with my girlfriend on the way to the restaurant.

I found out the hard way that my parents weren't foolish. They knew that I had a car, a pretty girl that I was into, and a typical 17-year-old mischievous attitude. They gave me a daunting punishment that would be sure to eat up every free minute I had that wasn't already dedicated to school or work. My punishment was picking the sprawling walnut orchard all by myself!

To be clear, harvesting that orchard took our *whole* family an *entire* week to complete. How the hell was I supposed to do that all on my own, while still going to school during the day and bussing tables at the restaurant at night? I was pissed off, even if I had to admire their ingenuity in choosing this penalty. Picking walnuts is a downright depressing task for a teenage boy. The weather during walnut harvesting time was typically rainy and cold, and the walnuts stain your hands yellow for a solid month. I was not looking forward to it in the least!

My parents left town on a Thursday. I went to school that Friday, feeling pretty sorry for myself. I knew my entire week was going to be shot, trying to accomplish an unachievable task. Not to mention, I wasn't going to have any time to see my girlfriend. I was fuming with frustration and life was feeling pretty unfair... until I noticed a note on one of the school lockers about a fundraiser the seniors were doing. The graduating class had a goal of raising $1,000 for their senior trip.

I'm not sure what caused it or that I would have known what to call it back then, but something ignited within me when I read that note. I saw an opportunity unfold before me, an opportunity that would not only solve my problems but would also help those around me. I realized that what I needed and what others needed could be combined to create a benefit for all of us. Looking back now, I recognize this was the ignition point—that pivotal moment that awakened my entrepreneurial spirit!

I figured out that if I could get the senior class to 'help me' harvest the orchard and sell the walnuts for a share of the profits, I would be able to raise the $1,000 they needed. More importantly, I would also gain some free time during the week to spend with my girlfriend while my parents were away. With the concept in place, I set out to execute it. The president of the senior class was an easy pitch, and plans were crafted for a Saturday morning harvest.

Saturday morning arrived. I was setting up wheelbarrows and prepping for the seniors' arrival when I began stressing, wondering if anyone was actually going to show. What if no one came? What if my idea failed? What if I still had to pick and clean all of those walnuts by myself before my parents came home? I started to worry and doubt my newly-formed entrepreneurial spirit.

Then a car arrived, and I thought, "Thank God!" And then another car, and another, and another. A couple of vans showed up, and then a couple of pickup trucks. Before I knew it, the entire senior class (which was about 35 people) had shown up. But they didn't show up alone, they brought their brothers, their sisters, and their parents. There must have been 100 people there ready to harvest walnuts!!

Those people picked, shucked, dried, and bagged every walnut in the field. They raked under the trees, cleaned the tools, and tidied up after themselves. The bare and harvested orchard looked the best it ever had. Better yet, I didn't touch a single walnut and my hands stayed clean. I instantly had the realization that maximizing others' abilities is what maximizes outcome. I saw that if I did what it took and made sure people showed up, *then* showed them what they had to do and gave them the tools to do it, success was guaranteed. It was there in my family's walnut orchard that I learned the power of having a team to maximize my impact.

At the end of the three days, people were asking to buy the walnuts. My parents needed $5,500 for tuition, and I needed to contribute $1,000 to the senior trip. I made up a price I thought would earn enough money to cover both. With my 2.4 GPA and poor math skills, I picked a price that resulted in $8,500. It was a fabulous outcome for everyone and I was thrilled! The orchard was harvested, the senior trip was funded, my reputation was boosted at school, and I still had a few days to spend with my girlfriend before my parents got home. Best of all was that I was absolutely certain they'd be delighted with the extra money I had earned. I imagined the positive things they'd say:

"You earned more money than we ever have with the orchard!"

"Your idea means no one in this family is ever going to have to pick walnuts again!"

"The orchard looks better than it ever has!"

Well, it turned out they weren't delighted at all. They were very unhappy because I didn't do what they told me to do. They wanted to teach me a lesson by having me spend the week laboring at a depressing task and ruminating about what I had done wrong. They wanted me to see the error in my behavior and change how I was acting. I will admit, I did learn plenty from that experience, but not the lesson my parents thought I needed to learn. Instead, it wasn't hard labor and punishment that incited a change, it was from ingenuity and creativity that I felt inspired.

After making up the walnut price, I learned that price is only an issue in the absence of value. The actual thing we did that Saturday was create value for peoples' lives. Those parents and family members wanted to show their seniors that they loved them. Buying the walnuts was a value-creating, tangible manifestation of their affection. I also learned that price is elastic; if you create enough value, you can fix whatever price you want.

I also came to understand the power of people and the power of messaging. The more people you throw at a problem, the bigger, better, and faster your solution will be. When attracting people to your side, emphasize the *why* and the *impact* of joining your endeavor.

I often meditate on that Saturday walnut harvest. I reflect on the powerful force of the mind — its ability to subconsciously influence that Ignite moment in front of the school lockers. When I got to school that morning, I was so focused on not wanting to harvest that orchard; I just didn't know how I was going to circumvent the task. By focusing on the outcome I wanted (spending the weekend doing anything *but* picking and shucking walnuts), my mind designed and manifested a solution.

My walnut orchard lessons have helped me to harvest many other "walnut orchards," solving problems and positively impacting those around me. As you reflect on the Ignite stories in these pages, reflect on orchards from your own life. Identify lessons from the experiences of others and from your own experiences. Be confident in your ability to shape the outcomes, the solutions, and the successes you *will* attain. Have confidence in your ideas and go after what you want; not just for you but for others. When we find ways to include others in our endeavors and provide ways that enrich their goals, then we've created not just a business but an environment of true success. That is the joy in being an entrepreneur.

Brandon Dawson is a scaling and turn-around expert, serial entrepreneur, and real estate investor who has a passion for helping business owners and their teams amplify their vision and impact through belief, strategy, execution, and team alignment. At only 29 years old, Dawson became one of the youngest people to ring the opening bell, listing his company, Sonus, on the American Stock Exchange. After Sonus, he self-funded Audigy Group with $500K, taking on zero debt, no outside capital, and growing annual revenues to over $35M through organic growth. Dawson exited the company at 77X EBITDA for $151M. As CEO of Cardone Ventures, Dawson's mission is to help business owners and entrepreneurs maximize their value and quality of life through the attainment of personal, professional, and financial goals.

IGNITE THE ENTREPRENEUR

DIDI WONG

INTRODUCTION BY DIDI WONG

I absolutely love the world of entrepreneurship. Why? Because of the people who are in it. Ever since I was a little girl, I have always loved connecting with people. People are what makes the world go around. I embrace every opportunity I get to meet new people, make a new friend, and network. When I was nine years old, I was sent away to an all-girls Royal boarding school. I exchanged the bustling energy and heat of Hong Kong with its lush mountain views bordering the South China Sea for the cool and rainy region of Kent in southeastern England. The school was housed in an elegant Victorian manor overlooking rolling green lawns, but what struck me most about it was how different everything around me was. There were no mountain peaks planted solidly in the background, the shopkeepers' voices rose and fell in an unfamiliar lilting accent, and all around me were people who didn't look like me. Looking back now, I could say that my childhood was all about meeting people who don't look like me; therefore, I had to be comfortable being in situations where I was not the majority and not the most at ease. As I grew up into adulthood, I loved meeting more and more people who were from all over the world. I wanted to understand their culture, where they came from, their ethics, and their family dynamics. Each time I meet a new person, I want to know the essence of who they are in their circle and their world.

Reflecting on this, I realize that I am armed with a very strong asset to conquer the world as a serial entrepreneur, a business and speaking mentor, an international keynote speaker, an angel investor and real estate investor, a venture capitalist, a TV and movie producer, as well as a mother of four. That very strong asset is my fearlessness in connecting with people from all walks of life, from different countries, different religions, different beliefs, and even in different languages. I see the world as one place for all of us.

In the world of entrepreneurship, the entrepreneurs are the ones who give it pizzazz, give it life, and give it the fun and challenges we need to propel ourselves forward. My fearlessness in meeting anyone anywhere around the globe is because I possess the most important characteristics an entrepreneur needs to have: self-confidence and self-worth.

Nobody can tell me I cannot do something. I learn the rules to break the rules. My brain operates consistently on how to do something better and more efficiently with the most accuracy. My mind likes to think about how a business scales and how to create something unique that no one has seen or felt before.

I am so blessed to get all of my 'go get it' and 'get stuff done' attitude from my parents, who are both very strong entrepreneurs themselves. My mother is a hustler in her own right; she finds a way to monetize every which way she can when she doesn't need to. My father is one of the top criminal defense lawyers to the tycoons, multimillionaires, and billionaires of Hong Kong. He also has been successful in the music industry where he wrote songs for the popstars. Talk about a great, royalty-making side hustle! My parents have never let me down. And I sincerely mean it when I use the word 'never.' With that kind of upbringing, I have developed true integrity and strive to be a woman of my word to everyone I meet. Trust is what you need in business because business is all about relationships. If I make it a habit to have integrity, I will build trust, and I will attract clients, customers, business partners, and a tribe of good people around me.

And that is really what it's all about; enjoying the people around you who make you happy and share the same values as you.

As I write about good people and attracting your 'tribe,' JB Owen, the Founder and CEO of Ignite and the publisher of this book, is one of them. She is, indeed, one of the good people I attracted. She is a good friend who is strong, ambitious, and powerful. You know how the amazing motivational speaker Jim Rohn says, "You are the average of the five people you spend the most time with"? Well, JB is one of those five YOU want to surround yourself with.

I met her through an interview I was asked to conduct to have her join the main cast of a TV show I was producing. Within minutes of the meeting, I already knew she would be the perfect fit for the show. It is not often that a phenomenal woman like JB comes your way. She shoots for the stars. And in her own journey, I love that she also loves to inspire, share, and give back. One of the ways in which she does so is by giving some of the great entrepreneurs whom she surrounds herself with the opportunity to become an author.

Each one of these entrepreneurs are experts in their own field; they are of that caliber with a strong sense of determination and resilience. They embody the spirit of entrepreneurship in the true sense of the word. Their stories are inspirational and life-changing. If you find yourself reading this book, you have embarked on a great journey through a doorway to the wonders of being a successful business owner, of being your own boss. Some of them will talk about mindset. Some will dive deep into how their stories have impacted them and how they are now bringing those stories out into the world to help others by becoming speakers. Some of them learned from their failures but picked themselves up again to be at the top of their game.

Failure is a big part of being successful. It is something that every successful entrepreneur experiences. As for my own failures, I was able to turn them into my Ignite moments. The moments where I turned inward and told myself I can and I will. Those inner voices I always talk about when I speak, called 'The Devil Voice vs. The Angel Voice.' And 95 percent of the time, I let the Angel Voice win.

It is so easy to let the Devil Voice talk you into believing the negative — that you are incapable and not good enough. This happened to me at the end of 2018 when I lost over $250,000 in just three days when an event I produced did not receive the return in investment that I had projected. It was definitely the biggest financial failure I have had in all my years in business. At that time, I could have whined and pitied myself; given up and let myself curl into a dark hole. I could have started complaining about my team and pointing fingers and blaming others. But I didn't. Instead, I took the whole of 2019 to pick myself back up and turned it into the most profitable year yet in my entrepreneurial journey. Perhaps that was the ignition that I needed!

The true entrepreneurs who have the 'never-give-up' attitude; the solopreneurs who believe in themselves so much that they are ready to tackle all that is required of them to run their businesses; the mompreneurs who — despite having one of the hardest jobs in the world, to raise children — still go out there to put their mark in their communities; the serial entrepreneurs who can't get enough of just one business but have to have several to ease their hunger… these are all remarkable people. They are the people that I said I loved at the beginning of this Introduction.

Entrepreneurs are the job providers. They are the leaders and the game changers. Just look at Jeff Bezos, Mark Zuckerberg, or Sara Blakely. They are all entrepreneurs, just like the authors in this book. They started somewhere and just climbed all the way up to the top. The personality traits of a successful entrepreneur include intuition, perseverance, mental strength and stamina, resourcefulness, open-mindedness, tenacity, passion, creativity, discipline, generosity, competency, and so many more. How many of these traits do you have? The only way one can become exceptionally wealthy is to become an entrepreneur. And I am proud to be one.

HOW TO IGNITE AN ENTREPRENEUR

There are a lot of books on the market about becoming an entrepreneur, but not a single one of them is as diverse as this one. *Ignite the Entrepreneur* brings together unique and inspiring stories from entrepreneurs in all kinds of industries and from all over the world, along with providing the fundamental tools each entrepreneur needs to grow themselves and build their brand. Inside this book, you get the best of both worlds: the honest sharings of individuals along their entrepreneurial journey and the key pieces of knowledge you need to ascertain and heighten your own success.

Being an entrepreneur is a journey with many complex layers to it. One must undergo their *own* incredible self-discovery to even be willing to take the first step. They must push past not just outward obstacles but overcome an array of inward self-limitations. Entrepreneurs are the makers of their own fate; constantly redefining who they were and who they want to become. It is both a physical and mental voyage into what is possible in the mind — in themselves and among the rest of the world. This constant dual effort in growing Self leads to the joyous experience of growing a successful business. That is what makes entrepreneurs a breed all their own, and why they function in both infinite and idealistic ways. Entrepreneurs see life differently; they evaluate and go after what others deem impossibile. An entrepreneur is often born out of necessity, forged from a burning desire. They are birthed from a cosmic convergence of ideas, wishes, and dreams. There is little that is common to every entrepreneur, but one thing is consistent: they persevere.

You are about to embark on a journey into the lives of those entrepreneurs who have made the leap into this amazing way of life. Each daring individual in this book has braved the ups and downs of being an entrepreneur and has experienced many trials and tribulations while getting there. They have courageously chosen to tell their story, the steps they took, and the hurdles they overcame in the hopes that their journeys will inspire your own. They have also shared the many golden nuggets of learning and wisdom they've gained, and the powerful insights that have given them the ability to carry on and follow through. Every story has something magical in it that you can benefit from in your own entrepreneurial quest.

A lot of business experts speak about 'drafting' behind someone who is just a little bit ahead of you, including the illustrious writer of our foreword, Brandon Dawson. The notion is that you can gain great momentum and get there faster when you follow someone who is already there; someone who has achieved what it is that you are going after. That idea is part of the reason this book was formed. The authors inside these pages have walked over burning coals and transversed choppy waters in their own lives, and now they want to help you do the same. You will find more than just the hardships and trials here; these authors share with you the serendipitous successes, the chance encounters, and the nerves of steel needed to risk it all as they give you their personal accounts of how they pushed through limitations both external and internal to overcome what someone else said was not possible, so they could reach their goals.

It is common knowledge that entrepreneurship can be filled with unknowns. There can be a multitude of worries and unexpected stresses. But as you will read, you will see how entrepreneurship is also filled with the most beautiful moments, a deep personal pride, and the makings of helping thousands of others be better, safer, and happier in themselves.

The world loves entrepreneurs for their initiatives, inventions, creations, and plans. We admire them for their fortitude, determination, and beliefs. The true entrepreneur is a manifestation of their own making, and although the road to get where they are going looks different, the passion they carry with them is always the same. We seek both the thrill and the success. We long for the freedom intertwined with the knowing that we are impacting others. It is an adventure we choose and when we arrive, we feel we have fulfilled our purpose.

The purpose you have as an entrepreneur is coursing through your veins. That is why you have begun reading the book. I invite you to devour each and every story inside these pages because each and every one is filled with powerful wisdom and helpful tools. They all have great insight and profound learnings that will encourage you to step into your own success. They are designed to get you thinking, motivate you to take action and push you past any obstacles that may be in your way. They all have steps you can take to support you and ideas you can implement immediately to make a massive change in your life. This isn't a book to casually consume; it is a guidebook and inspirational utopia that will inspire you along *your* way. Study it, absorb it, adopt the practices, and *do* the suggestions. Take from it all that it has to offer, and catapult yourself into the greatest (entrepreneurial) version of you.

Being an Entrepreneur means working on you

The biggest part of being a successful entrepreneur is being successful at working on yourself. Your growth and your greatest accomplishments are 100 percent contingent on you overcoming your biggest weaknesses. That means the work you do on yourself is paramount. How you adopt new ideas, factor in winning practices, and learn new skills will fundamentally reflect the level of long-term success you will achieve. The great news is, as promised, this book is going to support you in doing just that and uncover what key differentiators you need to accomplish all that you envision.

As you continue reading, you will come upon a few exercises designed to inspire you and remind you of the core reasons you started your business (or are wanting to start a business). Your *mission, purpose, vision*, and *values* are all key components in your ultimate success. Many entrepreneurs skip this introspection, feeling like they know it already or it isn't necessary to complete; I assure you that just isn't true. These vital components are the framework and the foundation for the business you wish to have. Be it a small home-based micro-niche or a multinational mega brand, knowing each one of these pieces of your dream business is a mandatory part of your long-term success.

Understanding what you stand for, why you do it, and what you aim to achieve will be the difference between hitting your targets or easily getting derailed. It will also be the beacon that guides your customers to trust and value what you deliver. The key components of *mission*, *purpose, vision,* and *values* will not only inspire you, but inspire those around you, those who work for you, and those wanting to work *with* you.

Take a bit of time right now to walk through your *mission, purpose, vision*, and *values*. You may have done this discovery in the past, but I assure you, these elements need to be reviewed and updated as you grow your business, face new challenges, and evolve. If you have never done this exploration, then get excited because this is an opportunity to dive deep into your reasons and get committed to your cause. Your business needs to be an internal passion for you to keep plowing ahead time and time again. That passion is Ignited when you write down and formulate the exact reasons, internal desires, and glorious impact you choose to gift upon the world.

Our authors took the time to write their stories in these pages and now it is *your* turn to add to this book by writing a little yourself. Grab a pen and have some fun defining or redefining the reason *why* you want to run your company and *who* you choose to impact. Use the next few pages to get crystal clear on what in your business matters most to you. Uncover your big audacious vision and define your masterful, heartfelt intrinsic goals; all while blazing a trail with what you stand for and every stake you are willing to plant in the sand to get there. Your business has to be yours, all you, and richly intertwined with what matters most to you. Every entrepreneur knows that the road they have chosen is not paved with ease and comfort but is instead laced with shards of personal delight and layers of extreme joy. It is an unknown path with pits and potholes, so having those gigantic ideas and magnanimous aspirations clearly in your sightline will be precisely what you need to make sure you triumphantly and successfully get there.

WHAT'S YOUR MISSION?

Think big. Think bold. In defining your mission, you get to throw back your arms and be like a little kid lying on the grass, looking up into a star-filled sky. You get to imagine the Universe is all yours to enjoy. This means you get to think as massively as possible and dream as outstandingly as you can. When it comes to your mission, there are no limits. Just as a child dreams of going to the moon or catching a shooting star, you too get to envision anything and everything in your entrepreneurial dream.

A **mission** is that megawatt idea you have to do something galactic, unprecedented, and profound! It is the statement you make and the decision you define that has all others shaking their head in disbelief. It gets to be as out-of-this-world as you can dream up, as unbelievable as you can muster, and as fantastical as you can foresee. There is no limit as to what your mission will entail. But you need to declare it. You need to state what big and wonderful hope you have for yourself and the world around you.

Your mission will often be about more than just you. It is usually centered around your wishes for humanity, the planet, the ecosystem, or even pure existence. It is the grand utopia of a better life for all others *and* you. Mission statements often speak of the collective, the human race, society, and the world. It aims for a better future on a grander scale. It is that one precious and powerful thing you wish for that benefits us all.

It's time to establish your mission statement. It starts with you taking the time to write out exactly what you wish to achieve in the biggest way possible. Mission statements often begin with, " I see a world where..." or " My mission is to create a world that... " They have impact and, at the same time, they have the elements that we as humans all long for: better, more connected, inclusive, and united.

Here are some examples of powerful mission statements from some of the top companies in the world.

- The **mission statement** of **The Walt Disney Company** is to entertain, inform and inspire people around the globe through the power of unparalleled storytelling, reflecting the iconic brands, creative minds and innovative technologies that make ours the world's premier entertainment company.

- The **mission statement** of **TIME Magazine** is to tell the stories that matter most, to spark conversations that drive global change, and to provide context and understanding to the issues and events that define our **times**.

- The **mission statement** of **Amazon** is to continually raise the bar of the customer experience by using the internet and technology to help consumers find, discover and buy anything, and empower businesses and content creators to maximise their success.

- The **mission statement** of **Life is Good** is to spread the power of optimism.

- The **mission statement** of **Sweetgreen** is to inspire healthier communities by connecting people to read food.

- The **mission statement** of **Patagonia** is to build the best product, cause no unnecessary harm, use business to inspire, and implement solutions for the environment.

- The **mission statement** of **JetBlue Airlines**: To inspire humanity – both in the air and on the ground.

- The **mission statement** of **Netflix** is to entertain the world.

A good mission statement has a clear, concise declaration about your business' intentions. The **mission statement** defines what industry you are in, why your business exists, and what purpose it desires to achieve. Your mission statement must be relatable and inspiring for all people at all levels. Don't underestimate the value of a mission statement. Every entrepreneur should write a mission statement early on in their endeavors because your mission provides you (and your employees) with the framework and deep reasons to proceed.

Use this space below to begin formulating your own powerful mission statement. Know that it will take a few drafts and a lot of introspection. This is not a quick exercise and may need countless revisions and adaptations. The great news is that once you nail your mission statement, you will feel it in your core. You will want to speak it often and will dare to plaster it on your office wall. It will be so true and so innately within you that you will feel moved every time you read it. If you don't feel that visceral connection, keep working it until you do!

My overall MISSION is:

_____

_____

_____

_____

_____

_____

Mission Statement Draft #1

_____

_____

_____

Mission Statement Draft #2

_____

_____

_____

Mission Statement Draft #3

_____

_____

_____

Mission Statement Draft #4

_____

_____

_____

Mission Statement Final/Favorite

_____

_____

_____

_____

_____

_____

_____

_____

_____

WHAT IS YOUR VISION STATEMENT?

Mission and vision go hand in hand when it comes to knowing the direction for your company. Often these two very different statements are misunderstood and confused with each other. People use them interchangeably and blend them into one. A proper vision statement describes where the company aspires to be upon achieving its mission. It shows the '*where we want to get to*' goal for a business. The vision statement is specific. It defines the company's objective and exact position it wishes to have in the marketplace. Impactful vision statements cast a vision or promise of the *results* your company will materialize in the future. A vision statement is not an endpoint or a status boost; it is a clear construct for what you are moving toward and want to be known for.

Getting clear on the vision of your company will set you apart from the other entrepreneurs who are chasing the shiny object or doing what takes to just make some 'quick' coin. Vision means you have an end point and a clear intention to go after it. While we dream about our *missions* in the long term, we see our *visions* more closely and more attainably. We know we can make it there in some capacity. We may not be the best, nor the only ones. We may not be doing it 100 percent or mastering it completely, but the vision is a facet of our company that we keep working toward and finding more and more of it as we go.

Below are some vision statements from well-known companies to give you a sense of how a vision represents a brand and defines just what it does in its industry.

- **Teach for America:** One day, all children in this nation will have the opportunity to attain an excellent education.

- **LinkedIn:** Create economic opportunity for every member of the global workforce.

- **Zoom:** Video communications empowering people to accomplish more.

- **Tesla:** To create the most compelling car company of the 21st century by driving the world's transition to electric vehicles.

- **Southwest Airlines:** To become the world's most loved, most efficient, and most profitable airline.

- **Habitat for Humanity:** A world where everyone has a decent place to live.

While the mission statement focuses on the high-level purpose of your company, the vision statement looks more at how you want to fulfill that purpose and how your company uniquely does just that. Both mission and vision statements are vital elements of your organization, but a vision statement should be seen as your company's driving force. Your vision is your tangible achievables, while your mission contains the more altruistic aspirations.

Given the impact that a vision statement has on a company's overall and long-term success, it is worth taking the time to craft a statement that encapsulates your ideals and inspires your team, colleagues, and future clients. Make your vision something people will remember because it needs to capture the heart of everyone you do business with. Yet it should also be concise; don't make it longer than a sentence or two. The best visions statements are ones people can quickly repeat and, more importantly, fully understand. Don't be too vague, nor too overly focused on one specific product or service. Your vision statement should answer the question, what ultimate impact do I want my business to have on my community, my industry, or the world?

My ideas for a VISION STATEMENT are:

_____

_____

_____

_____

_____

_____

Vision Statement Draft #1

_____

_____

_____

Vision Statement Draft #2

_____

_____

_____

Vision Statement Draft #3

_____

_____

_____

Vision Statement Draft #4

_____

_____

_____

Vision Statement Final/Favorite

_____

_____

_____

_____

_____

_____

_____

_____

_____

_____

_____

_____

_____

_____

_____

_____

_____

_____

_____

_____

_____

What are your Values?

If your vision statement is your destination, and a mission statement is your map, then your values are your guideposts. **Core Values** are the fundamental beliefs that guide the decisions you make and directly influence the actions you take. They can be both your own values and your organization's values. Many people have personal values and separate company values. For the purpose of this exercise you can choose which one you want to focus on. Ideally your personal values and corporate values crossover and interrelate. What you stand for personally is often the same for what your company stands for, so knowing what they are, is the key.

I like to say, values are what you 'ride and die' on. They are what you will say yes to with glee and excitement and what will cause you to adamantly disagree with. They are what you strive for, then push each day to accomplish and uphold. They help you make choices on who you work with, who you will hire, then must fire, and eventually what you will walk away from. They also define how you do business, make decisions and what you openly commit to. Your values need to be aligned with everyone you work with. Otherwise what starts out as rocky in the beginning, will only get worse. If values are misaligned, communications breakdown, emotions flare, and the entire direction of the company can suffer.

Knowing your values establishes a great sense of freedom for you and your company. Once you decide what your values are, you systematically act in accordance to them. When a new idea comes up, you see if it is in tune with your company values. When a partnership emerges, values must align. Troubles, challenges, and difficult personnel must all hold to the values you created. From big decisions to small modifications, acquisitions to borrowing funds, all that you do is filtered through your unrelenting commitment to your values.

Needless to say, defining your values is a big part of running your business. Once you do it, you likely will be set as values are core to who you are. Your values are deeply rooted in your personal beliefs and then transferred to your business's directive. According to good old' Google™, Core values *are the fundamental beliefs of a person or organization. These guiding principles dictate behavior and can help people understand the difference between right and wrong.* Core values *also help companies to determine if they are on the right path and fulfilling their goals by creating an unwavering guide.*

There are dozens of ways to map out your core values and hundreds of words that represent the values you resonate with most. You can do many different things to decipher your core values and spend a lot of time dissecting every option available. I like to start with what matters most… you. You are the driving force in your business, so what you need, want and desire matters to the highest degree. That is why, instead of looking at all the ways out there to find your values, I want you to look inside of you.

Use the following exercise to help you begin mapping out your values and be willing to have a little fun in the process..

1. Write out your name on a piece of paper in a vertical formation. That means stack each letter of your name on top of one another, in a line going down the left side of the page.

2. Then write down three to five powerful words that represent a value that starts with the same letter as each letter in your name. For example if your name is Bill, you would pick three to five values that start with B, then three to five that start with I, and then three to five that start with L, and so on and so on. Write down three to five words for each letter of your first and last name. Allow the letters of your name be the guides to help pinpoint the values that are important to you.

3. Once you are done, you can circle any repeated values, if you have any.

4. Then go through the list and pick four to five that mean the *very* most to you. Narrow down your list to your favorites and those that inspire you on a visceral level. You will know which values resonate with you when you feel them in your gut, not in your head.

NOTE: Don't choose values because they sound good to your ego or are on trend with your friends. Values are not just what looks good on paper or sounds impressive. True core values are something you'd stake your entire reputation on. They are the flags you put in the sand and the soap box you will stand on because they absolutely mean everything to you. When picking your core values, ask yourself if you'd be willing to 'ride and die' to uphold this value? If you don't feel that way, then keep searching.

Your top four or five values may not be those qualities that have the same first letter as a letter in your name, but this is a fun and easy way to Ignite the thoughts and spark your thinking to discover what values *do* matter most. Doing this exploration in a creative way from the right side of the brain triggers more abstract thinking instead of a linear analysis. I encourage this as it activates more of your internal beliefs rather than what your brain 'thinks' you should choose. We often read over a value list and pick something that looks good or sounds important, but it isn't the value we hold most dear. When you choose your values, they have to connect to you on the deepest level for you to make sure they are upheld in every aspect of your business.

Once you have defined your top values, refer to them often. Put them somewhere you can see them. Read over them, add them to your website, and teach them to your team. Knowing your core values off by heart is important, as you can filter everything you do through them to see how it aligns. Letting your customers and colleagues know what you stand for is an important distinction in business as it shows exactly what you cherish to uphold. Most importantly, your team and all the people who work with you should know you honor those values and commit to them on every level. Running your business according to your core values builds confidence in what you offer and fosters a true sense of pride in who you are as an entrepreneur.

The core of you is the core of your business.
— JB Owen

WHAT IS YOUR PURPOSE?

The word **purpose** often intimidates people. It feels so broad and even superficial that many negate the process of uncovering and discovering it. Humans have been conditioned to believe we are just here on this earth to do what we do. A purpose feels like an indulgence and defining it an irrelevant distinction. Most people think their purpose is to live, take care of their families, and work hard. But a purpose is so much more than that! You are born into being to live out the very essence of your magnificence. You are allowed to have everything you desire. The Universe wants you to live in bliss and splendor. A life of ultimate euphoria is truly your purpose; to know thyself utterly and to bask in all your gifts and glory while giving freely unto the world.

Yep… it sounds big and audacious, privileged, and profound… and it is divinely true. That's why so many people skip knowing their purpose and instead get stuck just living within the facts. Having the freedom to *have*, *be,* and *enjoy* all that you are meant to is a huge concept to adopt. It is also a massive responsibility: to live on purpose. That's why a lot of people simply avoid defining their purpose.

Instead of glossing over your purpose, let's take a bit of time to delve into the delight that 'living in purpose' brings, *especially as an entrepreneur*. You've decided to undertake this huge assignment and live in this unique atmosphere of entrepreneurship. You've devoted your time and energy to this decision. Knowing *the purpose* behind it is essential. Why do you feel compelled to stay up late, give it your all, endure the hardships, and prevail? The answers to these questions are the underpinnings within your purpose.

It is obvious that you have a list of things you are good at and a multitude of joys that lift your spirits and make you feel alive. You like to be a certain way and you aspire to be even more than you are now. Beyond the intellect, you feel driven to do certain things and perform in a particular way. You gravitate toward a definite inclination and know when something just isn't a good fit. Understanding all these nuances of you is a major part of clarifying your purpose. Let's begin by uncovering those first.

What makes you truly happy? What do you just LOVE doing?

_____

_____

_____

What lifts your spirits and makes you feel alive?

_____

_____

_____

How do you like to show up in the world? What are your attitudes, reactions, feelings, and behaviors toward yourself and others?

_____

_____

_____

How do you aspire to be? Who do you want to become?

_____

_____

_____

Defining these answers establishes the framework of your inner desires and the feelings you have inside that fuel your fire and Ignite your spirit. This is how you innately choose to be. Given the freedom, this is how you were designed to flourish from conception. You came into this world blissfully allowed to be exactly these things. No one is stopping you from being or living your life in this way… right?

Unfortunately, more often than not, many people struggle with those questions and most of us answer them the way we *think* we should. We are so programmed to *think* about what makes us happy, *think* who we should become, and *think* about what we love within the confines of reason and practicality. In fact, we *think* about it way too much.

Living on purpose goes beyond 'thinking' and far surpasses what we can conceptualize from an intellectual standpoint. (Another reason why many of us skip discovering their purpose.) Purpose is within your soul. It lives 'inside' your Being and is not something you can chart or map because it isn't sensical and logical. Your purpose was given to you on a deep cosmic heaven-and-the-stars molecular and cellular level that supersedes facts, data, and what your brain can perceive. It is so *within* you that it *IS* you. And for many, living a life of purpose means taking a journey into a deeper level of self to override the practical and 'trained' way of thinking.

Our minds have been taught and conditioned to want solutions, rewards, and guarantees. Humans seek survival over all else due to our primal and prehistoric upbringing. This survival instinct causes our minds to always kick into gear to save us, protect us, and keep us from being eaten alive. Although entrepreneur clichés included 'being out on the savanna alone,' 'swimming with the sharks,' and 'kill or be killed,' this is not really the case. In the 21st century, conditions are vastly different from those of the Stone Age days. In truth, nowadays many entrepreneurs are known to have 'the cushy life' and are 'living high on the hog' and have 'the Midas touch' while enjoying their 'Unicorn' business. It is far from sabre-tooth tigers and neanderthal conditions, but the brain still 'thinks' the same.

To find your real purpose, you have to dig far deeper into you than what your rational thinking deducts. That means bypassing the brain, the safety guard, and dipping into the emotional and spiritual you. It requires a much more personal exploration that triggers the soul to speak up, not the mind. Your purpose will conjure up feelings that tickle the very fiber of you, enliven your spirit, and awaken a tsunami of truth within you. Yes, it is big and audacious, privileged and profound, AND… it is divinely powerful!

Living in purpose means you have tapped into the steady flow of your *soul's* desires. That is far more invigorating than anything we 'think' we should do. Many entrepreneurs have found this personal nirvana; that is why you see them boundlessly successful, inventing life-changing widgets, and developing globally inspiring thing-a-ma-dos. They are living from the elixir of their life's purpose and basking in the power of an endless supply of Source energy.

Now it is your turn to open the valve and release the continuous outpouring of all that is available to you. Possibilities, opportunities, joy, freedom, bliss, and beauty are just a fraction of what is at your fingertips when you choose to find your purpose and live within it. All that you have ever dreamed of is just wanting to transpire because if you dreamed it up, then it was meant for you to experience. Nothing comes to us that isn't *for* us. Your ideas, wants, wishes, and aspirations are in your mind because they are just waiting for you to make them happen. Each one is destined for you to experience when you live your purpose full out.

What is your TRUE Purpose?

When you answer the questions this time, answer them from the very essence of you. Circumvent the mind and go straight to the heart. FEEL the answers; don't think them. Let your cells tingle and bubble the answers up to the center of your Being. Close your eyes and ask your soul to answer. Wait for as long as you need to HEAR what your spirit wants to tell you.

This may be new for some of you and the mind may be saying (at this very moment) how foolish this is; to negate it's instructions. Just try it. Ask your brain to pause its chatter just for a few minutes. Tell it that all is safe and no danger is near. Explain to the mind that it can rest for a few minutes because for right now, you want to connect with the essence of you and hear what the very core of your Being has to share. Allow your brain to take a short vacation while you nestle into the truest truth of you. With your soul at the forefront and all your emotions wide open, ask yourself these questions:

What truly makes me happy? What makes my heart sing?

_____

_____

_____

What lifts my spirits and makes me feel extraordinary, on purpose, and contributing to others?

_____

_____

_____

How do I enjoy showing up in the world? What are the real attitudes, reactions, feelings, and behaviors I have toward myself and others?

_____

_____

_____

Who am I truthfully? Who was I born to become?

_____

_____

_____

When you answer all these questions from your true self — your divine being — and have discovered who you are and what feels best for you, you have arrived at the doorstep of your purpose. You have found out your soul's desires and how your sacred essence wishes to live on this earth. You can now fulfill your purpose by bringing your soul's splendor and wishes into your human experience. Your purpose is to live in such a way that the divine part of you — the part that matters most — is existing in that beautiful state each and every day. Once you are doing that, you will be living your life on purpose. As you bring the soul's purpose forth into the human realm of the 'now,' you awaken your ability to live your purpose here on Earth.

You may be wondering what this all has to do with business and why are speaking about the soul and spirit in a book for entrepreneurs, but I assure you they go hand in hand. You see, your inner wishes are the very root of your outer desires. They are the starting point of all that you do; the ignition, the flame, and the fortitude that will keep you going in your business. No apple was produced, moonshot completed, or virtual highway invented without the unrelenting desires and unequivocal conviction of the business owner. They had to dig deep within themselves to not only to *know* their mission, vision, and values, but to clarify and identify with their soul's purpose. Otherwise they would have never made it. The stakes were too high and the journey too uncharted for them to take it on without a burning, yearning, super-connection to the very core of who they were and their purpose for being on this earth.

When you look at all the 'Greats' in business, the ones who have made it big, you can see the all-encompassing passion inside of them. You can feel their convictions and almost taste the blood, sweat, and tears they put into their businesses. They don't do any of that because someone told them to, nor because they want to see the numbers on a year-end fiscal report. They do it because they were born to; they have to! Inside of them is a bone-gnawing, banshee-howling, volcano-burning *knowing* of what their purpose is, and they decided to live doing that. It is undeniable: the most successful people on the planet know their purpose for being here and that *becomes* their business.

An Ignited Entrepreneur

My hope is that as you read this book and complete the exercises that are included, you begin to formulate a richer understanding of who you are as an entrepreneur. As you dive into the stories, and read the many experiences one can have as an entrepreneur, I hope you begin to see ways that you can improve your business, awaken your ideas, and get connected to the essence of why you chose this vocation for your life.

Everything inside *Ignite The Entrepreneur* is designed to Ignite something more in you as a business owner. Maybe a winning business practice or a slight change in how you see things; maybe a sense of pride from your accomplishments wrapped within a connection you feel toward someone's journey. May this book propel you forward. May the words and inspirations inside it touch you in a motivational way. May it excite you to work on your business and yourself.

I always say, "You have to grow *you* to grow your business," and this is what this book is all about. You, learning tools and techniques to implement into your business, but also the ideas and aspirations you can inject into your heart. Heart and hustle go hand in hand in business, as do conviction and connection — with self and others. Business is a symbiotic dance you have with yourself, your customers, and the world around you. It is an ecosystem of giving and receiving; serving and being served. Never underestimate the influence your business has on you and everyone around you. That is why working on yourself, improving your business knowledge, and accelerating your entrepreneurial mindset benefits not just you but everyone you know and meet.

May there be something inside this book that catapults you forward. May one idea, one suggestion, one hint of inspiration be the catalyst for that next iteration of you and your business. No matter where you are in your entre-preneurial endeavors, may you learn great things from your fellow business owners and the courageous authors in this book.

We are all part of the collective consciousness and our businesses, brands, and messaging need to speak to a better world going forward. As business owners, part of our responsibility is to create a better place for all the future generations while building a wonderful future for ourselves. May every day of your entrepranal adventure be filled with that which you love and cherish. A happy entrepreneur is a prosperous entrepreneur in all aspects of their life. May what you read here stay with you forever as it touches your heart and Ignites the magnificent and outstanding entrepreneur in you.

MANIFEST

TAKE RISKS

GO ALL OUT

LIVE YOUR PASSION

IGNITE THE ENTREPRENEUR

JB OWEN

JB OWEN

"You have got to be it to become it."

Wherever the entrepreneurial spirit lies within you, it is my intention that this story helps to bring it forward. It is no small feat to choose to be an entrepreneur. The road is filled with the most unknown ups and downs. But it is also filled with the most joyous triumphs and the greatest transformations. Who you are when you begin is not who you become. May this story awaken your inner desire and encourage you to shout a resounding, "Yes!" to the magnificent entrepreneur you can undoubtedly become.

WE ALL DESERVE TO BE SEEN, TO BE HEARD, AND TO BELONG

I am not sure if it is normal or if it is a rare thing to have your Ignite moment at the age of 9. I doubt I knew what to call it at the time, but I remember very distinctly having this life-changing feeling that awakened my desire to adore doing business. I was sitting on the curb of the sidewalk right outside the doors of a local tavern my father would visit. I was holding a rectangular piece of cardboard in my hands. Strung around the cardboard and knotted at the back were a dozen necklaces I had made out of braided brown leather and multi-colored macrame beads. I had taken to making jewelry, chokers to be exact. It was the latest fashion in the late '70s and I knew my designs were just as good as anything I had seen in magazines and on TV.

That confidence in the beauty of my designs is what had me sitting on that curb watching for patrons coming in and out of the bar. When a couple holding hands would walk from the parking lot toward the building, I would stand up eagerly and launch into my pitch, "Hey mister wanna buy a pretty necklace for your pretty lady?" When a man would exit the building, rushing to go home after a few drinks with the fellows, I'd use that opportunity to share, "Excuse me sir, how about a pretty necklace to take home to the missus?"

My approach was a combination of appealing to their emotions, seizing the moment, and being a solution to a problem they didn't realize they had. As soon as I made my pitch to the man holding hands with his girlfriend, she'd smile at him with big wanting eyes, waiting to see if he agreed with my question. As soon as I asked the tardy husband looking worriedly at his watch, he would immediately see the sense in my proposal. Of course the first man thought his girlfriend was pretty and deserved a necklace expressing his love. Of course the second man wanted to see a look of delight in his wife's eyes at the gift. Time after time, person after person, they'd stop, take a look at what I had, and realize they just had to buy one.

For me, it resulted in a gleeful sense of euphoria. I'd ask one simple question and then watch the magic unfold. It was like turning on a light bulb in a blackened room and revealing a litany of lost treasures and precious art. For the man with the girlfriend, there was this emotional dance that took place as he'd let his girlfriend pick the necklace she liked. Then he'd gingerly brush her neck with his fingertips as he tied it to her neck. She'd giddily hold up her long hair, patiently waiting while he fumbled to secure the braided leather around her neck. She'd then turn and smile at him with sweet validation in her eyes and he'd lovingly smile back with doting approval. The sale was cemented.

It was the same with the man rushing to get home. He'd stop to take a quick glance at my items as my question stirred and percolated in his mind. Within minutes, he would be picking a necklace and I would watch his emotions play out on his face as he shifted from being worried about arriving home late to being eager to get home to present a spontaneous gift to his wife. Each time I asked a prospective customer, I stood back in awe, watching the art of the transaction occur. I saw it time after time — the change from not knowing they needed it to absolutely having to have it! The men were happy that their girlfriends were happy. The women were happy with their new presents and I was happy with the $2.00 I got to neatly fold in my pocket from doing something that I loved; making jewelry. It felt like making money from my jewelry was something akin to magic.

Everything about it was a win, win, win. That feeling of pride and joy from selling something I had crafted. The appreciation from the customers and the residual in knowing that I had done something that brought so much happiness to others. Not to mention how impressed my father was each time he'd emerge from the pub to find that my cardboard displayer was empty and my pockets were full. At a very young age, I learned the joy in making things from my own volition, the delight in providing something that made people happy, and the power of sales and being an entrepreneur.

That triple-win mentality pushed me to always be thinking of ways to make something that provided joy to everyone. From group babysitting at the age of 12 to a pay-as-you-go art class at the local playground at age 14, I longed to be the solution maker and the provider of delight, all while making money resulting in that triple win. At 15, I was busing tables so I could buy jewelry bits to sell at the farmer's market on the weekends. At 17, I was certified to do acrylic nails and subleased a table at the mall in the back of a makeup shop. At 18, I dove into selling clothing while attending fashion design school in the big city. I spent the next two decades starting business after business, selling everything from metallic-molded jewelry to leather-patched clothing; from forgiveness workshops to cruise ship training; from folkloric handmade santas to paper-mache art pieces and smashed teacup mosaic-tiled coffee tables. Making things became my passion. If I could make it, I knew I could sell it.

I'd see something on the cover of a magazine and be inspired to start a clothing line. I'd find something I admired and knew I could make for half the price, so I would. A friend would make an off-the-cuff remark about wishing for a product and before you knew it, I had come up with a name and was hashing out a plan to produce it. I become an industrious 'if I can think it, I can make it' machine and, with my background in design and self-taught graphic skills, I could have a logo and business cards made and a whole new business launched in a week.

My self-driven mindset and diverse skills in creating has kept me in the entrepreneurial space for most of my life. Nine-to-five jobs have never fit me. Getting a paycheck at the end of the month was so unrewarding compared to dollars handed to me and stuffed gleefully in my pocket. I loved the interaction, the transaction, and the exchange with my customers. I adored how they handed me their money with a smile on their face. Being a cog in a big wheel of employees was arduous to me. Mundane tasks at an office, working with no end in sight, was a disaster to my psyche and drove me back to my design room. I craved the delight and sheer satisfaction of tallying the income my efforts had earned me, calculating what I had spent on supplies, and seeing the resulting profits grow.

In my 30s, married to an equally ambitious entrepreneur with two small kids and a house bigger than what we needed inspired another amazing idea: to start a kids' clothing company. I saw how the market was lacking in clothes for boys and, living on the west coast of Canada, it proved difficult to find good rain gear in the winter and clothing that would protect their skin from the hot summer sun. Solving a problem that parents didn't know they had soon became my company mantra. UV-protected clothing with stain-resistance and wick-away properties were an easy sale to parents who wanted the best for their kids. Once again making things that I loved, selling to happy parents, while protecting kids from the harsh ultra-violet sun, I was in my glory.

It was the best triple win ever! My company soared from starting in my basement to hitting a million dollars in sales in less than four years. We expanded into multiple countries, sold to stores around the world, and my house became the epicenter for all my employees. I had a large workroom in my rumpus room, office desks in every corner, and a 30-foot shipping container in the backyard as our distribution center. We scaled, grew 300 percent, and moved into absolute overdrive.

You'd think it was an entrepreneur's dream, but it wasn't. The thrill of selling was no longer up to me. The team took over. The marketing department, IT guys, and new social media gurus all had a say in how we pitched the product. I saw the customers less. My in-person sales calls to the local stores were replaced with factory visits to China and fabric shows with vendors. I never got to look anyone in the eye or see their smiles anymore. It was all emails and invoices; paperwork and deadlines; shipping quotes and backorders. I had lost the interaction I had enjoyed with the customers; I no longer saw the delight on their faces. I was forced to simply make what others were selling. My triple win was gone.

As the company grew, I became a machine. All people wanted me to do was design. They asked me to forget about everything else and just let them handle it. My job was to put my head down and create. They took away from me the one thing that I loved the most and I was required to look at forecasted marketing trends and analyze consumer demographic reports instead of seeing the sparkling eyes and smiling faces of my shoppers. If something was hot in the market, I was expected to replicate it, even if I didn't enjoy making it. If something had a big profit margin, we were doing it regardless of how I felt about it. The executives I hired insisted the company had to be known for dominating the market and crushing the competitors. Over time, the constant demand for big wins in market share and bigger wins in industry influence dominated my days and left me feeling depleted and void of any entrepreneurial ambition.

I can look back now and say that I had entrepreneured myself right out of my gifted talent, and eventually out of my marriage and away from my friends. The stress, unhappiness, and pressure tore away at me and left me little to talk about other than work at the end of the day. I was lost, deflated, and disconnected from myself, from my customers, and from the very reason why I had begun making anything at all. I had removed myself from the front lines, the place where I could listen to the clients. Gone were all the interactions that were laced with purpose and passion. The company had indirectly vanquished all of my joy.

On a fretful day in June, with nothing left in my spirit, I dismissed my staff, locked my doors, took my two kids in my white mommy van, walked out of my 5,000-square foot warehouse with its $780,000 worth of inventory... and I drove away. I left it all. I let the bank, the landlord, and whoever else wanted a piece, to have it, fight over it, and carve it up like a pack of rabid dogs. I didn't have an ounce of energy left in me to keep going, reinvent, or pivot. Nothing felt like it once had and I turned my back and gave up on all that I had built.

Some say entrepreneurs are like gamblers, throwing it all in on a hope and a dream. Entrepreneurs are well-known for coming up with a crazy idea and risking everything they have, believing it will undoubtedly happen. They are willing to go all out, doing whatever they can to chase after an idea until it comes to be. I can't say I am like a gambler — I'd rather swallow my quarters than give them up to a greedy slot machine, and seeing so many people sitting at a blackjack table foolishly losing their money is tortuous to see. And yet, I have spent a king's ransom chasing after all of my dreams and entrepreneurial ideas; both the hits and the misses. I have thrown in the dice, doubled down on a gamble and gone back time and time again amid the losses and gains.

I'll admit it took a few years to recover after that devastating decision to walk away; both emotionally and financially. I could hardly say the name of my company without tears welling up in my eyes from the shame and the loss. I wish at the time I had been stronger, wiser, and had found a mentor to lean on. I wish someone would have helped me through the anguish of what I didn't know and guided me to act more wisely. But everything happens for a reason and that loss was the foundation of something more. I had to look at what I had sacrificed, and why. I had to decide what truly mattered to me and define what non-negotiables I was willing to adhere to going forward.

When I started my next business, I decided to do it while learning from my past and focusing solely on the onward and upward; because that is what entrepreneurs do. They brush themselves off and return to the fray. They say "Yes" to the exciting elixir of the entrepreneurial life that compels them to start over and try again. In doing that, I went all the way back to the beginning. To that very day when I was bit by the entrepreneurial bug at nine years old and felt enamored by the look in my customers' eyes. I needed to reconnect to the meaning behind what I was doing. The real reasons, and the right reasons.

What surfaced from my deep introspection was the powerful emotion of the triple win. The glorious feeling that I was winning, they were winning, and other people were winning in the process. I made a clear declaration that from that moment on that any business I created had to be centered around the triple win; otherwise I wasn't doing it. Everyone benefiting became a mandatory component in anything I was going to do. In fact, the triple win became both my corporate mission and my personal mantra in everything I aspired to accomplish. I knew it was what got me started way back then and it was what was going to keep me committed going forward.

Now I have the pleasure of having not one but three thriving businesses all centered around the triple win. That concept has since grown exponentially into the 4x and 5x win. I win, my team wins, my client wins, the people my clients touch win, and humanity overall wins from so many people benefiting and transforming. When I give full-hearted and genuinely, it creates a ripple effect in everyone I serve. That grows and magnifies in the people I connect with. That transformation uplifts humanity on the whole. Seeing the benefits when everyone wins is, to me, the fundamental essence of a winning business.

This is the philosophy behind IGNITE, a global publishing house and the leaders in Empowerment Publishing. You and so many others get to experience this kind of triple win in every book that we publish. The authors, the readers, the readers' families and friends, and all of their families and friends benefit. Since we have authors in every corner of the world, I believe we are manifesting wins on the planet every minute of every day.

'IGNITE' came to me in an Ignite moment. I was sitting at a conference while a speaker was up on stage telling a personal and emotional story. As I witnessed their vulnerable sharing, what I realized was the fundamental and incredibly important need everyone has to be seen, to feel heard, and to belong. Speaker after speaker came up on stage and, as they expressed their life-changing moments, I saw how those moments did not define them, but instead refined them; catapulting them in a new and more amazing direction. I also noticed how there was a single powerful moment that put them on a new trajectory in their life and IGNITED a path toward something greater; ultimately a greater version of themselves.

When each speaker was done, the crowd stood up and applauded. Many received hugs when coming off of the stage. Telling their most intimate moments of heartache and sorrow didn't repel the audience, it brought them closer and formed a new level of authentic connection. I instantly saw how important it was to tell your story, share your truth, and do it in a way that allowed you to express how it made you a better person. The speakers felt amazing in sharing, the audience felt moved by listening, the entire room felt more connected with each other and left feeling more willing to be honest and open with the people in their world. For me, it was the triple win magnified.

I believe that telling our stories transforms us, transforms others, and can ultimately transform the world. I feel this in every fiber of my being. I know that every person on the planet has a story; that every person has an Ignite moment in their life. I believe more than ever that if we all can build businesses where people can relate to one another while experiencing a triple win, then we could all connect, transform, and heal on a global scale.

Imagine your business Igniting others so that all your customers are winning just as much as you are. See your business not as a business but as a way for people to come together, connect, create, and care about one another. Triple wins in business are endless and when you start seeing that in all that you do, it will not just benefit your business but benefit your life and the lives of generations to come. Ask yourself what would the world look like if we all were seen? Felt heard? Knew we belonged and were winning together? Be the kind of entrepreneur who will do whatever you can to make exactly that happen.

Use that powerful gift you have to do all you can to uplift and empower everyone around you. Focus on the triple win and stay true to your passion. Let others be seen, be heard, and feel a sense of belonging. A business is a life force and as its custodian, do everything possible to Ignite as many people as you can. A triple win benefits us all.

Ignite Action Steps

Define the triple win in all that you do. Be it with your kids, your spouse, your employees, a neighbor, a friend, a person at the market, or a stranger on the bus, find the triple win where you win, they win, and those around you win. Map out procedures so that everyone you work with always feels the win. That keeps customers and clients coming back and doing more business with you. No one has to lose for you to win. Everyone can win!

JB Owen – Canada
Speaker, Author, Publisher, CEO of Ignite, JBO Global Inc. & Lotus Liners
www.jbowen.website   www.igniteyou.life   www.lotusliners.com
 jbowen *jbthepossibilitymaker*

IGNITE THE ENTREPRENEUR

TANJA JADE POWELL

Tanja Jade Powell

"Change your perspective, change your life."

It is my wish that you will realize everything you need is within you. You don't need to look outside for satisfaction or validation. We are all more powerful than we have ever been led to believe or often tell ourselves. By reading my story, I hope you will see that winning at the game of life is your birthright! And it's all achievable, if you get out of your head and into your heart.

Get Out of Your Head and Into Your Heart

"You will never amount to anything." These words can define you. Your reaction to words can make or break the person you are meant to be. I learned this because it became one of my greatest driving forces toward achievement.

My dad grew up as an army brat and was surrounded by confinements. In turn he tried to rule me with a 'do as I say, not as I do' mentality. But, he was a rebel, so it was hard to follow rules when I was witnessing rebellion occur within the person trying to force that structure upon my life. The rebel in him created the rebel in me. I was going to prove him wrong. I was not only going to be free of his rules, I was going to be free of his patronization.

That wasn't all I was determined to leave behind, though. Ask my mom and she'll say I became an entrepreneur so I could earn my own money because I didn't want to wear Kmart™ clothing. At 13 years of age, I had a job working in a theater becoming a lifelong popcorn addict and witnessing entrepreneurs run a business. There I learned the hard work, systems, and operations that it took to succeed in business.

One night, I was walking through the aisle during the film *E.T. The Extra Terrestrial* to check for security and people's feet up on seats when something fell to the floor from my skirt. Horrified, I kept walking as the place was packed. On the next round through the aisle, I discreetly picked up what had dropped — OMG it was one of my dad's socks, stuck to my skirt with static cling. It took everything to get back to the lobby before I burst out laughing. I had rushed out of the house, as always relying on a ride, and had quickly grabbed my uniform out of the dryer and thrown it on. This was just proof, though, that I was more concerned about getting to the job and doing it well than I was about checking my uniform. I had one speed: go, go, go. It was all I ever did. That job is where I got my first taste of being an entrepreneur as I watched the owners work tirelessly, and they slowly trusted me to take over the front-end ticket sales, cash, and end-of-the-night locking up.

The moment that changed it all for me, however, occurred in high school, at Dawson Creek, mile zero of the Canada–Alaska Highway. That was where we had the pilot high school program for Entrepreneurship. Leading up to that, I had moved out at 16, worked more, and told the school I had to work to pay rent. I had passing grades but was much more interested in living life. They built an outbuilding at my high school just for this program and I was curious. It was the only class I attended full-time and I became enthralled! We did Dale Carnegie sales training, cash flow statements, and business plans; and in order to graduate, you had to have a business launch and be successful.

I decided to create a graduation dress shop with one-of-a-kind samples. Dawson Creek was a small town, population 12,000, with few places to shop so my idea was a big hit! My store sold out and I had a unique grad dress all my own. This was in 1988 — picture big 80s rocker hair, including sky-high hair-sprayed 'wall of bangs.'

The retail industry was exciting and something I wanted to continue working in. I found out that many major fashion distributors had sales representatives who sold samples once a season was over. After reaching out to several sales representatives and negotiating prices, I was flown 1,200 kilometers to shop in Vancouver; a city of millions with a variety of styles to witness. It was an insight into behind-the-scenes retail and I was excited about it. This was an opportunity to have unique clothing before all my friends and I no longer had to wear boring brands.

That successful buying experience in the dress shop made me want to keep exploring. I asked the owner of the coolest clothing store in town if I could work there. Through my story of launching my own successful sample sale store, I got the job. Being employed at this store taught me that to be successful you had to work hard and impress others in order to move up and make more money.

Each time the sales reps came to our store on their routine visits I would pester them to connect me to a job in Vancouver — a city I knew was full of more exciting opportunities than my hometown. Andy, an action sports clothing rep, connected me with a Vancouver store and I was on my way. One of the things I loved about retail was being allowed to merchandise windows. It was like playing dress up as a kid. I spent the next several years working retail as a buyer, merchandiser, and manager in sport stores.

At the height of my retail career, I was spending a million dollar company budget each year on shopping. I became an expert in ski, skate, and board sport clothing and accessories. Over seven years we went from $700,000 to $7 million yearly. The wonderful experiences I got to have included heli-skiing, cat boarding, trips to Alaska and Montana, and biyearly buying trips to Vegas and California. I got to go to the warehouses of the companies we bought from and fill bags with clothing for free!

The theme of freedom kept recurring for me. First it was freedom from my parents' strict rules, then the freedom to live where I wanted, and now the freedom to work on my own company and do it my way. From those experiences I knew it required diligence and having to be 'on' all the time, but I knew it was possible. Although I loved the freedom, success, and autonomy that the action sports store gave me, it was always for someone else: someone else's company. It wasn't my company or my vision, and that's what I truly wanted. To be an entrepreneur and create my own lifestyle. My schedule. My reality. My way.

I spent a year consulting to retail managers and helping them expand and improve their stores. But I quickly realized that this wasn't an industry where I could grow. It stagnated for me and I became bored. Even though retail ultimately wasn't for me, I realized one of the things I loved about merchandising was the impact my decisions had when I saw potential in something. I could look at a wall of clothing and immediately see how to improve it. I knew I had a talent.

That led to my next endeavor.

I would look at friends' houses and immediately see the cosmetic changes that could be made to improve it considerably. I have a gift for seeing the power that color, styling, and changing the look of a space has for shifting someone's emotional psyche. I saw possibilities everywhere!

In my determining next steps, I was working for a painting company part-time, learning hands-on about everything from protection and preparation to application and cleanup. I was shocked at how the clients were treated in their own home, as it was normal for workers to treat a space as their jobsite rather than someone's sacred sanctuary. I knew I could do it differently; do it better.

Meanwhile, my partner at the time quit his union painting job sandblasting the inside of new watershed pipes. It felt like a sign; a time to change and to finally take the leap. With new conviction and no hesitation, I said, "I guess we are starting that painting company!" Hence, shortly after my daughter arrived, six months later, Powell Painting was born.

In 2006 I was on the tools as well as doing sales, marketing, bookkeeping, production managing, color consulting, cleanup, and client management. Sometimes, it felt like I was driven to succeed despite circumstances. I can still recall the big push it took to complete this one particular job. I was working on beams on a construction job for a contractor and I was hustling! Up and down the ladder reaching as far as I could, popping off the ladder, moving the ladder, over and over. In my haste I stepped into a five gallon bucket of paint and gave myself a foot soaker. That was a small illustration of when moving too fast does not make things happen faster.

However, I did not get the message just yet.

The business grew, I had to add team members, and work myself even thinner. Managing people remotely to execute work to your standard is pretty much impossible. Testing painters involved me giving them a room to paint so they could show me their skills. When I would return after 30 minutes and all they had done was tape all the cut lines, instead of freehand, I knew they were not a fit. When you use tape for a cut line it will bleed under the tape and leave a cleanup nightmare. A good brush and patience will always supersede tape.

Having started with all subcontractors this was a huge learning curve, as most cared only about cutting corners and making as much moola as possible. This taught me how to be a paint inspector, with high standards and an eye for every detail. I can look at a home now and tell how many painters worked there by how they applied the paint. Clients think this skill is a magic trick. :o)

My sales and customer service background served me well, as I was trusted because I cared and was honest. In order to get clients I verbalized at daycare and mommy groups, and wore painting whites about town. It was networking that worked! I also would fix anything I did not like whether the client cared or not. In my opinion the only way to complete something is the right way! I believed eventually each client would see things as they lived and cleaned their home, and I still do.

Powell Painting grew and grew like the little engine that could. I was completely and utterly addicted to work as I believed you had to work hard to be successful. It was what I knew and it felt comfortable — until it didn't.

When we hit $3 million in sales I melted into stress. Everything was happening to me and sitting in this victim mentality was not a good place to be. I took action by finding a coach to support creating systems within our business. A master coach worked with me on my mindset and one day when I kept saying, "I am just sooo busy," he said, "Well, your brain is just giving you what you are asking for."

HUH? I didn't get it.

He explained that like a CPU in a computer, your brain collects information and gives you what you ask for. By keeping myself so busy my brain was making sure I could not focus! After my session I wanted to know more. I googled retraining your brain, came across Marisa Peer on the Mindvalley™ platform, and took the *Uncompromised Life* course. This was the beginning of my personal development journey that actually led me to find IGNITE!

Personal development only led me so far before I realized countless teachers were telling their hero journey and then expecting people to emulate them through the course or program. I couldn't get behind that, knowing that really we all need to be ourselves, remaining true to becoming the best version of ourselves. It took me half my life before I FULLY realized we are all energy beings having a human experience. Just like I refused to let my parents, my education, or my previous careers dictate who I was meant to be, I wanted to keep pushing others to find their own definition of success and happiness. I am now a Master Certified Trainer with Mindvalley™ and grateful for all I learned and all the beautiful souls I have met around the world.

TRUE FREEDOM is what it's all about! If we are on Earth for only so long then let's have fun. This is a game and we make up the rules. Part of my success is my energy: it is infectious for some and draining for others over the years. We are all truly made of energy and it took me years to figure out little tricks to preserving mine and not collecting too much of others' as I moved through my day.

In my stress meltdown, my nervous system was shot and adrenal exhaustion became my reality. Enter yoga, pilates, meditation, journaling, along with hiking, mountain biking, rock climbing, and back country snow touring. Now I take 10 deep breaths before seeing a client and wish for it to be the best outcome for everyone involved.

Life is about balancing yourself and balancing with others, and grounding yourself makes your life adventure a lot easier. I learned to love myself first, taking care of my own needs so I can be better at serving and supporting others. I haven't abandoned working hard, but in finding the freedom to work for myself, I also found the freedom to BE myself and play.

No matter where you put your energy, don't let it be defined or controlled by someone else. When you slow down and pay attention to your body, versus your mind, you will get the answers you are seeking. Often we have to slow down to speed up. We have to trust our heart and intuition. You will amount to amazing things, when you do your life, and your business, your way.

Ignite Action Steps

- Active meditation — whatever inspires movement in nature, walking, biking, rock climbing etc. Experiment with guided or silent breath meditations as you grow your practice.

- Take 10 deep breaths before meeting a new client. Clear the energy from where you were to where you're going and focus in on them. When your breathing is concluded, say to yourself, "May this meeting be the best outcome for all involved." It will ground you and give you a positive intention toward the client.

- Be the observer of your brain and questioning thoughts. Observe and do not react for the only thing you can control is your actions.

- As humans we each have the right to have an emotion and to act as we choose. By committing to be the observer of others, you refrain from taking on their energy or adopting their opinions. Be a good listener and don't get your ego involved.

- Connect with your intuition, which is nonverbal (this is your ego). Take 10 deep breaths, be still, and ask a question to which you know the answer is yes. Pay attention to your heartbeat. You cannot explain intuition with your mind.

- Educate your clients rather than sell — listen to their needs, reiterate what they are saying, and include the solution.

- Create a mantra for your business. One I have learned is: "I have a wonderful business that serves in wonderful ways to wonderful clients for wonderful pay." Find or create your own. Mantras help lock in positive thoughts.

- When it gets tough, just remember… when you change your perspective, you change your life.

Tanja Powell – Canada
SheEO
www.powellpainting.ca

IGNITE THE ENTREPRENEUR

RAVI MUTI

RAVI MUTI

"Vocation is your personal legend; something that your heart desires and humanity needs. Keep searching until you find it."

My personal intention is for the reader to learn that anyone can be an entrepreneur; yes, anyone. More importantly, we can be whatever we desire. We should take the necessary time to find what it is that we are on planet Earth for. A one-size-fits-all model doesn't apply and it's up to us to dig deep within ourselves to honor our greatest passions. Then, not *adapt* to the world, but *create* the world you're inspired to build.

THE MAVERICK DO-GOOD MANIFESTER AND CREATOR

My motivation to become an entrepreneur was never about status or money. I've always wanted to help others, make the world a better place, and provide service to those in need. Entrepreneurship is in my blood. It's the environment I've grown up in. My dad has been an entrepreneur my whole life, driven by the necessity to survive and provide. Starting from 12, I always questioned my dad's lifestyle. As an entrepreneur, he worked long hours, 16 to 18 hours daily. He has an inspiring story of passion, drive, creativity, focus, determination, and longevity. He inspired me.

My dad sacrificed a lot for us, spending so much time and energy just so we could live a better life than he had experienced in his childhood. And it worked. Our family is in a great place, and I have the opportunity to carry on his legacy. I remember telling my mom that I'd never want to do what he is doing. As I got older, I started to appreciate his work ethic, ethos and desire, but I wanted to be like him in my own way; by defining what my work and life looked like. I saw the power of the entrepreneurial drive, and what it can create positively.

I always wanted to be a superhero. My addiction to heroes was admirable, to say the least, but okay, you cannot actually put on a cape and start jumping off of buildings. That isn't allowed, not to mention how ludicrous it really is. My sister once asked me why I had such an obsession with superheroes. I just laughed, didn't respond, but knew deep down that I wanted to 'save the world.' What did that even entail? I wanted to save the world from killing itself — I grew up watching and reading about crime, wars, and poverty and responded by wanting to make a difference to the world by living a good, honorable, and decent life. My sister said to me a few times that my fascination with these heroes was odd. I wasn't sure. Later, I learned that heroes can be anyone, even someone who lent you a hand during tough times.

When I went to university at 17, I started learning more about the world. I learned material ways of how large-scale institutional changes can cause big social problems. I chose to study Criminology, a wonderful discipline that I selected because of my interest in crime and criminal behavior. I love the subject, but I needed variety and more breadth in knowledge. A program that really caught my eye was Sociology! 'The study of society.' To be honest, I didn't know much about this discipline. All I knew was that I had this curiosity about the world we live in, and an eager desire to learn more about it. I decided to pursue a second major in Sociology.

Studying Sociology turned out to be a key aspect of my personal growth as a conscious human being. I was inspired to dig deeper into the interplay of humans and our institutions and how they both shape one another. I learned that on the surface, we may come from different backgrounds and cultures, but at the root, WE ARE ALL ONE. I saw in a new way how we are all connected and how our actions and behaviors impact each other — negatively and positively.

At 25 years old, I was ready. It was time to emerge from school and learn more about the world via hands-on experiences.

I had always desired to be a part of something bigger than myself, global, connecting the world, and helping others, but I hadn't imagined that the route to that was entrepreneurship. I saw entrepreneurship as most did at the time — long hours, the pursuit of profit, and the lack of consideration of wholeness. Then, I learned about a pretty successful fella by the name of Richard Branson, a global, maverick-like entrepreneur, daredevil, and world traveler. Safe to say, I wanted to emulate his lifestyle. I wanted more from life and with Branson as inspiration, I now knew that entrepreneurship can be used to not only do good, but also live a joyful and satisfying life.

During university, I worked side-by-side with my father in our family's real estate business where I got my first taste of entrepreneurship. It taught me that I wanted to work for myself in a way that would allow me to pursue my passion. Instead of following a generic path, I wanted to work diligently toward creating ventures that would have a positive impact on more people than just myself. The plan was to follow my passion and start being an entrepreneur at age 33. What type of business was I going to run? I had eight years to hone my skills, yet I had no idea what the business was going to be.

Enter business school. The idea of 'start-up' was new to a Criminology and Sociology major. I was just five when my dad started his company, so I don't remember that phase of it, but I fell in love with the concept after taking an entrepreneur course. I was inspired by various companies that were built after 2010. At the time, I was enrolled in a CPA and MBA course. After learning about creating start-ups, I wanted to drop out and start a business. Eventually, I decided to complete the MBA, and drop out of the CPA. As I've learned, this is a typical entrepreneur's story, dropping out to pursue a business venture. It made me feel like some of the greats who have done the same.

This is also the time I started to travel, curious to find my place in the world.

During graduate school, I started exploring ventures to help others with my schoolmates. Ideas ranged from a marketplace that supports small businesses, to a marketplace for artists, to a finance-lending hub, to a Planet Sub™ franchise — a healthier, higher-quality alternative to Subway™. I learned a lot, especially that entrepreneurship requires commitment. You have to be all in, because anything less than that will most likely lead to failure. More than anything, I learned that since ventures are so time and energy consuming, it is essential for me to be passionate about the cause so I have the fuel to drive me through the challenging times. Also, researching an idea is key; relying on others and jumping into something without doing due diligence is risky. I experienced this firsthand. My biggest lesson came from my Planet Sub investment. I was young when I invested. We could have definitely made the business work if we moved to Arizona, United States, but we hadn't factored in the regular four-hour flight from Vancouver, Canada that nobody was willing to do. This led us to relying on others to run the business, and that did not work out well. I moved on. I had thought I was immune to the laws of what makes a business successful, but this experience made it clear I was not. Furthermore, I realized that if you don't pursue something from the heart, there are low chances of success. I did not do this with the Planet Sub investment. My heart yearned to help others, and the business I was working on initially did not align. I kept pursuing my personal legend.

I wanted to make the world a better place. How would I do this? I kept going, my vision intact. I desired to connect the world, bring humanity together as one. My idea was to do this by offering multi-perspective tours of cities and cultures. I set up a low-cost venture, and after running some tours, found that tours did not excite me. But the idea of connecting the world and making it a better place was still where my passion laid.

It was time to now find my personal legend. The failures, the education, and the experiences had now prepared me to take the next step. Travel was the vehicle where this aha moment would occur. I've traveled to many countries in search of the meaning of life and who I am; in each trip, I found a piece of me.

It's December 2017, five years into my eight-year plan, I decided to embark on another adventure. This time, my heart felt that it was the right time to explore village life in Nicaragua. We ended up staying at Maderas village, it was like a retreat.

Maderas Village is tucked away at the end of a dirt road in the jungle off the coast of Nicaragua and it is one of the most beautiful places I've ever been to. Our first day there, I decided to check out the sunset. The water, illuminated by the setting sun, was glorious and I walked in up to my waist. Five minutes later, I felt something go into my foot and I immediately yanked my foot forward. Right away, I knew something was terribly wrong! Once out of the water, I could see how I was bleeding uncontrollably from the back of my foot. It was bad! My heart raced and I started thinking, "I'm going to die!"

I honestly did think my life was over! Luckily, paramedics were on-site. They told me I had been stung by a stingray and quickly patched me up before things could take a turn for the worse. Stingrays inject poison into your body and you can die from the bleeding or infection. As I sat there being tended to by an entire cluster of paramedics, a gentleman walked by. Sarcastically, he threw out, "Need any help?"

Once patched up, I headed back to the village to rest. Coincidentally, the individual who offered his assistance was staying at the same village. Nothing is ever a coincidence, because over the next three days, during my convalescing, we spent endless hours sharing food, drinks, and our most deeply desired goals and aspirations. He told me his life story and I told him mine. In that short time, as I regained my strength, we became like family. I was moved to realize that what I once thought was my path, was no longer it. In fact, my time with him made me see that there are people like me who want to do good in the world and that by working together we can accomplish it faster. I hadn't seen before how easy it was to find synergy with another person and his passion for helping others was equally aligned with mine. It was both exciting and Igniting!

We had a very powerful spiritual connection, and the more we talked over the months that followed, the more it grew. Eventually, he pitched an idea and a few months later, we agreed to start creating a business called *Imiloa*, a place where people connect, learn, become themselves, align with nature, and heal. A retreat center!! Help people and the world?! I'm in!

Over the next 12 months, we worked together, found other heart-centered investors, and resurrected an outstanding conscious environment for people to come and reconnect with themselves. It was both a place of sanctuary and a haven to give back to the local community. Everything about it proved I had found my true calling on Earth! Social entrepreneurship! I've always wanted to help people, and change the world, and now I had the chance.

Imiloa has opened up many opportunities and connections. Recently, I launched a new socially-driven project called *Mazlow*. It builds on the understanding of 'Oneness' that I embodied and was first presented to me at Imiloa. It is a social impact venture focused on meeting the basic needs of people and the planet through Oneness to create stronger communities and a better world for us all. *Maslow's hierarchy of needs'* postulates that if basic needs are not met, other life-enriching needs and desires are difficult to achieve. This can also be related to Earth. If we do not take care of our planet's basic needs, our planet cannot serve us to its fullest potential. Another aspect of the business is to help people self-actualize, by raising their consciousness and vibration. Once people are at this stage, we are naturally inclined to help others. *Mazlow* offers sustainable, recycled material, and eco-friendly fair trade products that when purchased, donate a basic item to someone in need. We also invest in systemic issues, beginning with hiring those who need work, for a more equal, balanced world.

This is exactly the work I dreamed of and the impact I have felt passionate about since I was a child.

Recently, I invested in a bioceramic domes company, becoming a shareholder and minority owner. *Geoship* offers sustainable, eco, affordable housing options, connecting us to nature and the geometry of the Earth. Furthermore, I'm involved in start-ups that focus on solutions for mental illness

and conservation. I am working with a company, *Zambezi*, to fight poaching, and protect wildlife and animals. My desire is to make my family's real estate company green and sustainable. While at Imiloa, we have started to offer transformative content to anyone who wants to better themselves from the comfort of their own home. Finally, I have just recently invested in two social impact movies, one of which is a documentary. When I started on my entrepreneur journey I didn't know that these specific start-ups and businesses would be in my life now, but I did know that if I followed what I most desired, I would make a difference to the world. And not to mention the like-minded connections I've now created.

In my life, I have witnessed many people unfulfilled with their jobs and the way they lived life. I often heard, "Gosh, I wish I did this," or "This isn't what I wanted." I didn't want to go down that path. I do sympathize with the regret, as I've realized in life, it's very difficult to get life 'right,' or even perfect it, and now that I think about it, I'm not even sure if this is possible. I haven't heard of anyone who has lived a life with no regret. But, I believe that we have the power to align our lives with what we truly desire. Now I truly feel like a superhero.

I have become a social entrepreneur who develops, funds, and implements solutions to social, cultural, and environmental issues. Motivated by my father's hard work, Richard Branson's adventurous spirit and business acumen, Nicola Tesla's creativity, and the Ignite experiences in my life, my life has come full circle. My goal is for the world to come as close to a version of heaven as possible, it's achievable, yes. We have to believe it.

I wanted to be a social entrepreneur, and I did that. I wanted to create and be part of ventures that bring the world together to solve humanities pressing issues, and I've done that. There were some challenges along the journey, and I did not let them phase me. I worked with many people in the past that ended up giving up on their dreams. I, however, committed to following my passions to make this world a better place.

If you deeply desire to be someone or do something, and you put in the hard work, you will accomplish what you set out to do. Your heart already knows what you are, and what you want. It'll all make sense. Just let it flow, tap into your curiosity, explore, and then, watch where you will be in three to five years. Ask yourself, what is it that you want to do? What do you want to give back? What do you like doing? Then follow your passion, work at what you love, give more than you recieve, and know that the world needs more superheroes just like you.

Ignite Action Steps

Manifest your reality. Opportunities will come your way. Be ready for them as they will disappear as quickly as they came.

Constantly keep learning. Also work on the intangibles: persistence, hard work, creativity, dedication.

Entrepreneurship takes energy — Fuel your mind, body, and soul.

The ride is not linear. Buckle up, you're in for an adventure. As a result, enjoy the journey, and celebrate the small wins.

Entrepreneurship isn't your entire life. There is more to life; family, relationships, and health.

What are you waiting for! Go get it. Entrepreneurs are afterall, go-getters.

Ravi Muti – Canada

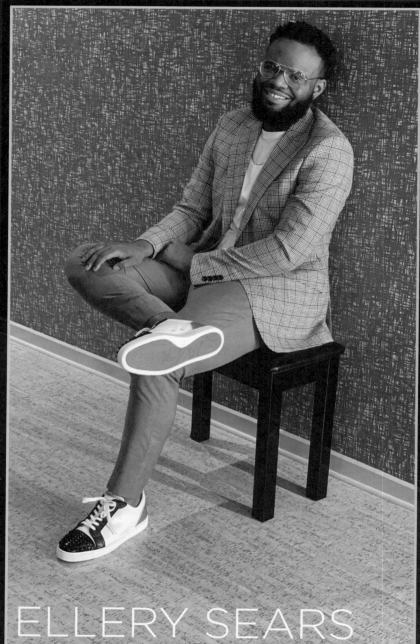

IGNITE THE ENTREPRENEUR

ELLERY SEARS

ELLERY SEARS

"If you are able to accomplish your big goals as the person that you are right now, without improving anything internally, then your goal is too small compared to the potential that is locked inside of you."

The purpose of this story is not to brag or boast of my personal accolades. It is to first, through transparency and vulnerability, highlight our similarities and to inspire you to take action on your big dreams and goals. One thing that science and theology agree upon is that we become what we think about. Decide what your dream life looks like and go after it. Think of your dream often and *become* who you need to become in order to make the dream a reality. Believe me when I say there is nothing particularly special about me or what I've done. We all have the same God-given powers to CREATE any experience in life that we desire.

WE CREATE OUR WORLD FROM WITHIN

I grew up in a suburb of Cleveland, Ohio, a unique city established right on the banks of Lake Erie, where you could potentially experience weather from all four seasons in a single day. The model of success I grew up idolizing was: find a reputable company with good benefits where I could work for about 30 years, get married, have kids, find 'stability,' and retire. Starting a business wasn't even in the cards. I grew up hearing the glory stories of my grandfather retiring from Ford Motor Company™ with full benefits and a healthy retirement account, and my grandmother too, retiring from the United States Postal

Service® with her pension. It meant they could now spend their time doing things they loved. My mother is on a similar trajectory and has been working for the government since I was a toddler. With these examples of success as part of my paradigm, this is what I began to pursue.

In my early 20s, I received a job offer from an up-and-coming alarm company after working several frivolous jobs and dropping out of college. Once I got started, I fell completely in love with the security alarm industry. I wanted to make this my career and decided to overcommit, picking up extra shifts and sharpening my skills to become one of the best field technicians at the company.

I made it my business to develop my ability to generate additional revenue for the company thinking that if I were to become a profitable employee, I'd be too valuable to ever lose my job. Feeling committed to being successful, I quickly began to make a name for myself as the top revenue generating employee company-wide (out of 500 plus employees). I set records, broke my own records, was promoted, won awards, and cleared six figures as a technician who only was getting paid $16 an hour. Finally I was successful in my own mind. I had it all; the good job, the benefits, the stability, even a girlfriend who had given birth to my first daughter and was pregnant with our second daughter. She had a daughter of her own so that would make a total of three girls that I was responsible for. I was committed to the company and being the provider for my family, and worked 80-hour weeks to make sure that we had everything we needed.

The company eventually went through a management shift which resulted in me getting a new supervisor. That supervisor was actually a peer of mine prior to his promotion, another name on the list of technicians aspiring to put up the numbers that I did. The supervisors were salaried so I didn't go for the promotion because I was making twice as much as a tech with less responsibility. I was comfortable… too comfortable. I didn't realize that my supervisor was jealous of my income and that he'd ultimately find a backhanded way to get me terminated. I was totally crushed by his actions. My sadness turned to spite which eventually would turn into anger and resentment. Combining those emotions with the intense apprehension I felt regarding my duty to provide, I realized that I needed to stop leaving the fate of my family under the control of others.

I decided to start my own security alarm company and compete against my former employer. In my mind, at least if I was the boss I could never be fired again. I was resolute and my company, Angelic Smart Homes, was born. I used my experience and began to build a company by knocking on doors with my partner and doing research on the internet about how to run a successful business. We began operations in 2015 and went through every entrepreneurial challenge imaginable, from hiring the wrong employees, trusting shady sales people, cleaning house, rehiring, filing taxes, repaying charge-backs, and probably a dozen other things that I am failing to mention. We almost went out of business a few times (more often than we would have liked) but managed to buckle down and save the company each time.

I persisted through these ups and downs for years. Alongside running the business, my girlfriend and I decided to elope and get married. It was a semi-rushed decision due to us being heavily involved in ministry and "shacking up" being frowned upon in the Christian community. Now I was locked into two committed relationships that I had very little experience with, a new business, and a marriage. As you can imagine, when things were good, they were great, but when they were not good, you had a perfect recipe for rough circumstances with either relationship.

Our marriage wasn't all sunshine and rainbows. We did our best to raise our children and cohabitate and had lots of great moments. But as with any marriage, we had our share of negative experiences as well. Without a stable foundation, these negative experiences eventually began to outweigh the good and we separated just before our four-year anniversary. 'Off and on' had been the nature of our relationship since it started. We had been repeating this cycle of good times, bad times, separation, and reconciliation for as long as I could remember. This time was different though. This was the first separation since we were married. I had moved out but only for two months because we ended up making up after New Year's, and I moved back home with her and the kids to give the marriage another shot.

That was in January of 2020, which was an interesting year to say the least. My wife and I attempted to force our marriage to work even though a lot of our deal breakers had been violated on both sides. Meanwhile, my business took a plunge due to the pandemic. When you mix financial issues with an unstable marriage you have the components for an almost unavoidable storm. In June, an argument we'd been having came to a head one Friday evening after being out for dinner. The meal had been my way of attempting to reconcile after not speaking and sleeping in separate rooms for a week.

When we got home we all went our separate ways. The children took over the family room and turned on their favorite Netflix™ shows while we prepared to go up to our bedroom to finish our leftovers and spend time together. While we were in the kitchen, my wife began to, out of literally nowhere, start saying some pretty terrible things to me which escalated into an argument in my office. The argument got to a point where she became even more verbally and physically aggressive and began to assault me and destroy my office. In one furious sweeping motion, she scattered everything that was on top of my desk across the room. The crashing of the miscellaneous items, including a printer, computers, monitors, and about a hundred other things created quite a ruckus. She then flipped my desk over and rushed at me with flailing arms determined to hit and scratch me in the face. I attempted to restrain her and calm her down, imagining the alcohol had gotten the best of her as she was completely out of control and not herself. I wrapped my arms around her to try to avoid being hit. My goal was to simply hug her to protect myself from bodily harm. The kids heard the yelling and tussling and eventually we stopped and she told me that she was taking the kids to her mother's house. She couldn't find her car keys so she took our three daughters and left the house walking. I stayed behind.

The next thing I knew there were three police officers at my front door. The tallest one said, "We saw your wife and kids walking alone at night so we took them to the station." Bewildered, I heard them say, "We're going to take you to jail."

"I haven't even committed any crimes," I explained, determined to express my innocence. Unfortunately, I knew enough about these situations to know that the man is usually the one to go to jail even if the woman is the aggressor and he is innocent. I learned this the hard way and was hauled off to spend my first night ever in jail.

After what seemed to be hours of going through the booking procedures; getting my mugshot taken, getting fingerprinted, and having my personal items confiscated, I was finally escorted to my accommodations for the evening. I remember that night like it was yesterday. Some of the many thoughts running through my mind as I lay in the eight-by-eight foot concrete cell, on a two-inch thick plastic mattress, atop of a solid brick frame was: *This is one of the most uncomfortable beds I have ever slept on in my life. My freedom has been stripped away from me, and this discomfort is the tip of the unpleasant iceberg. It's about 3 AM and I'm lying face up under a blanket that feels like it is made of cardboard or some type of paperlike material. It is completely ineffective and I am freezing. I am still in shock as to how I ended up here in the first place.*"

As I lay here physically and mentally exhausted, I was filled with so many emotions of defeat. I felt like a complete and utter failure. "Why am I failing?" I thought to myself. "Why does everything I commit myself to… fail?" I felt like I had failed my family because I couldn't keep my good job. I failed my church because my marriage was toxic. I began to allow these negative feelings and thoughts to consume me.

Then something in me awakened. I heard a voice — my own voice. It asked me, "Will you let these moments define your entire life?" I continued to lay there in silence. A few seconds went by. I was in so much pain, internally and externally. Then I had an epiphany. "No," I thought in response to the voice. "F**k no! This won't define me." I summoned all the strength I had left to leave the bed and buzzed the intercom for the guard, asking for some paper and a pen. The guard complied and gave me paper and a tube of ink to write with. I sat up and began writing furiously starting my paragraph with, "I am so happy now." Then I started to describe my ideal life in vivid detail. I was resolute that I wouldn't be able to work things out with my wife, so part of the description I wrote was, "that I have an amicable divorce with shared 50/50 parenting of my kids." Also among the many details on that sheet of paper were "successful businesses," "living in a beautiful downtown apartment," and "author." I was so emotional when I was writing that I spent the next day writing and refining this "perfect life."

I left jail on Sunday morning and went to stay with my mother. She gave me back my old bedroom from my childhood. It was exactly the same, except she had been using it for storage so there wasn't much space. I was grateful for the bed, but I felt so confined that I knew I needed to get away. I booked a flight to Las Vegas, and while I was there I kept noticing advertisements for something I never experienced before: skydiving. I decided to go for it. Next thing I knew, I found myself 15,000 feet in the air sitting on the edge of an open aircraft staring certain death in the face.

I hadn't lost the desire to live. On the contrary, I had the desire to create *more* in my life. Until that very moment, I lived my life in pursuit of a picture of success that was painted for me by everyone in my life… except myself. I was ready for this. I had done all the research, looking up skydiving fatality rates and paying close attention during the pre-takeoff training video. There was no way I was backing out. Seconds later, I was free-falling through the sky at 120 miles an hour, screaming at the top of my lungs.

When I first hit the open sky, it felt similar to jumping into a cool swimming pool on a hot day. It gave me a sense of calmness. After 45 seconds of free-falling, the parachute released, and I was floating in the sky. I had never experienced more peace in my life. I could see miles of God's beautiful world. "I'm free," I thought. It was so quiet. As I hovered above all of creation, I looked up and saw the plane I had just jumped from. To me, it symbolized my old life, flying off into the distance. I was ready to move forward; I vowed I'd never look back after this liberating experience. We came in for a landing, and I made a promise to myself: *"Today I am reborn. Today I release failed relationships, feelings of inadequacy, and of not living my life on my terms."*

I returned to Cleveland determined to make a complete shift. I had been studying the free material of a few authorities in the personal development industry and made the decision to go deeper and join a coaching program. I was being taught about how the results we see in our external world are a reflection of our internal furnishings; such as our mindset, our self-image, and our habitual behaviors. I learned how to align these things with my aspirations and once that happened, everything changed. I seemingly began to 'attract' a multitude of the right people, ideas, and resources into my life that were necessary to progress me toward my goals and vision.

Three months went by and I had been more focused than ever. I made a habit of writing my goals and describing my dream life every single day at the advice of one of my mentors. One particular morning, during my normal routine, I was writing my dream life for the hundredth time. It was a more refined version of what I composed in the jail cell with most of the same desires. As I was writing, I abruptly had to stop mid-sentence. Tears began running down my cheeks as I realized something incredible had happened. I looked over at my two daughters who were sound asleep next to me and realized this would be their first weekend with me due to the 50/50 shared parenting agreement that was now in effect. I looked out the window at the beautiful downtown Cleveland skyline from my spacious apartment on the 27th floor. My business had bounced back from the pandemic and I even started a couple other businesses which were equally successful. I also was in the process of writing my first book. Everything that I decided to go after on that paper, I had manifested in my life. I realized that by understanding the power of the mind, and shifting how we think, we are capable of accomplishing anything! The perfect life that I imagined internally had manifested into reality. I was so grateful.

Reader, I encourage you to make a decision. Do not delay. Do not procrastinate. Make a decision to seize the biggest goals, dreams, and desires of your heart. The circumstances of your past have no bearing on your potential in the future. It does not matter, even if you have abandoned most of your aspirations until this very moment. A decision is all you need. Decision is the catalyst to progression. Once the decision has been made, COMMIT to it. Commit to becoming who you need to become to accomplish what you want to accomplish. Remember, if you are able to accomplish your big goals, as the person that you are right now, without improving anything internally, then your goal is too small compared to the potential that is locked inside of you.

IGNITE ACTION STEPS

1. Using your imagination, create a picture in your mind of the life you desire to live without limitation.

2. List three to six 'must do' action steps each day and commit to completing these tasks no matter what. If you miss one or two, simply use them as the first to-dos for tomorrow. A reliable accountability partner is a great resource to have as well.

3. Write your dream life out in present tense, two times a day, and read it out loud. Continue progressing toward your goal until it is a reality. You will attract everything you need into your life to make your dream come true. I promise.

Ellery Sears – United States of America
Speaker, Author, Success Coach, Mindset Mentor, CEO of Angelic Smart Homes, Angelic Solar, & Ellery Sears, LLC
https://www.ellerydoesitall.com
www.angelicsmarthomes.com
www.angelicsolar.com
@ellerysears
@ellerysearsofficial

STEVE NEALE

"Having personal power means you start self-leadership
and take ownership of your life."

Your beliefs define your reality. After reading my story, I hope you step into your personal power and create the beliefs that will generate abundance for you in all areas of your life. Realizing you are not your thoughts, feelings, or actions is the first step to changing them. And, when you change the way you think, feel, and behave, you become the creator of your own life and will always feel powerful.

YOUR BELIEFS CREATE YOUR REALITY

I was afraid to go to the supermarket. I was too scared to leave my home. I lay on my safe haven, my sofa, day after day. I was ready to give up. As far as I was concerned — I was in hell on earth. You see, anxiety had taken over me. It had hijacked my mind and body. But there was one small thing that kept me going — one small ray of light in a dark, dark place. A *belief.* A simple belief that this was going to be the biggest learning opportunity of my life.

There I was, a 48-year-old successful entrepreneur with a dream life. Freedom to work when I wanted. A job I loved. Three houses, including a dream house with panoramic views overlooking the endless and free expanse of the Atlantic ocean. I was looking for the perfect spot for house number four in an exotic location in the sun. I was traveling and adventuring for six months of the year. I had helped more than 40,000 people in more than 40 countries achieve greater abundance and happiness in their lives. I had changed an education system so all schools in Lithuania now integrated my emotional and social intelligence training into their weekly lessons. I had a partnership deal with the United Nations, helping to spread my online learning program around the globe.

Then I crashed. And, it was almost overnight. I remember feeling abdominal pains. More than the pain, it was a gut-wrenching tightness of uncontrollable angst and within 24 hours I had convinced myself I was going to die. Adrenaline was pumping. I felt as if I was self imploding. Obsessive negative thoughts that were completely foreign to me and my greatest friend, my imagination, had turned on me. An extreme anxiety reaction took over my mind and body. I couldn't sleep. I couldn't focus. I couldn't function in the "real" world anymore. Going to the local supermarket was suddenly terrifying. I was instantly housebound.

Looking back, I didn't see the flags that were waving. I had retreated to my holiday home in a small Cornish fishing village and had begun to isolate myself. I had stopped my busy lifestyle of classroom training, travel, and working from country to country. Fueled by the success of my online program, I had gone to a more virtual life. I withdrew from seeing my friends around Europe and spent day after day with online meetings and walking my dog. And that's how the crash sneaked up on me. Step by step, I had removed my busy lifestyle — I realized that my busy lifestyle was my way of avoiding some hard inner truths.

For me, success in terms of helping people and making money was always going to happen. My childhood belief that anything is possible made sure every day I saw opportunities and acted on them... my belief that I never wanted to have a 9-to-5 and be in a routine became my reality, steering me down an entrepreneurial road. Both beliefs formed from seeing too many people in my hometown seemingly unhappy with their work and lifestyle — already at the age of 10 I had decided this was never going to be me. It seems I was always destined to be an entrepreneur, first motivated by a fear of being trapped in something I didn't want and later fueled by the fun, openness, and rush of trying out something new that was a win-win. Helping other people live more fulfilled lives and the silent applause of money as the reward.

Then it started: the demolishing of all the years of work I had done to take me from feeling worthless to valuing myself and an apparently successful life. The negative self-talk was relentless. "You are a fake." "How can you teach others to be more emotionally intelligent when you are not?" This crash was *hard* when it hit. I battered myself endlessly. I endured over a year's worth of sleepless nights, extreme anxiety, and bouts of feeling like I wanted to give up.

Add to that a loss of appetite, low energy, and weight loss for which all medical tests drew a blank. Oh, and let's not forget the ruthless negative self-talk.

Yet, I found a way back.

My Hungarian dog Odi still needed his daily walks. He became my trusted protector. No coincidence as Odi means prosperous protector in Hungarian and I marvel at the role he has played in my life. I somehow managed to find the strength to take him to the woods and beach every day. The only place I felt safe was, in fact, in nature. After a year of walking in the woods with Odi, constantly feeling that my daily life was full of fear, anxiety, and had become my reality, this one walk was different. It was a dark, cold, and wet winter's day. I wanted out of this daily hell. The next moment, in an explosion of pure frustration, I started running. I had full winter gear on including my muddy walking boots and thick winter jacket, but these didn't stop me. I ran... and I ran... and I ran... And I realized that for many years, I had been running. No safe love. Wounds I had not healed. My work and success globally had helped me run away from my childhood trauma for years. Running was my way to slowly step back into the world. On the surface, I had a happy life and was a huge success. My subconscious brain had another view — this was the time for me to heal so that I could make a difference like never before.

The running gave me hope. The small kick of serotonin in my brain was enough to momentarily lift the storm clouds. Even if only a glimpse at first, I could see blue sky and I felt hope. My imagination, which for too long had focused on negative, destructive thoughts began to serve me once again. *Possibilities. New ideas. Opportunities.* A glimpse of that entrepreneurial spirit had returned.

With each squelching footstep that day in the woods, the path to my recovery became clearer. Healthy eating. Naturopathic doctors. Therapists. Amazing friends I had not been able to phone and share my suffering with. My supportive partner. They all played their unique role in helping me come out of my cocoon. A rebirth at the age of 50 — letting go of the past and slowly moving into a new level of consciousness and energy.

Three years after that wintery walk in the woods, I am still running every day. Running has played a small but significant part in this rebirth process alongside other healing modalities. I do it for both the physical and the mental benefits that it gives. Together with therapy, yoga, and lots of new and healthier habits, it's key for my health, my fitness, and my vitality. The authenticity and freedom that comes from being open about my truth as well as sharing my vulnerabilities is huge. And I'm teaching again. Around the globe. Trips to California, Estonia, Denmark, Finland, and UAE all in recent times. Once again helping individuals and organizations transform themselves and become more emotionally, socially, and spiritually intelligent. My love of people and adventure and different cultures is back. But not like before. Now, it's with renewed energy and wisdom and I'm resonating from a much more authentic place. I'm no longer afraid to share my truth. My vulnerabilities and my story. This renewed openness and honesty brings more and more valuable connections, opportunities, and love into my life.

What of that simple belief I had? The one about the crash being my biggest learning opportunity so far? Well, it became my reality. This was the biggest learning opportunity of my life. I am back. Loving life. New global projects. Stronger and wiser and fitter than I have ever been. Ready to embrace the next 50 years without the need to control, fix, or micro-manage every small area of my life. I am so much freer. And the anxiety and negative thoughts? Well sure, they show up from time to time because I'm human, but now I don't run *away* from them. I know they return because my learning is not yet complete, and probably never will be. And that's okay. I believe it's the same for all of us to some degree, constantly learning is a significant plus of the human condition.

What you believe really does become your reality. If you truly believe you deserve and are worthy of love, abundance, and financial freedom, the Universe will resonate with you and give you opportunities to make that a reality. When your senses take in information (you see, hear, feel, smell, taste, or touch), your subconscious beliefs 'filter' that information and only allow a small amount of it to enter your conscious awareness. You notice what you believe to be true in this world, and that becomes your reality.

I, just like all of us, am a human data projector of my internal thoughts, feelings, and beliefs. My experience of reality is a mirror of what I think, feel, and believe inside. For example, I love dogs, but when I was overpowered by anxiety, Odi's barking would challenge me beyond good reason. I'd think things like, "Why is he so irritating, I don't need this stress." When I am in a calm place, that same barking triggers thoughts like, "He's so funny, barking at a plant. I am so glad I have a dog with so much character."

If I believed this world is an unfair place, full of suffering, sadness, and injustice, and, if I believed I would l never be happy, never find the love I only dream of and never create financial freedom and abundance — guess what? This will become my reality. Your subconscious belief filter will only allow you to become consciously aware of things that are consistent with these beliefs.

And the more you 'see' this evidence, the more these negative beliefs become even stronger.

Beliefs are just neuronal pathways in your brain. They have developed because of the experiences you have had until now in your life. They can all be updated and reprogrammed to provide your foundation to a happier more successful life with less suffering and more fulfillment. This is pure science and the thousands of people I have helped over the years, including myself, are living evidence of this.

From everything I have learned, my key messages are... firstly, don't be afraid if you have challenges. They come to teach and give an opportunity to grow. Secondly, know that you can create the life you dream of. Your dreams can become your reality, but first you've got to believe it and believe you are worth it!

As I see it, the key elements to a happy life are:
- Healthy self-belief.
- Healing from and accepting your negative past experiences.
- Allowing yourself to be vulnerable and accepting yourself fully.
- Defining what true success means for you and creating purposeful goals in line with your core values and healthy beliefs.
- Learning to let go of control.

First up, I had to learn to love and accept myself. Many of us didn't get the ideal gift of unconditional love as a child, and emerged from childhood believing we are not enough. I can assure you that you *are* enough. A daily practice of learning to accept and love myself proved to be a vital foundation of my happy life. Don't be afraid if you have periods of worry, sadness, or anger in your life. You are human, and your subconscious beliefs are triggering emotional states that are connected to negative past experiences. That's okay. The emotion needs to come out. It's not bad — it's honest, raw, and, well, just human.

It's okay to share your worries, concerns, and negative feelings with others. It's okay to be vulnerable at times. True friends will support you and not judge you. And others who don't accept your vulnerabilities? Well, do you really want them in your life?

Once you have healthy self-belief as a foundation, you are free to go make a difference in this world. Connect with something that you believe is important. More than that. Something that makes your heart sing. Something you want to jump out of bed for every morning. Then go do it, live it, and experience it with all your heart! Enjoying and embracing every moment and experience on the way. Including the challenges and setbacks. They are *always* learning opportunities there to help you grow.

Strive to live life as a gardener, not a carpenter. You see, carpenters of life try to produce the perfect chair. They know how it should look. They know how to make it. And they strive to get their life to fit that perfect chair. But life is not this way. Life is unpredictable. It surprises us and creates twists and turns we could not imagine. A gardener of life realizes this and knows that they need to let go of control in many situations. Sure, it's important to create a healthy environment by building nutrient-rich soil foundations and managing the weeds (negative beliefs) before they take over and kill your favorite flowers. So much of the garden of life is unpredictable. You don't know if the daffodils will bloom in March or April. You don't know if the weather will always be kind to your garden. And that's okay. Letting go of the need to force a life of happiness by micro-managing all the small details is in itself an important step to a happier life.

I was forced to let go of control when anxiety took over. I had to make changes. I needed to let go of being a control freak. Many people may have experienced their first taste of this when facing a serious illness or living through a global pandemic. My anxiety-crash forced me to go within and stop running away from my past. In accepting this and facing up to my fears, I found renewed energy, freedom, and wisdom. I learned to love myself despite my insecurities. I choose to accept myself for not always being strong and positive. I forgive myself for actions I have made and choices I have taken. I learned to embrace each day with a sense of gratitude and acceptance. I decided to love myself at a deeper level. And, I awakened to gratitude, compassion, love, and kindness, that are the core ingredients of a happy life, for yourself and then for others.

I believe that everyone in this world has the right to live a happy and fulfilled life. Everyone has a right to be treated with respect. This is your birthright. This is what you deserve. If you believe it too, your life will change in ways that you maybe can't even imagine. Start with yourself and love yourself — the good, the bad, and the ugly! And then connect with a purposeful cause based on virtuous goals — goals that benefit your mental, emotional, physical, and spiritual energy, and goals that also benefit others and the planet we share.

Your beliefs become your reality. Your life. Realizing you are not your thoughts, feelings, or actions is the first step to changing them. When you change the way you think, feel, and behave, you will never again feel powerless. You will become the self-leader and personal-creator of your own life.

Ignite Action Steps

Challenging your beliefs

Write a list of your good and bad habits. For each habit, write down the underlying belief connected to it (it may take a little time to dig deeper and identify the belief). For example:

Good habit: I start each day with a green smoothie.

Underlying belief: A healthy body means a healthy mind.

Bad habit: I avoid speaking up in meetings.

Underlying beliefs: Others are more intelligent than me. My ideas are probably silly.

For each of the beliefs, think of other examples of how they may be affecting your life in either good or bad ways. Make a list of the beliefs you would like to change. For each belief, write down the opposite, positive belief statement that would serve you better. Imagine the positive habits and outcomes you will get from these new beliefs. Try to be specific in your images. Visualize the details of how you can carry out these new habits. Close your eyes and identify how you feel with these new habits in your life.

Next, answer these questions…

- *What were the old bad habits and beliefs? Why were they not serving you?*
- *What are the new beliefs and habits, and how are they serving you?*
- *What benefits does having these new beliefs and habits bring to you and others?*
- *What are the costs to you and others of not developing these new beliefs and habits?*
- *What steps will you take to make these new beliefs and habits your new reality?*
- *What could stop you from doing this?*
- *What will you do to make sure this does not stop you?*
- *Who and what do you need to support you in creating this new reality?*
- *How do you feel now that you know you will succeed?*

Steve Neale – United Kingdom
Psychologist, Hypnotherapist, Coach,
Psychotherapist, International Author & Speaker,
Creator of the Limbic Performance System for Abundance
https://limbicperformancesystem.com

IGNITE THE ENTREPRENEUR

SALANA WHITEHEAD

SALANA WHITEHEAD

"Commit, Connect, Give, and Grow!"

So many of us don't know our purpose — we're just wandering. I have learned that you don't have to have everything together to reach your purpose. I hope you will realize you're building your story every day, if you just take notice of all that's going on around you. Everyday you are connecting with your purpose. May you never give up finding your WHY — it's usually right in front of you.

CONNECTING ADVERSITY AND PURPOSE

Have you ever felt like you were meant to do something great? I mean really, really, great. The kind of something great that leaves a legacy that is even more than you had planned for. That deep gut feeling has been inside me my entire life and the search for the answer has been an adventure. At 47 years young, I am finally seeing the beautiful mosaic that has been created through years of challenge and persistence. I am a solid believer that our life experiences, both great and horrible, are gifts given to us to connect with, share, and grow from.

Many of us are lucky enough to have parents and role models who told us when we were young that the world was ours to conquer and that ANYTHING was possible. I remember hearing this message loud and clear from just about everyone around me. Being an only child, I spent most of my time around other adults. I now understand that the older you are, the more you want to give counsel to the next generation. Although I remember hearing this consistent message, it somehow never really sank in. It's like I knew it had to be true, but the feeling was not there. I had spent most of my adult life not truly knowing what my purpose was or what my value was in this world.

I grew up with a strong desire to have approval and performance-based attention. This was great for academics, staying out of trouble, and keeping up with the status quo, but not for connecting with who I really was. My parents moved to a new state about every three years during my childhood until I finished high school. That adventurous upbringing gave me the gift of meeting new people and the skill of building new relationships quickly and I loved it. I was always on the search for connection, gathering groups of people together. I'm not sure if it is because I always wanted a large family growing up an only child, but I have always been drawn to bringing people together.

The earliest memory I have was in elementary school. Recess was my favorite time to socialize and play outside. I used to hang out with everyone, but one day I was cornered and asked to pick between friends by their skin color. I couldn't understand why there had to be any separation and remember going home that day frustrated. After talking it over with my Mom, she agreed that it didn't make sense and encouraged me to find a solution. The next day, I brought the two groups together and said I wasn't choosing between them because it was more fun to all play together. And it worked! We all made a decision to choose fun over separation. That is my first memory of showing people that we are better together than apart.

The downside to this upbringing was always having to say goodbye and not creating long-term deep relationships. Constantly changing locations meant also changing myself. Oftentimes I would just morph into what others wanted me to be to gain acceptance. It felt great to be included, but slowly I began learning that allowing others to make choices for me kept me further from my purpose. Trying to guess what each new person expected me to be was stressful. Even when I was able to figure out the path I should take, I never felt like I was actually in the driver's seat.

When I reached high school, the pressure to fit it was very high and the consequences of not being connected with my purpose began to appear. I chose a controlling and abusive boyfriend as my first real dating relationship; a person with whom I would eventually have three children. In hindsight I believe I was yet again allowing others to make my decisions. I am so thankful to God for the strength and courage he put inside me to leave that toxic relationship and create better opportunities for myself and my children. It was through that experience of being a bold, courageous, and resourceful single mother that I learned about faith, persistence, perseverance, giving, connecting, and growing. These tough and tearful years would give me the muscle and strength to face the even more difficult challenges ahead.

Life refines you through pressure and slowly turns you into the diamond that you were meant to be in the first place. The past five years have been another layer of challenge, frustration, and uncomfortable times, yet have provided the most clarity I have ever felt. In the fall of 2017, life was great and to most outsiders looking in, it would seem "set." I was remarried to a wonderful husband and our blended family of five children had all moved out of the house. I had a great corporate job with incredible benefits, and our goal of owning and reviving our local pizza and sports bar restaurant had been attained. Most would say that I had everything going for me but internally something was missing. I had no passion for what I was doing daily. It was an interesting time in my life when my kids left home — both a mix of excitement and reflection.

Along with this new freedom came fear and doubt, not knowing which direction to go. That same feeling that I had as a child was even stronger now; a belief that I was meant to do something great, but I didn't know where to begin. I found myself wavering back and forth between staying in my comfort zone and jumping into the unknown where my gut was telling me to go. Once I connected and started listening to that inner voice, it felt like torture to continue in a profession that I was not passionate about, and I knew that resigning from my comfortable corporate career was inevitable.

Then the winds shifted, and really stirred things up.

One fateful night in early October we lost our family home to the California wildfires, and that disruption started a series of events that would forever change my outlook on life and connect me with my true purpose. I will never forget the drive toward our neighborhood that night: the smoke-filled air, sirens blaring outside, and the shocked quiet in the car that came from knowing everything was already gone. It was hard to breathe, and our disbelief was just as much to blame as the smoke. We had no idea what we were supposed to do next, or how to move forward. All we knew was that life had just taken a major turn. I had sensed that my life's direction was meant to change, but I never thought it would come about like this.

When you lose everything, you appreciate everything.

Losing our family home opened up my eyes and gave me the opportunity to work through barriers that were preventing me from living as my full self. I saw and appreciated time as much more precious than I had ever before. I made a decision to listen to my heart and my gut, follow my inner peace, and not care what others' opinions were about me. Leaving the corporate world took several months of writing resignation letters and crushing them up before I had the courage to spread my wings, jump, and learn how to fly!

When opportunity appears, you have to act immediately. I've always known that I'm meant to bring people together. I truly believe we are all unique puzzle pieces that when connected make a beautiful piece of art. Turns out I wasn't the only one who thought that way.

Years ago, my bonus son, Clark, invented an incredible product solution that we thought was brilliant. He grew up outdoors on the lake and rivers and was frustrated with always floating away from his friends and family. He invented a puzzle-shaped interlocking floating inner tube that allowed you to connect and disconnect safely on the water. We watched him take this great product to market but lose interest in it a few years later. I loved his idea and wondered how far it could go if someone was to pursue it.

My husband and I already had set the precedent of taking businesses with potential and turning them into successes. Our restaurant was proof. With no restaurant experience, we applied courage, tenacity, and showed up daily with purpose. The success was fantastic and we had reached our goal of creating a fun and thriving restaurant where the community could come and connect with each other. We had worked so hard for seven years building that business. Taking it from failing to success was one of the most rewarding challenges I have been a part of. However, our five kids were finally out of the house, I was spreading my wings, and my husband was ready to travel. After we lost our home in the fires, we decided to retire.

After taking a year to enjoy traveling, I was itching to be a part of something bigger. Our initial plan was to partner with our son to reintroduce his creation, Fluzzle Tube™, to the market. It turned out that he was more interested in working on his next invention and encouraged us to go ahead and relaunch without him. Initially I was intimidated, not knowing much about watersports or bringing a product to market, but my gut reminded me that I also didn't know about being a single mother or how to run a restaurant either, but had managed to succeed at both through my tenacity, adaptability, and hard work. The Fluzzle Tube, which stands for 'Floating Puzzle,' was not only puzzle-shaped but also brought people together outside to have fun. This product had the power to connect people, and I knew this was meant to be my new passion.

I originally believed bringing this new and exciting product solution to market was going to be a fairly easy business, but boy was I wrong. We were coming off a great success of restoring a failing restaurant business and thought by applying the same principles we would have the same results. Although some of that is true, running a brick-and-mortar business with a team of 25 people is totally different than creating an e-commerce business with just two people! There was so much to learn about digital media, online sales, finance, and the retail market. The one thing I did have naturally was the ability to commit first and figure the rest out later.

Our first year in business, we made great improvements to our product and thought all we had to do was put them on Amazon™ and the sales would take care of themselves. That did not work! We only had $20K in sales and ended up having to send back all of our inventory from Amazon so we didn't incur huge storage fees. At that point I was really starting to wonder if we made the right decision to leave our comfortable life. It was not looking good, but I did not want to go back to the corporate world. I dug deep and called on that courage and grit that had gotten me through an abusive relationship, being a single mom, and losing our family home in a fire. I was still here, and there was a purpose to be lived out, so I doubled down on that strength and began investing in business education, expanding my mindset, giving more, and deepening relationships. There was clearly something I didn't know, but I was determined and committed to finding out what was missing. I applied persistence, solid and unwavering vision, and belief in the goal for our company.

When you are disrupting a market, so many people will think you are crazy and will try to discourage you. We had our share of doubters and others that told me I didn't know what I was getting myself into. But teachers will appear as students are ready to learn, and I was discovering new lessons all the time. For example, staying connected to your WHY is what keeps you focused and allows the negativity to bounce right off you. I learned this from the first mentor I was drawn to, Grant Cardone. Through his guidance I began writing gratitude, goals, intention statements, and wins twice a day and attending all the training courses and conferences I could find. I learned that this dedication and consistency were the keys to the success in our start-up. Having the discipline to stay on the path even when it's not comfortable is where the muscle is made. I attended a boot camp later where I first heard his new business partner, Brandon Dawson, sharing the early days in building his first start-up. Brandon became one of the most impactful mentors for me after that day.

Our second year into our business started right at the beginning of the Covid-19 pandemic. We had just moved the Amazon inventory to a new warehouse in Arizona. To save on expenses, our plan was to live in our motor home inside a portion of the warehouse while we hired a team of two and promoted our product to the world. This was a complete 180 degrees to how we had lived less than two years ago, and it was tough. I took all my showers at the local gym, and worked long days and nights building our business in one of the most run-down towns in the Arizona desert. This environment kept me hungry and motivated, striving for more. I knew it would be temporary and was a part of the sacrifice needed to launch us to where we wanted to go. Just as I was acclimating to my new living conditions, COVID hit. At that point I asked myself — is this a sign that we are not moving in the right direction? The day after I asked myself that, Brandon delivered his *Emergency Business Response Training*. I applied the lessons and took massive action. By mid-April, our sales were going through the roof. We ended the second year with close to a 2000 percent increase in revenue!

We are now entering our third year and have won multiple large retail chain pitch contests, landed nationwide retail contracts, and have sold to every state across the United States. More importantly, we are bringing people together outside to reconnect and have fun.

The beautiful part about this success is the WHY. The reason I left the comfort zone to live in an RV in a warehouse was because of the belief I have in my WHY. This incredible journey has removed all the distractions that the comforts of life give us and created a clarity that I am so thankful for. I now see everyday as a new opportunity to move in the direction of this purpose and cannot wait for what is in store. I have always known that my purpose is to connect people, and now I have found so many ways to do that. I do it through my product, I do it through sharing my story, and above all, I do it through always striving to help inspire others to connect with their purpose.

You, too, can connect with your purpose, your passion, and your why. Knowing this allows you to give it to other people and create your legacy. Once this connection is made, doors will open and your entire journey will make sense. What once felt like a puzzle will all start to fall into place. Commit, connect, give, grow, and you will find the path to your greatest success.

Ignite Action Steps

Commit — Embrace life's tough times. Instead of wishing them to be over, ask yourself what they are trying to give you that you will someday be able to give to others. Make a decision to believe that you are enough; capable and blessed with unique gifts. Recommit to yourself daily with positive affirmations.

Connect — Intentionally schedule time for yourself where you have no distractions and can hear your inner voice. All the answers you need are already inside you. Don't wait for life to cause a disruption. Use this time to fully connect, take inventory, write down what you are grateful for, what your massive goals are, and what legacy you want to leave. When you know 100 percent who you are, you will be able to fully connect with others.

Give — The law of reciprocity works. Write a list of people or events where you have been on the receiving end of something awesome. Remember that feeling — it feels great right? That feeling is gratitude, sometimes you may feel like you didn't deserve it and sometimes it may feel earned and appreciated. It is said to whom much is given, much is expected. We all have unique gifts inside of us and what good are gifts that aren't given? Everyday look for opportunities to share your gifts with others. The beautiful part about giving is it opens doors of gratitude and blessings multiply.

Grow — Most parents keep a growth chart to track how tall their kids get year after year. It's fun to remember how little they once were and how much they've changed. Measuring growth shouldn't stop once you've maxed out your physical height. You should measure your mental and spiritual growth. Write your time-specific HUGE goals down in the morning when you rise and right before you go to bed. It's important that your goals are *GIANT* to pull you out of the mundane day-to-day goals and stretch your belief in yourself. Next to these goals, list daily achievable targets. These daily wins remind you that you are winning and capable. Keep these plans in a journal so that you can go back and measure your progress. Knowing that you are growing and improving creates the momentum you need to push through the challenges that are part of climbing the mountain.

Salana Whitehead – United States of America
Co-Founder of Innovative Water Products & The Fluzzle Tube
www.fluzzletube.com
@fluzzletube

IGNITE THE ENTREPRENEUR

THERESA
ALFARO
DAYTNER

Theresa Alfaro Daytner

"Unstoppable! Remember, the fire in your belly is your Superpower!"

I am Unstoppable and so are you! No one wishes to encounter trauma, challenges, setbacks, or pain just to *test* our resiliency. On the journey of life, it's easy to get lost or take a detour, like I did. Remember the dreams you've always had. Believe in your uniqueness. Listen to the fire in your belly and let this propel you into Action.

Unstoppable: Re-Igniting the Fire in my Belly!

For some reason, I had always felt I was meant to do big, impactful things in the world. I grew up just outside of Washington, DC and, even as a child, knew how important that city down the road was to many around the globe. I knew big decisions that impacted so many lives were being made by important people in DC. I felt a certain kind of reverence for the Capital City that I didn't notice my peers having. In high school, I felt so bored in the classroom that I often took myself on "field trips." I would head to the Smithsonian Museum, inspecting every square inch of its hallowed halls. I would talk to everyone I met, indulging a fierce desire to interview everyone I encountered about what kind of work they did, how they got there, and what they were doing to improve the world. But there was also another curiosity deep inside that led me to cruise through the most expensive neighborhoods and dream that I would one day have that kind of wealth.

Despite being a student with poor grades, my parents had always believed in me. In fact, when I was 17, my mother gave me a little self-help paperback, *Seeds of Greatness,* by Denis Waitley. The messages in that book have stuck with me to this day; the most impactful one, a quote paraphrasing Viktor Frankl, "You choose your response," has influenced me more than I could have imagined when I first read it.

Even as young as 10 years old, I knew down to my bones that I would be a business leader and make big decisions that improved people's quality of life… and that I would make a LOT of money doing it. Yes, I always dreamed BIG! That's why, at 20 years old, not enrolled in college, married too young to an unsupportive partner, living in the agricultural breadbasket of Lincoln, Nebraska, and working full-time for minimum wage at a hospital cafeteria… I stopped in my tracks, right in the middle of the kitchen halfway between the sink and the cooler, my hairnet on my head as I carried soup to the serving area. I don't know why it happened at that precise moment, but I'll never forget where I was standing and what was happening around me. It was prep time, not mealtime, so the place was rather quiet. Celia, an older woman who had escaped communist Cuba and landed here as a refugee, was nearby. I could see her profile as she washed vegetables in the sink. Mrs. Smith, the lead dietitian, was in her office behind me doing paperwork. Betsy, who was a little older than me and had worked there several years, was chopping apples for a Waldorf salad and I could hear the clack, clack, clack of her sharp chef's knife on the cutting board. I remember the pungent scents of onion and garlic filling the air from that day's ingredients, yet knowing the meals would still all be a little bland, despite the delicious smells.

I don't know how long I just stood there, but THIS happened: I remember thinking, "Theresa, is this the life you have always dreamed of? Is this who you thought you'd become? Where did YOU go? Do you remember your dreams of becoming an entrepreneur and using that success to make lots of money, living a dream life full of adventure and travel, and having a positive impact on many people?"

The thought was painful. It was like when you sit on your foot and you don't realize you've gone numb. It hurt to wake up and realize where I was at that moment, like I'd just been slapped back into reality by a rush of uncomfortable prickling pins and needles. But, it was just the wake-up call I needed. In that moment, I remembered that young girl with the big dreams and I charged forward and never looked back. That fire in the belly burned so strong, I thought I smelled burnt flesh! It wasn't all sunshine and rainbows, but I decided it was time to go back to the east coast, enroll in school, and create the life I had always envisioned.

For a 20-year-old, it's not like I had completely failed, but it felt like I had. I was proud of my work ethic and having always had a job. This was the definition of success for me. I had no desire to end up living in a housing development with a house full of kids and no job. To me, that would be the ultimate failure. And yet, in that moment in the cafeteria kitchen, I *knew* there was something more just waiting for me to grab it. I remembered the feeling of *knowing* that I was meant for something bigger, something exceptional.

I didn't know what that was going to look like, I just had to prepare myself. I had to put myself in a place of most potential.

So, trust me, when that moment hit me like a lightning bolt in that hospital cafeteria kitchen, I was so excited and fired up to remember my dreams! There was a fire in my belly and I was going to get into action before it went out!

I knew I wanted to be an entrepreneur, but I didn't have a specific product or service in mind, so I decided I was going to study accounting and learn the language of business, to prepare myself. I saw accounting as a marketable skill set and liked the idea of working for a CPA firm after college. I'd have access to a variety of business owners, cultures, and business models. In later years, I would come to call that my "scratch and sniff" years. Friends and family who knew me well believed I was foolish to think that I could be an accountant. They were even more concerned when I shared that I didn't want to actually be an accountant, I just wanted to learn the language of business and money and that seemed like a great place to start! I knew where they were coming from and listened to their logic and their reasons why it didn't make sense for me to study accounting. I had barely graduated high school due to missing so many days scratching my curiosity itch with "field trips." I don't have much energy for things that aren't fun and interesting and although I haven't been officially diagnosed, I've known I have ADHD since first grade, when everyone else in the classroom finished their work and I had to stay during lunch to complete my assignments. But in this new journey, the fire in my belly made me unstoppable.

This is not a story where I became Valedictorian, or even rich overnight! It was hard! I had stayed in that unsupportive marriage, worked part-time at numerous jobs through college, did two full-time internships, had a baby two weeks after my Junior year college finals, and finally graduated with a two-point-something-low GPA at 25 years old with a one-year-old in tow.

During that last year of college with my baby on my hip, I convinced my husband that we could start a residential roofing company. He was a great technician and knew what he was doing so I told him, "You just do what you do and I'll build a business around the skill." Leveraging the skill sets of others would become a theme in my life, as my third business, commercial construction and project management, was the same. The roofing company was a great starter business model. Get the work. Do the work. Collect the money. Rinse. Repeat. I would strategically pick a target market and apply my skills to decrease risks, increase profits, and provide a steady line of continuous referral business.

By 26, I left the husband and the roofing company. I took the baby and the accounting degree, but it was not smooth sailing yet. Two weeks into reveling in my newly rediscovered energy as a single, I completely shredded my knee playing soccer one day with friends. With a broken knee and a toddler, I had to bail on the CPA firm and so I moved on to a steady nine-to-five paycheck job.

I accepted the new job from my hospital bed on a Friday and made my doctor discharge me so I could start my new job on Monday. On day two, I met the man who would become my second husband, father of four more of my children, and my business partner. He would be the most supportive cheerleader I could have ever hoped for or felt I deserved.

Riding the wave of energy that comes with a shiny new, supportive relationship, I sat for that CPA exam and PASSED the FIRST TIME!! I stopped arguing with people who said, "Oh, you must've been an A student all these years." I believe in timing and riding those waves up! I was a newly minted CPA and decided to build a solo accounting and tax business. Working for myself was night and day compared to working for someone else, for sure!

Ten years later, I gave birth to twins. I decided to close my practice to dedicate my energy to raising them, my teenage daughter, my stepdaughter, and our 5- and 3-year-old daughters. I was also dedicated to caring for my parents who were both in poor health and living with us; Dad with prostate cancer and Mom with progessive MS. Life was really busy and I felt I had lost track of that dream again. I remember having a flashback to the cafeteria moment, and recalling the thought that "if I ever end up living in a housing development with a house full of kids, I've failed." Yikes! That was my life now! Did that make me a failure? No! My definitions had changed. I had the same desire and urgency for impact, but I measured wealth differently.

I just knew there was more work to do, more places to go, something new that needed to be created. I wanted to build something positive and family friendly that would have a ripple effect on others. By the time my twins were

18 months old, and my husband was working at a job he hated to support all of us, I said, "Hey, you're such an awesome Project Manager, why don't you let me build a business around your skill set?"

The fire in my belly was back. I can. I *must*. Don't count me out yet!

We sat at the kitchen table and talked about risk and our non-negotiables. He was in his early 40s and hadn't had much of an appetite for becoming an entrepreneur, but realized that this may be his only window of opportunity to give it a go. More importantly, he knew about my entrepreneurial dreams and was happy to help me in any way he could. We sat there, in between feeding and changing and entertaining our kids, and reasoned that both of us were employable. He trusted me to manage our money and sound the alarm if we were in danger of losing the roof over our heads or the food on the table. The backup plan was for one of us to abandon the business and get a paycheck. It felt like a rational and logical handshake deal.

Two years after that kitchen table talk, my father died. I wasn't prepared for how draining mourning the loss of my father would be and it felt like my tears had put out the fire in my belly. I just did not have the energy to put into scaling a business.

I needed a break, so I took our four youngest children to Idaho for a month of fresh air, rodeos, white water rafting, and various other adventures at "Uncle Woody's Ranch," my brother's house. It's amazing what a little fresh air, adventure, and change of scenery can do for my energy!

My brother still talks about how fascinating it was to witness my energy process in that month. It took the first week there to slow down my pace and just settle into "country time." The second week, I took the kids exploring all kinds of ghost towns, back roads, local diners, swimming holes… and it was just amazing. By week three, I was looking for real estate and prepared to tell my husband to pack everything up and "head West, young man!"

And in week four? That familiar unstoppable fire in the belly Ignited yet again! This time, though, it felt like someone had poured rocket fuel on the fire!

I came home with the kids and we grew to become a $20M business, earning awards and recognition, finding new opportunities, building new relationships, and gaining media exposure. I finally felt that we could stash money away for retirement, take our family on nice vacations, put all of our kids through college, buy reliable new cars, AND positively impact lots of people by being an awesome employer.

There was so much I loved about that ride. So much. Validation, Achievement, Recognition, Financial Reward, Positive Impact, and fun meetings with

people like President Obama, Tyra Banks, Warren Buffet, Arianna Huffington…
and some of the most amazing peer entrepreneurs on the planet who I still
cherish in my life.

All that, and yet, there was still something missing… something left for
me to contribute. I wanted to help others to remember their dreams and
help make them UNSTOPPABLE, too! It was time to stop doing and start
coaching others. I wound down the construction company after 13 years
to help others to focus their energy on creating the amazing life of their
dreams, like I have.

I am often reminded of the words by Viktor Frankl, a holocaust survivor,
and his experience of having had everything he held dear taken from him,
including his family, his career, his belief in humankind, and his *dignity*. I
interpret his words as, "No matter what happens to you, you still are responsible for choosing how you respond. That is the one thing no one can take
from you, ever."

I'm excited about this chapter in my entrepreneurial journey as a Coach. I
get to leverage all my years of experience in business, as a working parent, as
a caregiver to my parents, helping others lead the high-quality and intentional
life of their dreams. I have such compassion now for myself and that young
girl who stood in that hospital cafeteria, wondering if she'd ever amount to
anything.

I carry this compassion over to my work. I create a safe place where
people trust me with their successes, failures, doubts, and dreams. People
judge themselves so harshly and just need someone to listen and clear the
space for them to remember and rediscover who they really are so they can
start building the path to who they're meant to be and fill their lives with
beauty, love, and joy.

I have learned to be unstoppable. Success comes when you take action.
Overnight success is actually someone who has plugged away at it for over
20 years. On the journey of life, it's easy to get lost or take a detour, like I did.
Remember the dreams you've always had and know that they are just waiting
for you to claim them. Believe in your uniqueness. Listen to the fire in your
belly and let it propel you forward. Know that you are unstoppable! Remember,
that the fire in your belly *is* your Superpower!

IGNITE ACTION STEPS

Believe in your uniqueness. Think back to your youth and remember the dreams you had. What issues were you passionate about as a teen? What excited you as a child?

Open your eyes. What choices and actions can you start taking responsibility for? Is it a need to spend more time with your loved ones? A need to take better care of your health? Are you creating a supportive work environment for yourself that exudes positivity?

Listen to the fire in your belly and let this propel you into action!

Theresa Alfaro Daytner – United States of America
Executive Coach
www.tadcurious.com

IGNITE THE ENTREPRENEUR

JUDY (J.) WINSLOW

JUDY (J.) WINSLOW

"Fitting in is not a recipe for success."

My intention is to move you to look for your own delicious recipe. This magical intersection merges our definition of success and its expression. It's where you will find the path, the words, and even the business, services, and products that will not only inspire you, but motivate you to do so for the good of humanity. In doing so, you can rest assured you will leave a legacy that reverberates throughout the cosmos. In this place, you are able to live joyfully, resting in the knowing that WHO you are is perfectly perfect for a time such as this.

YOU HAVE EVERYTHING YOU NEED TO SUCCEED

There I was, a youngish 30-year-old woman, way up in a New York City skyscraper, sitting in a meeting with people I never imagined I'd meet. Each one was someone I found to be inspiring, intelligent, accomplished — rockstars in their own right. Looking around the table at these dynamic professional women, I was kind of thrown. I wondered… how can this be? How did I end up here?

It felt wildly ironic that we were there (my biz partner and I) to share with them the value of standing out and the positive impact that having this perspective would have on their marketing results. In that moment, I could feel all the pain of my past clicking into place like pieces in a puzzle in a way I had never ever visualized. Hold on, I'm jumping ahead of myself. Let's go back a couple of decades to see the twists and turns of the unlikely path that brought me there.

Like some of you reading now, I'm a rather sensitive soul. I was the kid who didn't fit in. You know, the typical last-to-be-picked-to-be-on-any-team kid who wasn't invited to parties and sat home on a Saturday night watching TV while my parents went out more than I did. I was someone on the fringe wanting to be 'seen' and be 'popular.'

Knowing you're valued — the sense of belonging — begins at home. For myself, growing up in an environment that was filled with anger, arguing, and toxic energy was more than detrimental. My parents were such micromanagers that my ability to speak for myself or make decisions about my life was stifled, making it truly challenging to access my own true desires. Only years later would I understand the effects of this pattern and control on my psyche.

Life was miserable and I had no idea why. It looked normal and nice from the outside, yet all I knew was that being at home was awful. Nothing I did was 'right.' Humans are wired to be pleasers, but that strategy wasn't working for me. Fitting in with my family wasn't going very well. It was crazy-making and, by the age of 11, my biggest, most compelling wish was to die. To check out. I'd spend hours hidden away in my mom's car crying big buckets of tears. Home is supposed to be safe. Mine wasn't.

School wasn't much better. If anything, it amplified my feelings of being a weirdo. Everything school-related seemed to be a struggle. In first grade, I was denigrated at the hands of a teacher, something which sticks with me a bit today. Perhaps those were little things, yet to me, they were a monster spotlight on my oddities and I craved relief from my pain. I often fantasized about that perfect moment when our car would veer off the road and crash into a guardrail, ending it all. I yearned for teachers to lift me up, not suffocate my soul. No one was helping me to embrace my special qualities, see my uniqueness, and appreciate the truth that was me.

When it was time for college, I applied only to get away from home. For a long time, I had aspired to be a hippie. I was hungry for an environment of mutual trust, love, and respect. Does that sound crazy? To me, it was totally sane. After all, hippies do good. Spread love. Disdain money. They live in a world of their own creation. I was *all-in* to this concept; the perfect credo for me as one who was yearning for something very different than my upbringing. That felt like a solution to the madness.

Little did I know that university would afford me the biggest changes to my world, none of which I had ever anticipated. First, though, I had to drop out a couple of times. Because? Because I didn't want to go to college! That didn't fit at all with my version of being a hippie… did self-respecting hippies go to college? According to me, Hell no.

I finally decided to apply to the University of Denver, in Colorado. I fell in love with its beauty. The crisp air and blue skies were mesmerizing. The campus was easy to navigate. The mountain views surrounding me were incredible. Another shy friend who was attending school there seemed to be blossoming and that gave me hope that I could also thrive there, find friends, and discover my way. All good indicators. Starting classes mid-year had its own challenges, not the least of which was the cold in snowy January. Packing up and heading to Colorado from New Jersey was scary. And exciting. And scary. So much was new, unknown, unplanned. Not at all like the little world that I was used to.

Something happened that first year. A switch was flipped that would begin to alter everything for me. Life was so very different, and as with many leaving home, was more of a gift than I realized at the time. That one year would lead me to: finding my voice, lifelong friendships, and my first husband — more on that in a bit — all life-altering, transformative, and hugely impactful.

But wait, there's more! I discovered my true path in life. Being on my own for the first time was liberating!!!!!!! Any fears I had dissipated almost immediately as I took my first deep breath of the cool mountain air. It cleared my head and lungs simultaneously. Suddenly I could hear my own voice, follow my own heart, play with my own desires, explore my own concepts. It was amazing!

This delighted my hippie soul. It seemed so idyllic. However, there was a glitch. My intention was to be a celebrated ceramicist, yet it turned out that my skill as a thrower-of-pots was not good. Okay, it was terrible. Awful in fact. The head of the department somehow felt I was faking my lack of ability. What?! Who would do that? Nope, I was actually bad at it. Couldn't seem to throw a pot to save my life. For hours I would sit at the potter's wheel and create lopsided alien objects. Not pots, not anything! No matter how many hours I spent trying, nothing seemed to work. It was quite pitiful.

Thankfully there was what seemed (in hindsight) a divine intervention. As a requirement, I had signed up for an introduction to design class, which turned out to be more like an awakening. An immediate epiphany! Design was THE most powerful force I could be involved with on this planet! WOW! I was finally more focused here than getting out of my toxic home environment or dying in a fiery car crash. That is how my 'making a difference' driver was awakened and set on the road to fully express my values through my work.

After all, everything is designed. Without shouting or pretending. From our waking moments until we go to sleep, all we encounter has been designed. The bed we sleep in. Our toothbrush. What we see out of our windows. How we work, travel, and dress. EVERYTHING has this underpinning. I was seeing that design influences our entire planet! For the first time, I could see beyond my present into a future of promise and joy as I lived with true purpose. I was on the precipice of these emerging concepts that would begin to unpack themselves.

Those discoveries began to be the critical foundation for my life's path and reminded me that we are here as unique creatures. We don't have a one-size-fits-all recipe for success. Many of us spend a lot of time mimicking others rather than finding our own way: a path that is easy, fun, and promising. (A stark contrast to those attempts at ceramics.) With this newfound feeling of ease, I could move forward in flow.

Flow is critical to success.
Flow is where we create with ease.
Flow is where we move toward life.

Moving with flow and purpose began to change my entire life experience. Over the next few decades, this would come up time and time again. This didn't mean I was no longer sad or lost or confused. Nor did it mean that I had suddenly found happiness. Oh no!

This was a process. A journey I'm still on. Back then it was a seesaw. Some days I was elated, hopeful, involved with my new 'art.' Other days I was dark, sad, scared, and felt trapped. Still the idea of death would seem viable. A good idea. How would I change that — and did I want to — were questions yet to be answered.

Another big event was meeting a guy with beautiful blue eyes. A guy who would become my husband. He was the first to reach out a hand to me; to truly see and listen. He liked me. And we laughed. Lots. We were together on and off for all of university. The summer before my senior year, the week before I turned 21, we got married. For a young spirit like myself, this wasn't my best idea.

Many years later, I realized that I had made it his job to bring 'happy' to me, which was so unfair of me. And (surprise!) it never happened, which caused bitter resentment, more fear, and deeper depression. No wonder that didn't end well! We split up and, because of a decline in the economy, my job designing packaging for an international brand was eliminated. It seemed time to leave Denver. I had to find a new direction.

Again, my internal guidance intervened. In short order I moved to New

York City — a place that I had sworn I would never live. Never! Yet in that moment, it made sense. After all, where else would there be plenty of work for a designer? NYC seemed to be the answer. My best friend lived there too, which helped, so off I went.

As planned, I arrived in NYC on New Year's Eve and immediately started making new connections. That first night at a party, a man mentioned a course he had taken — one that other friends had told me about and I had been skeptical of, but for some reason, this time, I heard the message. The Universe conspired to make it possible for me to attend the next session, and that was the next BIG game changer for me. One course over two weekends changed me forever. Literally. The 'life-lens' I looked through was altered, never to be quite so clouded again. During that course, somehow my desire to die was no longer a choice, an option, a thought. It vanished. It wasn't that I gave up the idea of it; rather that I chose to *live*.

My career took off, too. After many weeks of interviews, I found freelance work at *Woman's Day* magazine where eventually my boss became my business partner after I pitched her with a clear and determined vision. It was the beginning of an incredible chapter. We started with $500 and grew the business to over a million dollars in less than two years. During the 80s! It was the beginning of gathering proof — evidence, if you will — that not only was I more capable than I ever knew, but that my instincts gathered on the fringe (which I thought were so useless) were some of my most valuable assets.

In that meeting room in that New York City skyscraper, sitting with people I never imagined I'd meet, face-to-face with those I admired for their strength, passion, and leadership, I knew I had something worthwhile to give them that they needed: Me.

Me! My uniqueness. My quirky qualities that were so undervalued yet important and significant to what they were trying to do. It was the first realization that all my experiences were translatable *and highly valuable* for people who are ready for their own version of impact.

Every single business and person has a T.W.I.S.T. — *"The Way I See Things."* This is how you begin to access YOUR recipe. You're here because you're not like anyone else! You're a lovely unicorn and that's an asset, not a curse! Everything you bring to the table contains your unique blueprint. Revealing that is your life's work.

In the boardroom that day, I realized that the years of misery were actually *important*. That going through all that was my journey. Fitting in was not for me. Standing out was my truth — my secret weapon. Insisting on 'doing me' was now translating into the ability to see a similar path for others. This new perspective gave my journey a new and useful directive that was easily applied to the businesses I worked with. And in applying it, they access their 'thrival muscles,' which ultimately leads to certain success.

Since then, I have gone from graphic designer and business owner to brand specialist, business strategist, consultant, and speaker. I am always hungry to learn about myself and ways to up-level my game. This pursuit has aided in my ability to help others as my commitment to making a difference in the world. It's been far from a smooth ride, but what shifted has been my ability to deal with the roller coaster; to manage my emotions, my thoughts, even my habits to be FOR me, rather than against my own heart's knowing. Even the bad times don't last as long. And I am SO glad to be alive, living my purpose and helping others blossom and grow.

It's my great joy and honor to work with CEOs and business owners as they learn to align with their true selves. Together we design a path for their business and teams — adding value to customers, revenue to the business, and allowing their employees to contribute their best while infusing their dreams, values, and talents. It's completely invigorating and energizing!

Over the years, I've developed my own unique and individualized recipe for success. I am who I am because of all that I went through. My own definition of what a rich, successful life looks like took time to create. Doing so has allowed me to forge my own way, to find my own happiness, to connect to my own definitions to live fully.

After all, we spend many years learning and yearning to be like everyone else, but what matters most is listening to our own guidance. It can be challenging to break the habit of looking outside for validation and direction. We spend the first 18 or so years of life as followers and now, suddenly, there's a new expectation. It takes time to learn that when we are our true selves and express that through our work, we then attract those we can serve well. You then access a part of yourself that has been suppressed: your best Self. Most of us have forgotten how to be our best selves. As adults this is a wonderful gift — to self-express through business. To give our best selves as we share what we are here to contribute to this world.

It's not exhausting. It's invigorating.
It's not limiting. It's freeing.
It won't stifle us… it will give us wings.

I invite you to do the same. Stay aware. Follow your heart. Pay attention to your inner guides, knowing you are the one we've been waiting for. This magic will never let you down. Find the intersection of your gifts and where they will serve humanity. Use them. Let them fuel you. Let them guide you. And be grateful for it all. It is that *All* that makes you *You*.

When these pieces come together, your life becomes a scrumptious treat, a delicious concoction, where others enjoy you and value you for your unique contribution. You are tasty. Yummy. Uniquely you. Go. Succeed and thrive by your own definition, living your own magical recipe.

Ignite Action Steps

The Power of Two is a great way to access and understand how others see you. It gives you some of the ingredients to your recipe; those pantry items that you can always go to and integrate into your offers, your products, your services, your marketing. The power of two will yield language that showcases your brand, your strengths, your special sauce.

Ask two vendors, two clients, two colleagues, two friends, and two family members to share (in writing) three words or phrases that come to mind when they think about you. Compile the results into one sheet. Then see how you can use these words and/or the actions implied to integrate into your content, offers, and services. These are the brand attributes you're known for and can build upon. Your platform begins here. Your recipe lies within.

Judy (J.) Winslow – United States of America
Brandologist
UnforgettableBrands.com

IGNITE THE ENTREPRENEUR

KATHLEEN SINCLAIR

KATHLEEN SINCLAIR

"Dance with your life every day."

Every day I wake up thinking about how great it would be for everyone over 60, or even 50, to know they are looking forward to the most wonderful and creative years of their lives. I dream of you realizing you have the tools, experience, and motivation to use your skills for meaningful change in the world. I want you to know you aren't alone and that there are people all over the world looking forward to working with you on life-changing pursuits. Most of all, I want you to enjoy, have fun, and realize that contributing to the goodness of all is the grandest legacy you could leave for your loved ones and the world.

AGING — THE BEST BUSINESS IN THE WORLD

When I was 25 years old, my dad died. We weren't close, but he was my dad. There was too much drinking and hitting for him to be someone I trusted. For several weeks, he had been having chest pains and, without much education or experience, my parents didn't see many options. They didn't go to doctors. My mother would call me to go with her (about a 30-minute drive) to take him to the emergency room. Time after time, they would check him out and send him home.

One evening, she called about 11 PM; he was having another episode. This time she didn't want to bother me and just took him in on her own. Because of the lateness and needing more tests, they decided to keep him for observation.

He died during the night. I felt guilty for not going with her. I felt that, if I had been there, then maybe he wouldn't have died.

The next day, I was assigned the duty to go to the hospital and pick up his personal belongings. I sidestepped around dazed families and medical personnel. The lights blurred colors to gray. The smells were sharp with a mixture of sweat, disinfectant, floor polish, and stale urine. At the information desk, I told them my father had died during the night and that I was there to pick up his things. The receptionist made a phone call and soon a woman came up to me and handed me a large brown paper bag. My dad's name was written on the side. I took it.

Outside, I squinted in the morning sunlight. Heat radiated in waves off the pavement. I stood there in the parking lot for a while, letting it all wash over me. My dad was dead. This was all that was left of him. In this brown paper bag. Sweat poured off me. I couldn't hear or see anything as my fury and anger bled out. At him. At myself. At the hospital and the doctors.

He smoked three packs of Camel cigarettes a day. He never exercised. He never walked the dog. He would only eat fried food. Salad, to him, was cottage cheese with sugar on it. He never weighed over 125 lbs. When he was home, all he did was sit and watch TV.

My anger was not because he died; it was because I never cared to know enough about him to ask him about himself — his dreams, hopes, aspirations, and disappointments. Whatever they were, he never felt he had choices; the choice to do anything that mattered nor to share with me. He only went to eighth grade and couldn't read very well. I was not only angry at myself but also disappointed because I had been so wrapped up in my life that I hadn't realized my time with him was limited. And now he was gone.

I tried to determine how my father had fit into my life. When he wasn't drinking, I was the one who did things with him. We went fishing a lot, even though he never caught any fish. We developed camera film in the bathtub. He tied his own flies for fly fishing. When we did things together, we never really talked about anything. There wasn't much outward love or affection toward me.

Shielding myself from bad parts of my homelife, I became self-sufficient. My grandmother encouraged my independent quirks. She was also my role model. She never asked me if I could do something, she assumed I could, and I took up the challenge.

My memories did a dump on me right there in that lot. Determination reared to the surface and I made up my mind, sweating and red-faced in the parking lot of that hospital, that I would NOT be like my father when I got to be older.

It was a promise I made — I would take care of myself and have interests and hobbies and be independent. I would talk with my kids, tell them stories, and share my ideas with them. Mostly I vowed not to get stuck like my dad and feel like I had no choices. More importantly I wanted my life to be filled with opportunities and to go after my dreams.

When I turned 60, divorced for the second time, I moved across the United States from North Carolina to Bend, Oregon with four dogs, four cats, and a few rugs, books, and artwork. My youngest daughter was in a therapeutic boarding school and I wanted to be closer to her.

One morning as the sun was touching the tops of the mountains, I was walking along the Deschutes River with the four doggos in the near dark when, like a bolt from the Universe, that scene with my dad's brown paper bag at the hospital materialized in my vision.

I stopped dead along the trail. Whoa. What was I doing with my life? Was this some cosmic reminder that I was getting older and what the hell was I going to do about it? What about my promise to myself? Was I going to keep it?

I went home and sat my butt in a chair for three days straight. I made lists. What do I like about my life? What don't I like about my life? What is on my bucket list? Where do I see myself in five years? What about 10 years? What would I like to accomplish? What really excites me? Who are the most important people in my life? How can I get closer to them? Who are the people who need to slip off my list? When was I going to start this... this change? And how was I going to do it? Did I need help? What did I need to learn? Who could teach me?

And on it went, through a couple of bottles of wine, walking the dogs several times a day, staring out the window, weeding the garden, baking bread, and doing Tai Chi. Lots of Tai Chi. I felt energized and motivated. After three days, I closed up the house, called the pet sitter, and went nature rafting. I needed to clear my head. Staring at the Milky Way at night and listening to the river's current roll over the rocks helped put things in perspective.

The brainy fog morphed into a plan. I was working on a Master's degree, so I needed to finish that. I had always wanted to go into the Peace Corps, so I would look into that. I loved teaching but was tired of teaching the curriculum and not connecting with the kids. I wanted to be an entrepreneur, but I didn't know how to go about it. I wanted to travel, meet people, and learn stuff. Lots of stuff. Jeez, my list was full.

For the next 10 years, I followed my list: finished the Master's degree, did some teaching — kids and adults, went into the Peace Corps for two years in the Ukraine where I taught at a university. I traveled the world for a year and talked with hundreds of people, completed lots of courses, learned languages, and kept asking questions.

At 70, I felt there was still something missing. I had done amazing things, met wonderful people, stockpiled a Fort Knox worth of golden memories, taken 27,203 photos, became certified to teach Tai Chi, and made a shitload of money in the stock market. It looked like my life was going really well. Many of the things on my list were checked off. Still, I felt unsettled and unsatisfied.

I thought more challenges was the answer. I moved to Mexico. Sold everything and drove down from Oregon. Down there, I took an online course from T. Harv Eker called *The Spiritual Laws of Money*. I found him to be laugh-out-loud funny and smart, too. Who knew spirituality and money could come together so well?

During that course, we had an assignment to find our purpose. We went through a whole set of exercises which led us to forming our purpose or mission statement — something that captured the heart and soul of who and what we wanted to accomplish. What was valuable for me were the multi-day exercises of going through the questions and really thinking about my answers.

When I got through with that process, I could raise my hand and yell, "Bingo." I had found the missing piece to my puzzle. I had been missing my *purpose*. I thought back on the many conversations I had experienced with people my age for the past 10 years. There was a theme. *Many of them didn't have a purpose either.* Well, they did when they were younger and raising a family, working, paying the mortgage, etc. But, not so much now that they had begun their next journey in life. Wow. I became very curious to discover why that happened after a certain age.

I recalled the face of this lovely retired nurse I met on a boat going from Copenhagen to Germany. We talked about how she escaped years ago with her family from East Germany. I got goosebumps listening to her. But then she said, "I would really like to help the immigrants here but I am not an attorney and don't know where to start and I wish there was a community I could connect with to help me." All I could do was give her the names of a couple of NGOs I knew about who might give her some guidelines.

Then another memory came up when I was in the Peace Corps in Slavyansk, Ukraine. One of my professor friends from the university told me stories of living under Soviet rule. Hearing about what she endured cut me to the core. One night, walking through the snow to her apartment, she said, "I no longer feel useful or respected. I have no reason for going on. I have to retire, and I don't know what I will do." I thought she was a brilliant person and had a lot to offer. I didn't know how to respond.

There were others. One by one, each of these memories and conversations came flooding back. These people were looking for a purpose for the second half of their lives. I was too, but I hadn't named it at that time.

We were still being influenced by the old reality: linear thinking. First you do this, then this, then this = results. *Update!* A big shift happened because now we are in a time of exponential change, growth and, to quote Steven Kotler's new book, *"The Future is Faster Than You Think."*

Twenty percent of the population will be over 60 in a few short years. Ten thousand people a day turn 65 in the US alone. Every day. That's a shit ton of people. Holy smoke. And what are we doing about it? We have the skills, talent, and experience times 20 percent of the population. To quote the poet June Jordan, "We are the ones we have been waiting for." What a massive human resource. And, millions of us will live healthy, peak-performance second halves of our lives to way over 100 years old. I plan on it. Don't you?

I discovered my missing puzzle piece; my PURPOSE. It is to help people live a brilliant kickass second half of their lives with purpose, passion, and peak performance. The first question I needed to ask myself after I understood my purpose was, "Okay, Kathleen. How are you going to do that?"

I decided to challenge the stereotypes, culture, and language surrounding aging by living my purpose and passion and doing that through how I act, dress, think, and eat. Once I got into doing this, I would gain the tools to help others. My feeling is, if I did it then they could do it too.

What would I need to do to reach a lot of people over 50 or 60? Once again, I made my lists. Write a book. Write a course. Become a speaker. Write for publications and sites that catered to my demographic. Who did I need to know? What did I need to learn? How was I going to do all of this? How much time would it take? How much would it cost? I thought "Oh, shit. How am I ever going to do all of this?" It was so much bigger than me, I had trouble getting my mind around it. I realized that I had to take the 'how' and put it in a little box and put it off to the side. I told 'how' I would get back to it later.

I poured a glass of wine and did some research. I bought books on how to write books. I signed up for classes on how to write books. I read *Grit* by Angela Duckworth, *Mindset* by Carol Dweck, and *Start with Why* by Simon Sinek. Those books got me going in the right direction. That led me to other authors, lots of inspiration, and a path to follow.

When I started writing *my* book, I ran into questions involving publishers, agents, editors, designers, endorsers, etc. Those questions went with every single thing I needed to do to get my message out there and reach my audience. I became a speaker by taking workshops with Eric Edmeades, speaking at Toastmasters™, making videos, talking to individuals, couples, and small groups. I kept writing for any publication that would take my work.

Why would I do all of that and not just sit back and have a frosty drink with an umbrella on the beach? The reason is I want to Ignite your journey to find your purpose. I see you as a wonderful person of high intelligence and resourcefulness who has endured many hardships and challenges. And that is exactly what the world needs right now. Competent, skilled, resourceful, and compassionate people who care about the earth and all of its inhabitants, overcoming their setbacks. Collectively we have the knowledge it takes to create solutions to the world's problems. My goal is to make sure we do that and see the outcomes as our contribution and legacy. My heart races wildly writing this.

I took a lot of risks, spent over half of my retirement money, worked long hours, and attended seminars and workshops on leadership, marketing, and advertising. I also joined masterminds to learn from the experts. One of my mastermind leaders said that the journey I described is exactly what he did as an entrepreneur to start his online business and I realized that is also what I am — an Entrepreneur! AND, my products involve possibility, purpose, and peak performance. I am overjoyed by my vision which also includes a book, courses, an online magazine, webinars, and knowing I get to work with so many creative thinkers and doers.

Age doesn't matter! However, you need to challenge yourself that age *doesn't* matter. You can take responsibility for what is meaningful to you, regardless of how old you are. You can challenge the beliefs that don't align with you and find your purpose. In Japan the word 'retire' does not exist. We made that word up and all it does is dwindle our mindset. We have so many abilities despite the current opinions on being out of date. We have the power to make a difference with our skills and ideas. Age is just a concept.

Be gritty and go after it. If one percent of the older people went after it, the world would change for the better. We don't need technology to change; we need a mindset to change. Expand your mind and learn. Discover your passions, work on your performance, have fun, and more than anything LIVE your PURPOSE at any age.

IGNITE ACTION STEPS

Good people, listen up. I've said this before. The world needs us. Needs you and me and all of us to step up to our wonderful brilliance and talent and make the world a better place. Start by kicking traditional and conventional ideas of aging to the curb. Challenge everything you currently think that gets in your way of finding your purpose. Make those lists. Listen to your inner voice, the one that is quiet a lot of the time. Be compassionate with yourself and others. Tell the truth. Watch how you speak about your life. And let go of old habits and negative people.

*Have purpose, live with passion, and go after
a life filled with peak performance.*

*Kathleen Sinclair – United States of America
Author, Writer, Speaker
www.kathleensinclair.com
 @thekathleensinclair*

IGNITE THE ENTREPRENEUR

CHARLES HAI NGUYEN

CHARLES HAI NGUYEN

"Your self-worth is not your net worth."

It is my intention that this story reminds you of your true worth. True wealth is not about what you have accumulated but who you really are within. Going through difficult times may distract you from recognizing your true beauty, your true strengths, and your true assets. May this story awaken your wealth within and inspire you to tap into the source that creates a prosperous and abundant life. Your resources are within you. YOU are your wealth.

SUICIDAL TO SENSATIONAL: THE DISCOVERY OF THE WEALTH WITHIN

Curled up in the bed in the dark, by myself, the thought that I had never wanted to imagine actually crossed my mind, "What's the point of living? I've got nothing. I am nothing." I'd had dark moments before, but this was my darkest. I was alone and lonely, in despair. The pain was getting unbearable… I thought I would be better off not here, not living.

I pondered, "How did my life end up like this?" I closed my eyes and started to pray. I prayed to God for relief from my suffering. I prayed that what I'd gone through would give me insights into what I need to do next to survive and maybe even thrive through this. I started to examine my whole life, to see my past struggles and how I overcame them, hoping for the clue I needed to resolve my situation.

I thought all the way back to my birth. I was born in Can Tho, Vietnam, in early June of 1969. I recalled that my mom told me that I was born premature, weighing less than four pounds. It was uncertain whether or not I would survive. I was placed into an incubator and my mom wasn't able to see me until a week later.

I remembered the Vietnam war. I remembered that near the end of the war, around 1975, my family and I had to sleep on the lower floor of our home just in case bombs were dropped. I remembered the sound of artillery firing at night. It wasn't the type of fireworks I anticipated seeing, but rather it was the type that I hid from in fear. When the war ended, the communists took over the assets and homes of the rich and changed the whole monetary system overnight. Yet, our family not only survived the war, we actually thrived economically. As an electrician, my dad found his niche starting a repair shop fixing refrigerators, and did quite well providing for the family.

Several years after the war, my dad decided to come to America and it almost cost us our lives. He bought a boat. With our family of six and several other families, we made our first attempt to leave Vietnam and failed. When we got caught by the communists, my dad and sister escaped, while my mom, my two brothers, and I were thrown in jail for two months. At only 8 years old, I felt hopeless and unsure if I would survive, as I witnessed horrifying things happening to the other prisoners around me.

Several months later, we paid to board a ship to escape Vietnam again. Drifting in the sea for over seven days, we ran low on food and I was starving. I remembered my dad sharing with us the little rice pouch, barely anything to nibble on. The conditions worsened as the ship started to leak. I remembered standing on the deck seeing the water seeping through our sleeping area and from afar, seeing three Thai pirate ships chasing after us. Fortunately, our ship was spotted and rescued by a German oil tanker that dropped us off on KuKu, one of the Indonesian islands. We were among the first refugees to settle on that island. We stayed there for eight months till we got transferred to Galang island for another six months. Eventually, through a friend of my father's, we were sponsored to enter the USA..

Coming to America with barely any resources, my dad partnered with his two friends and opened the original Pho Hoa restaurant. Being resourceful, he got the capital for the business from a school loan my mom received to attend college. As the restaurant became a chain, he expanded to other businesses and invested in real estate. Inspired by his success, I pursued my path of going to college. Although I majored in business, with an emphasis on finance, I was not really taught anything about managing my money or creating wealth. I ended up getting my car repossessed and filing for bankruptcy at the age of 21. I got a job doing computer work at a company but was laid off during the 2001 recession. It puzzled me how my dad who couldn't speak English and didn't have a high school diploma became a multimillionaire. On the other hand, I was well educated with a four-year college degree, but still ended up in financial trouble. It was then I realized that a college education was not enough and having a job was not guaranteed.

Taking charge of my future, I studied wealth by reading books, attending seminars, and seeking mentors. I met a multimillionaire, Aaron Berger. He became my mentor; my second father for over 13 years until he passed away in 2014. Through him, I got inspired to obtain real estate and insurance licenses and began to make multiple streams of income.

Living the 'American Dream,' I had a house, a family with three children, and a financial services business. However, when the US economy crashed in 2008, my dreams became my nightmares. I lost my business partner to death, I lost my business, and I lost my house. In my darkest hour, I prayed. By the grace of God, I bought my house back for less than the market price and absolved over $400K in mortgage and credit card debts. This was a big weight off my shoulders. Things started looking up and shortly afterward, while in church one day, I took the opportunity to be baptized and felt so light for the first time in many years.

A lot of people were affected by the economic meltdown, including my dad's business, an Asian food and spice manufacturing company. My dad asked me to help. Trong Food In't. (TFI) was heading for disaster. The first year I helped restore TFI to neutral from a negative cash flow, and in the second year it grew to profit over $600K. With profits came tax issues which attracted lawsuits. Out of necessity, I was forced to learn about protecting profits, saving TFI several hundred thousand dollars over the years. I also learned to protect assets so we didn't have to incur these losses again.

While I was helping my father's company, not everything was perfect. I was realizing that my marriage was not bringing me happiness; something that ultimately caused me to stray. I tried to keep the secret so we could keep up appearances for the kids, but eventually I realized I had to tell the truth and let my wife know. I wanted to be true to myself, and honest with her so that we could both move forward in our lives separately. I put my focus back into work and traveling to create new business opportunities.

As a CFO of TFI for over 13 years, I thought my position was secured. However, when I came back from a cruise trip with my potential new business partners in November of 2019, I found the lock to the entrance of the company was changed. Then, I was dismissed from the company without any explanation. I attempted to ask my dad why, but he refused to give me an answer. Besides the cut of my income, my dad decided to keep my share of the profit from a real estate investment we had together. This was my greatest disappointment. I had idolized him for so long, then supported him. I not only helped his company but took personal care of him, driving him to doctor's appointments and tending to his needs. I was in shock, being treated like a criminal while I had no idea what I was accused of.

I was going through my divorce so the shortage of revenues did not help my contribution to my family. Several months later, the whole world economy shut down because of the Covid-19 pandemic. Not only could I not pursue other business ventures or find work, but my investment income payout also got delayed. I barely survived with the little savings I had left in my bank account. At one point, I only had $20 in my checkings account.

Going through a divorce, having a career change, and dealing with the pandemic were quite overwhelming for me. My children didn't want to talk to me nor did they want me to be a part of their life. My wife was angry as she felt betrayed that I had an affair and disappointed that I didn't find a way to work out the marriage. My dad disowned me. He said that no one in his ancestry ever got divorced or abandoned their family. He accused me of stealing his investment and giving it away to girls. He refused to listen, saying he didn't want to argue every time I tried to talk to him. Out of money and out of love, I faced shame, guilt, and despair. I didn't know who to turn to or what to pursue. I felt no motivation to do anything.

Although I prayed every day, desperate thoughts still bombarded my mind. The worst idea tempted me, "Am I better off dead?" I still kept my prayers, though, and one day I got a better thought — a reminder for me to watch the movie *It's a Wonderful Life*. It's the movie I usually watch every Christmas and sometimes during the year to remind me how precious life is. The movie showed a good man, George Bailey, who was about to attempt suicide because he got into big financial trouble. He was intervened by a guardian angel who let him see what would happen if he wasn't born at all. George got to see the negative impact on everyone around him because he wasn't there to do his part; make his contribution to his world. He realized that in his weakest moment he forgot all the great things he had done.

I started to see what God was telling me. One day I did my meditation and entered a dreamlike state. God spoke to me, "Why are you seeking from others your source of validation, love, and approval? I am the source of unlimited wisdom and unconditional love. I'm here within you. I never left you. Why do you keep turning away from me?" As I turned to Him, tears flowed from my eyes as I felt overwhelming love penetrate through my soul. I felt like a child receiving a big embrace from a parent. He said, "Your self-worth is not your net worth."

It took me losing almost everything, including my life, to realize this. God reminded me that I'm loved, that I'm somebody, that I'm one of his children, and that I matter. He reminded me that I have rich life experiences and wisdom and asked me why I'd want to throw all that away. He said that just because certain unfortunate things happened, and others found my actions despicable, that does not mean that I am a bad person. He further added that just because I made a few mistakes, I should not forget all the great things I have accomplished throughout my lifetime. There was a chance to redeem myself from my mistakes, and I could change for the better because of what I learned from them. Being true to yourself is not about simply looking good, but rather being authentic and real even in our flaws, so we can be our very best selves.

As I continued to embrace God's unconditional love, I stopped listening to people's opinions of me. I stopped allowing all the judgments. I stopped blaming my wife for sabotaging my relationship between my children and me. I stopped blaming the pandemic for my failure to produce income. I let go of my pride, of wondering how come I got into financial messes when I'm a financial professional. I started to ask for help and receive help without self-criticism. I opened myself up to receiving food from the food bank, benefits from the government, and personal loans from friends. I reached out to a few good colleagues for support. They helped uplift my spirits, clarified my thinking, and shared with me new opportunities they encountered.

My true worth is about believing and appreciating who I really am and who I choose to become. It's not about what I did, what I accomplished, and what I had. True abundance and wealth comes from my own realization that I'm loved unconditionally by God, that I can experience joy and happiness, regardless of my situation, and that I have the power to create new experiences and realities.

Therefore, I choose to remember. I remembered that despite the struggles, I got to experience much joy in the refugee camp — playing soccer using a coconut as a ball, strolling on white sand beaches with crystal clear water, and laying back at night on the docking boat conversing about life with my mixed race, blond-haired Vietnamese friend. I remembered and appreciated the times I spent with my mentor Aaron, sharing his wisdom. He told me that I was one of the five people he trusted in his life and that he appreciated all the things that I have done for him. I remembered how I enjoyed spending time with my dad and taking him to doctor's visits, for it helped me understand him better and that we both have entrepreneurial blood in us. I appreciated it so much: losing our home and getting it back somehow brought the family closer together.

The last two years gave me a chance to be by myself, to learn to love and accept myself, and to examine my life so I can create a compelling future. My daily walk to the park across the street enjoying the life of the fish, turtles, ducks, and other birds, reminds me of the miracle of life that I don't want to take for granted. All these ups and downs have brought me closer to God, developed my ability to love unconditionally, and clarified my purpose and vision of what I need to share with the world. I recognized that experiencing true wealth and abundance is about accepting that I'm already worthy. I know that I have my health, that I have people around me that I care about and who care about me, that I have the richness of experiences, mindset, and skill set, and that I can create positive possibilities for myself, my loved ones, and my community. My network, including Shannon Castello, Dame Lillian Walker, Brenda Tan, Coach A.M. Williams, and so many others, has been my most invaluable asset. They are my great friends and mentors who guided me through my darkest hours to help me see who I truly am.

As I'm realizing who I am and developing who I am committed to be, my thoughts and actions allowed me to see the abundances in my life and seize the opportunities presented in front of me. I'm enjoying training and coaching entrepreneurs to their journey to prosperity, having true freedom and a fulfilling life. I'm leveraging my past to prepare my future, taking what I've learned from my mistakes and advancing toward my mission in life with conviction and confidence. I'm recovering my relationship with my children. I'm reconnecting with my dad, knowing that we do love and care for each other. I'm nurturing my relationship with my newfound love and soulmate, who I'm excited to share my future with. I'm grateful that God reminded me that my life is precious, and that my self-worth is not my net worth. I know my true wealth, I am one with God, and God is in me.

I'm clear on my life purpose: To share my wealth of love and wisdom and to inspire and empower people to be, do, and have what matters most to them... all in serving God. I'm living my purpose each day, whether I'm taking the time to get to know my neighbor or counsel my clients on really mastering their money and utilizing their finances to fulfill their dreams and build wealth in every aspect of their life. Wealth is not just about money or finance, but rather your health, your wellness, your fulfillment. Joy can be found even in moments where we are struggling or seemingly have nothing, if you focus on the good and find meaning in it. Joy does not come from accumulation, it comes when you choose to find it in each moment that you live. It's not about your accomplishments or what you have made and done, it's about being true to yourself and who you are becoming. Learning from your mistakes, owning them, and growing from them is a big part of being authentic to yourself. When you know who you are and what is really important in your life, you design your work and the way you make money around you in a way that is most important to you. Discovering this freedom and purpose is what being wealthy really means.

IGNITE ACTION STEPS

Steps to a sensational life:

- **Define your compelling future.** Describe in detail your ideal life. Design it with the context, "If I have unlimited resources, what would I like to be, do, and have?"
- **Connect to the Source,** where you are supplied with unconditional love and unlimited wisdom — your power within, your higher being, your so-called "God."
- **Make peace with your past.** Fear and doubt are derived from the experiences that hurt us; from the mistakes of yourself and others. Learn to forgive these mistakes. Have compassion and embrace the whole you: the good, the bad, and the ugly. Your true beauty emerges from self-acceptance.
- **Create a list of your wins:** your accomplishments, the characteristics of you that you're proud of, the things you're grateful for in your life. This is to remind you of your worth when you're in doubt.
- **Access the resources you have:** skill set, mindset, network, finances, etc.
- **Determine the resources you need:** who do you need to become, who do you need to connect with, and what do you need to develop and get access to?
- **Create a daily self-care routine** for your physical, mental, emotional, and spiritual health.

Charles Hai Nguyen – United States of America
Prosperity Coach, Smarter Money Guy — American Dreams Company
www.CharlesHaiNguyen360.com

IGNITE THE ENTREPRENEUR

ASHLEY BAXTER

ASHLEY BAXTER

"Always embrace the joy along your journey."

Hard work and sacrifice have long been attributed with success. But, as burnout becomes a growing concern across the globe, we must ask ourselves, "Is it always worth it?" My truths are an invitation for you to step into yours and a reminder to feel joy every single day instead of waiting until you reach your goals.

TURN IN YOUR RESIGNATION TO MEDIOCRITY

"We need you at headquarters for the launch. It's now happening in May."

At that moment, I was faced with making a life-changing decision. A pit of anxiety dropped to the bottom of my stomach.

I was in my late 20s and had just been dumped by the man I thought I would marry. I jumped at a new job opportunity when an old friend from college pinged me to say she knew of a team that was in dire need of my skills. The company was a Fortune Top 10 conglomerate. They were launching a new subsidiary brand in their market and I was quickly hired. Despite being beneath the wings of a behemoth, they operated like a free-flying startup. There was little structure, no HR, and an understanding that as a team we should ask for forgiveness not permission when it came to breaking the rules.

Our division was small, but mighty. We were spread across the United States from coast to coast. That meant juggling impossible deadlines and schedules. Every month I was on planes and in hotel rooms meeting with the team at headquarters. However, I had no complaints — at least not in the beginning. We treated each other like family most days. Get to the office by 8 AM, high-fives in the hallway, say yes to the last minute meeting at 7 PM, and be grateful. If you got home, changed into comfy clothes, and savored a glass of wine before continuing the work day until 10 PM you were lucky. That was the mood.

For months leading up to the launch, I'd been near exhaustion. I was familiar with the energy behind launching new brands, and I loved the excitement. Yet, our rebranded social media presence had to be impeccable. I was there to do the dirty work to make things happen. I'd run out of fingers counting the times our lawyer screamed at me. I witnessed repulsive vulgarity while moderating our online communities. I questioned my safety after my personal Facebook profile was stalked by a brand 'superfan' who was also a convicted felon. I started to yearn for my life to feel just a little more normal again.

At the time, the only thing that mattered was hitting goals. I had to make it look easy while keeping an ear to ear smile slapped across my face. I hid my exhaustion, stress, and anxiety. If you could rate my ability to stuff down emotions, I'd have gotten five stars. But what goes down often comes back up. When those emotions began to resurface, I started to struggle.

Nearly a year into the project those stressful and demanding hours had begun to feel like more than I could bear. They were no longer a welcome distraction from my heart-shattering breakup. They were a trap. My time didn't belong to me anymore. Being single and childless meant everyone assumed I had 24/7 availability for work. No area of my life was left untouched. Not even nights and weekends.

Overnight our team's family-style dynamic morphed into a toxic high school drama. One of the directors took charge as the lead bully. Cross her and you'd be the butt of every joke and the center of every juicy office rumor. Even team happy hours became manipulated with arbitrary guest lists and whispers about who was or wasn't invited. I was told to shun certain teammates as if 'mean girl' was just another bullet on my job description. Failure to join in on the bullying meant I would also be on the list of rejects. I'd seen it happen to others. I'd even supported some of them through the tears and self-doubt that came along with being ridiculed in the office, but only in secret. I was frightened at the possibility of others finding out and becoming the next target.

The launch was my light at the end of the tunnel. The brand would go live. We'd ease into the flow of daily operations. Things would finally calm down. I had put my life on hold in dedication to bringing this project to life hoping that in some way it'd all pay off. I wanted to feel like all my hard work had a real purpose. If I was lucky, there'd be a financial incentive also.

When the rescheduled timing of a new May launch was announced, I was beside myself. My mom's birthday was May 14th, smack dab in the middle of it all. I knew I'd have to make a heart-wrenching decision on where to invest my time. Celebrating her birthday on a day other than her actual birthday would normally be okay. But, this was her 50th birthday and I had planned for it to be a grand gesture of appreciation.

My mother had gone from graduating high school with honors to pregnant college dropout by the age of 19. My dad had never been present so she raised me alone with the support of her parents. She was as smart as a whip, but no one was handing out second chances to black unwed single mothers in rural Texas where I was raised. Watching her sacrifice so much so that I could dream bigger than she did, fueled my drive for success. She was my best friend and making her feel loved was important.

To celebrate her birthday I'd planned the Hawaiian vacation she'd always dreamed of. This trip was a thank you that I'd never managed to put into words. We were planning to go to pineapple farms and a luau and catch the sunrise on top of a volcano. She was more excited than a kid in a candy store. How could I call her to cancel? I had to shake myself into reality. I didn't need to sacrifice every minute for work.

I felt in my gut that I shouldn't bail on my mom. So I called my boss to break the news that I wouldn't be in-person for the launch. I planned to use my vacation days, which had already been approved, but I was committed to still work the entire trip while I was in Hawaii. I would set up office hours and make myself available when needed for team meetings. Sacrificing my time on vacation felt like the best option because breaking my promise to my mom wasn't aligned with my values. My boss listened then dropped some news of his own. I was getting a promotion!

Our team had done so well on preparing for the launch that he was getting a new role. I was flagged to be his successor. I'd get a bump in title, a nice raise, and the chance to buy discounted company stock as a director. I thought about how this could literally change the footprint of wealth in my family. I was afraid that it would all vanish if I didn't come to the launch. My boss confirmed that I needed to prove my dedication. The senior leadership team wanted to see my commitment to the team.

I was in turmoil for over a week deciding what to do. The promotion was a carrot dangled in my face so I'd keep sacrificing my time and sanity. Yet, I realized the carrot had serious benefits. I began daydreaming of a better life with my future promotion. I wasn't aligned with my truth, but the massive pit in my stomach would have to sit there unaddressed. I reluctantly took the bait and made a difficult phone call to my mom.

"We'll just need to postpone our trip," I hesitantly told my mom over the phone later that night, while fighting back tears. She was disappointed, but she understood like any loving mother would. Her Hawaiian dream vacation got pushed to a later date and I fell back into working long hours to numb the guilt.

The launch was pure insanity. I was lucky to get three hours of sleep each night between approving content, responding to emails, and coordinating efforts with our agencies. Any doubt in my mind was calmed in knowing that no one could question my dedication. My reality was hell and highly-stressful but I was reminded that my sacrifices were securing my future success. I carried on despite longing to build a personal life like some of my co-workers had with their families.

Accolades for our team's work began to pour in the minute the launch was over. When I inquired with my boss about the timing of my official promotion, he dropped more news. If I wanted it to happen I had to move to another state. As the soon-to-be new team lead I had to be at headquarters full-time. "I'd have to prove my dedication," he said again.

This left me dumbfounded. Hadn't I already proven myself by bailing on my own mother? Wasn't that a big enough sacrifice for the company?

The pit in my stomach returned as I hesitantly agreed to move across the country to an unfamiliar place with no family or friends. My heart wasn't in it. As I packed up my beautiful high-rise apartment, I tried to imagine what life would be like after I got the promotion. I was convinced to make this final sacrifice and made my way across the country to my new home. I struggled to get settled in my new city. My boss had taken his own promotion and moved on. I was left behind waiting with bated breath for the details of when my promotion would finally happen.

I had a new boss in the interim. It was none other than the lead bully. I danced around her mood swings. I struggled to remain friendly in the face of her constant criticism. My only comfort was knowing that this hierarchy was temporary. I hoped that things would change once I got promoted.

Feeling left in the dark, I finally pressed her about my pending new role. She called me into a conference room to drop a bomb that killed every ounce of hope I had left… I wasn't getting promoted.

For a full hour I sat across from her as she riddled my self-esteem with bullets of judgment and insult. Each comment from her left a new wound. Her aim wasn't the quality of my work, but my humanity. In her eyes I wasn't chatty enough, didn't go to happy hour enough, and didn't smile enough. She opened a new round of ammo as she joyfully explained that there had never even been a promotion waiting for me. My former boss had taken the only available opportunity in our department for that calendar year. His request for my move was meant to secure his advancement, not mine. My fears had come true. I was the bully's new target. My face flushed with embarrassment, then sadness, then anger. Her words became the voice of crippling, negative self-talk in my mind for months.

She reassured me with all the empathy of a wet blanket that this was for the best. She offered me two years to prove myself worthy of career growth under her watch. During that time she was happy to load me up with director level responsibilities, but with zero acknowledgement. No bump in title. No raise. No options to purchase stock. I was once again told that "I'd have to prove my dedication." I left that meeting speechless. As all the life drained from my body, I headed straight to my car to cry and call the only person who would understand my pain, my mom.

"God's got your back. Sometimes things that cause us pain in the beginning are simply a blessing in disguise," she offered amid my sniffles.

She was right. That day I realized I had a choice. I *could* continue down the path of proving my dedication to others. Yet, I knew that I would continue to be exhausted and emotionally beaten down. It was a miserable journey. I realized that there was a good chance that I would never receive a promotion or the acknowledgment I deserved. It wasn't appealing.

Or, I could take a new path. I could start embracing my joy in the moment. I could own my truth that I was already worthy and fully enough. I could build the personal life I had craved and start new friendships. I could take the steps to start building the family I wanted. I could honor my values and get back into alignment with the things that really mattered to me.

For the very first time since I'd begun my corporate career, I decided to choose myself. My definition of success was rewritten. It was now centered on my joy. Fancy titles and material things could come and go. But, if I could find joy on my path in every moment, then the trip would always be worthwhile.

Just like that, I gave myself permission to abandon the miserable journey of climbing the corporate ladder. I started moving closer toward being my true authentic self. I had sacrificed all I could and hadn't received what I was promised in return. That was my biggest fear and I had just faced it. There was no longer a game to play. There was nothing to lose now and I felt free.

Instead of continuing to sacrifice my joy, I made amazing new friends. I explored every corner of the city and enjoyed life with people who accepted me for me. As the weight of being overworked and undervalued was lifted off my shoulders, I embraced true success in my day-to-day and this new way of being felt better than any acknowledgement I could have ever gotten from a job.

I continued on for a few more years in corporate with my newfound sense of self. But eventually my soul's calling to support impact driven businesses took over and I made the leap to start my own business. Some called my leap of faith a bold move, but to me it was necessary. I knew that being me, owning my truth, and embracing my joy were all I needed to win in life.

I challenge you to take the same approach as well. Maybe you're an entrepreneur at a point of confusion on your path. Or perhaps you're in corporate searching for the right moment to take your chance. I ask you to consider: Are you living your truth? Have you embraced the joy in your journey?

To step into your truth and embrace joy is the most generous gift you can give to yourself. It doesn't cost a dime. All you have to do is make the choice. Everything else will figure itself out from there. Turn in your resignation to the pity party and quit accepting mediocrity. You can design whatever life you want for yourself. Be really honest with what you want and share your desires with the world. That is how you can create the space for each and every one of them to show up in your life.

Ignite Action Steps

The first step to owning your truth and embracing your joy is to identify how they are currently represented in your life. It's easy to focus on chasing the future. However, when we're in this frame of mind we can become disconnected from our truth and the joy that's already present in our day-to-day life. In this exercise you're going to use your mind to visualize both your truth and your joy. Grab a pen and paper to take notes on what comes up for you.

STEP 1:

Start by taking four deep cleansing breaths. Close your eyes and ask yourself, "What is my TRUTH?" This may be done internally or out loud. Continue to ask the question until no new answers are revealed. If no ideas initially come to mind that is also okay. Simply repeat the practice daily until a vision appears.

You might picture colors, words, animals, people, or specific situations. Try your best to allow these thoughts to flow free from judgment. Write down or draw out your answers.

STEP 2:

Start by taking four deep cleansing breaths. Close your eyes and ask yourself, "What is my JOY?" This may be done internally or out loud. Continue to ask the question until no new answers are revealed. If no ideas initially appear that is also okay. Simply repeat the practice daily until a vision appears. You might picture colors, words, animals, people, or specific situations. Try your best to allow these thoughts to flow free from judgment. Write down or draw out your answers.

STEP 3:

Review what has come up during your visualization process. As you look at your realizations, list three steps you can take in the next week that would bring you closer to alignment with your truth. Then list three ways you can incorporate your joy into your life in the present.

Complete this process until you are aligned with your truth and embracing your joy. Miraculous things will find their way to you when you operate from this heart space.

Ashley Baxter – United States of America
Digital Marketing Expert & Educator
www.itsashleybaxter.com

IGNITE the ENTREPRENEUR

LAURIE H
DAVIS

LAURIE H DAVIS

"Money does not generate great ideas; it is great ideas that generate money."

Through educating, inspiring, motivating, and supporting others in their entrepreneurial journeys, not to mention my own, I have come to realize that we cannot climb the high mountains by ourselves. I am trusting that, after reading my story, you will know that you can do whatever you set your mind to and it can be accomplished regardless of the circumstances. Through my experience of setbacks, losses, and disappointments, I chose to be an entrepreneur through it all and not allow anyone or anything to stop me. You will understand that freedom comes at a high price but is well worth any sacrifice you are willing to make.

MY ENTREPRENEURIAL PATH TO FREEDOM

Chaotic energy flowed between the rooms of our small house; three kids shutting down in confusion as two adults desperately tried to figure out their next move. The year was 1962 and I was about to celebrate my 13th birthday. My dad had received "the golden handshake" from the large steel company he had worked for as a bookkeeper and payroll clerk; losing his job with no notice, compensation, or support. My family went from having everything to having so truly little that we struggled to put food on the table. This was my reality check that a J.O.B. means 'just over broke.' It can be here today and gone tomorrow.

I wanted to help. I told my parents that I could earn money to buy groceries.

Being the eldest, I knew I was capable of babysitting, housework, walking the dog, feeding the cat, mowing the grass: whatever it took to assist others and, of course, get paid. I proceeded to take my colored pencils and paper to create my homemade flyers to deliver to each household on my street. Being able to contribute, and knowing I made a difference to my family's mealtime, made me so proud. I know it was then that my entrepreneurial spark had first been lit.

Eventually my dad got back to work. I knew he saw my ambition because one day he handed me a book, *Success Through a Positive Mental Attitude*, by W. Clement Stone. I still have it in my library. I remain grateful to my dad, as that gesture planted the seeds for my continuous journey as an entrepreneur.

I was the first person in my family to not only graduate from high school but to continue with my education. I eventually became a teacher. So here I was with a JOB. My family was proud and excited even though it was something I may not have chosen if my familial circumstances had been different at the time.

In my first teaching role I was a shy, inexperienced young teacher. I drove up to the rickety old wooden building filled with children wanting to be educated. The poverty was overwhelming as I stepped into an environment where I had to quickly learn how to serve appropriately by meeting the needs of students in a marginalized community. I felt anxious and excited at the same time. I was appalled to see that children were coming to class hungry because many of them had walked three or four miles to school. Again, I saw that I could fill a need. I decided to provide a hot breakfast program for the students in my class. Little did I know, a fellow teacher reported me to the Department of Health for not having a food-handling permit. I was forbidden from serving the children a hot breakfast; but nothing was said about whether they could serve themselves. So, refusing to let my students go hungry, I adapted by having them help themselves to the breakfast I continued to provide.

My second teaching role was in a rural area with no restaurants or fast-food available and no hot lunch program or cafeteria in the building. We were a young teaching staff working on a special project and pilot school. Each day I took a packed lunch but I realized some of the staff were not eating; having no time to take care of that detail. A male colleague said to me one day, "You know, Laurie, if you would make me a sandwich alongside yours, I would pay you for it."

Well now, catering, hmmm, yes, I could do that. Pretty soon I was buying an extra cartload of groceries each week to take care of my lunch program which I was now selling to my teaching friends. I was earning money, but it was never really about that. I was ensuring everyone was looked after, and that is where I drew my satisfaction.

One day while I was serving lunch in the staff room, a colleague said to me that she was hosting a Mary Kay Cosmetics™ skincare and makeup party and wanted me to attend. Yikes! I was 30 at the time and did not wear cosmetics of any kind, so naturally I declined. It wasn't until the sixth invitation that I agreed to go. Even then, I convinced myself there'd be nothing there that interested me.

The moment I walked in, my mind was changed, and I knew I'd made the right decision by attending. Seeing the presentation and education that was being shared, along with the products in their pretty pink boxes, I knew I would probably be buying something. I learned that it was okay to pamper myself and to look prettier. I simply loved the whole process. I purchased everything that I tried, only after I raced home to pick up my checkbook, having brought no money with me in my initial closed-mindedness. Then, always one to see and act on an opportunity, I asked the Beauty Consultant if the company was looking for anyone else to deliver the program. She put me in touch with her Sales Director and 48 hours later I became a part-time Beauty Consultant. I was well on my way to fueling the entrepreneur inside of me.

I continued with my teaching career while running my part-time business. Only 18 months later, I was ecstatic to be driving to school each day in my first pink Cadillac™, a car I had earned since becoming a Sales Director. When my business income matched my teaching salary, I resigned from the school. I would continue with the company for a total of 12 years as a top performer, growing by leaps and bounds, and learning from some of the absolute best people in the industry including Mary Kay Ash herself. The time I spent in the organization was time well-invested. I was making money, traveling, and enjoying all the rewards.

Then tragedy struck, suddenly jolting me out of any sense of security I had. My childhood sweetheart, to whom I had been married for 14 years, made two attempts to take his own life in the span of a week. He would spend the next two years in a mental hospital. I was shocked and devastated that the love of my life, my friend since childhood, wanted to leave us all. He had no intention of coming out and six months later we amicably agreed to a divorce. Eventually he was released from the hospital, disappearing without a trace. He has been on a missing persons list since 1986.

Six weeks later, another blow: my six-year-old niece was struck by her school bus and killed. I was overwhelmed with the loss of our first grandbaby in the family. It fell to me to inform my parents on behalf of my grieving sister.

I can say that there has been nothing in business or in life that has compared to the anguish of that moment. That was the hardest thing I have ever had to do. Losing children is heart-wrenching, and I was not doing well as it was. That was a dark and sad time for myself and my family, and the experience changed my perspective and forced me to become stronger.

Being an entrepreneur is what made it possible for me to take the time I needed to heal and support my family. I had others working on my team and so my income continued whether I was working or not. Had I been working at a full-time job I would not have had that freedom. Up until that time I had not placed any value on all the risks I had taken to be an entrepreneur — it was only then that I knew the high value I placed on my freedom.

I was on my own for nine more years before I was introduced to my present love and husband, Ron Davis, by his daughter. Out one evening on our motorcycle, cruising to our favorite coffee spot, I heard him ask me something through our helmet microphones. He asked, "Laurie, what do you want to do next?"

I was stunned and overwhelmed by hearing this question I had never been asked... what was it that I wanted for my life? I had always spent my time taking care of everyone else's needs and drawing fulfillment from that, never thinking of my own dreams. Immersed in the feeling of love and support I had just received from him, I immediately declared that I was going to marry him one day. Then, giving my dreams even more thought, I answered, "I would love to create my own private training company." By knowing my answer and then speaking it out loud for the very first time, my life would be changed forever.

Dreaming soon turned to action. With Ron as my partner we formed our own corporation, and the next day I was launching my dream business. I had been a professional educator for most of my life, and I knew that all I had experienced was merely getting me ready for this. I was dedicated to creating and delivering my own lineup of products, programs, and services with the same entrepreneurial skill that had granted me the freedom to travel and work anywhere in the world: the freedom to live my life and support those who most need me. That confidence allowed me to say 'yes,' to a myriad of life-changing opportunities.

When I get up every morning, I am in awe of the surprises and gifts that flow when we choose to be all in and keep showing up. The minute I would give up on something, the next day might bring the phone call that could change everything. I had just finished breakfast and was sipping on a second cup of tea when the phone rang. It was rather early and I wondered who could be calling me at this hour. It was the Director of Health Services from Big Cove,

Elsipogtog, the second largest indigenous reservation in the eastern side of Canada. She invited me to come to the community, a five-hour drive away for me at that time, and present myself along with the empowerment programs I had developed. They were looking for some fresh and innovative workshops to support the community. I was excited and honored as it was my first chance to provide services to an Aboriginal population.

The community was, as most reserves are, off the beaten track. As I drove in, I could hardly take in the scenes of poverty; it felt like I was in a third world country. With a population of 2,500 people, it was even impossible to buy a cup of coffee. Most homes were in disrepair and many had 10 people living in a two-bedroom bungalow. The streets were not paved and there were no signs of business or economic development. The most attractive building in the community was the Health Center where I would be working. Despite these disturbing conditions, I was about to embark on the most beautiful project of my career to date.

The Mi'kMaq people welcomed me with open arms and I would get to create amazing, lifelong relationships with so many of them. With their trust, I rolled up my sleeves and went to work. I would travel once a week to the community, host my educational workshops, stay a couple of days, and then return home.

There are so many stories from this experience I could share but the highlight was piloting my youth program while I was there. We welcomed the youth of the community to experience 10 weekly workshops designed to empower them. Seventy-two children signed up for the workshops. I hired some women in the community to help me and they never missed a beat. The children loved it. We packaged their workbooks in a box and told them it was theirs and for their eyes only. That was when the empowerment and self-worth journey began for those 72 kids. It was exhilarating to watch the light bulbs go on and see their attitudes shift and change when they began to realize that regardless of their circumstances they had value and mattered. I was so proud of them, and myself also, for taking the risks that are involved when you have the responsibility to care for other people's children.

Here is the kicker. Twenty years after this project I was invited to come and visit the community. I had not been there in all that time. I drove in as I had done so many years before. To my surprise I thought I had taken a wrong turn. As I slowed down I realized I was on the road into the community. I did not recognize it because it had changed so much. All the streets were paved and curbed, and there were sidewalks. A shopping mall with a pharmacy and convenience store greeted me at the entrance. In town, a drive-through coffee shop:

yes, coffee. A community beautification program had resulted in delightfully painted houses and mowed yards with flowers all around. I could not believe my eyes! Would you like to take a guess who owned those businesses and got the community cleaned up and on the road to prosperity? Without giving all of the credit, of course, I am quite certain those 72 children had something to do with it all.

Entrepreneurship gave me the perfect platform to actually live out some legacies. My work is now into the third generations of families I have worked with and that has left me feeling very accomplished in the difference I have been able to make. Could that have happened in my role as a teacher? Absolutely, but I may never have been able to experience it at this level; actually seeing the fruits of my labor.

My business has evolved tremendously but not without challenges; legal, financial, personnel, and my greatest enemy, myself. Getting Laurie in shape for what is about to happen in my own business amid our difficult times is encouraging and exciting. As I look back over the past and see how much I have grown both personally and professionally, it boggles my mind. I have discovered things about myself that would have laid dormant had I not been an entrepreneur. Over the past 29 years in this business there were at least 100 times I could have thrown in the towel and gone to get a JOB. What kept me going? Why did I persist? Was it all worth it? These are questions I have asked myself repeatedly. The answer is always the same for me — I love my freedom. My freedom continues to put me in the driver's seat.

Fifty-one years after I stepped into that impoverished rickety school on my first day of teaching, I recently received a call from the Managing Director of the Helping Hands Orphanage, in Malawi, Africa. He said he was seeking my support to provide education and training for his teachers and volunteers to support the 450 orphans in his care. He had hardly finished his request before I said, "I'm in!" I have now stepped in as their Director of Training and Future Development. I have come full circle and my heart is full. I have come to know that if for some reason I could not help one more person, I have made a difference. I could not have done it without choosing to be an entrepreneur.

We often resist that which we actually need. We talk ourselves out of what we desire and listen to the intellect. The intellect will want you to do things 'right.' The heart will always show how to do the 'right' things. Your heart will give you courage and lead in the direction of what means most to you. So, listen to it. You intuitively know what to do so follow that.

IGNITE ACTION STEPS

You have within you an entrepreneurial spark that, when discovered, can grant you the freedom I have enjoyed. To begin unearthing it, put pen to paper and answer the following:

1. Why am I here on the planet?
2. What do I want? (Make a big long list.)
3. What am I willing to do to get what I want?
4. If I could change just one thing in my life right now, what would that be?
5. What have I done so far to make the change?
6. What parts of my story need to be rewritten?
7. Whom do I have in my circle who will support me no matter what?
8. What is it about *being* an entrepreneur that intrigues me the most?
9. What is my next step in my business or business start-up?
10. What am I the most passionate about doing?

Once you complete these questions, put a timeline on the tangibles you can accomplish. Let go of the things that no longer serve you. Adapt new patterns that will move you forward, and most of all, have fun.

Laurie H Davis – Canada
Founder and CEO Self Worth the Missing Link
www.lauriehdavis.com

IGN TE THE ENTREPRENEUR

MIKE LEDOUX

MIKE LeDOUX

"My survival story has been written; my success story has begun."

My childhood wasn't the worst, but the bad choices I made as a young adult, combined with a dysfunctional mentality, led me to a pain-filled way of life for many years. When parts of my life would be great, other parts would really suffer. Learning that I had to push through the pain and fear, recognizing that before I needed to take on the big problems of the world, I first needed to battle my own bad habits and stop the self-destructive behavior. My wish is that you can learn from my story and uncover the parts of your life that you need to give up so that you can have the success story that *you* deserve.

WHAT DO YOU NEED TO GIVE UP?

At a very young age, I developed a habit of finding myself in opportunities of work. I began a very disciplined work ethic. I would often hear people say, "I don't know how you're doing it; you always get so lucky." That would usually be followed with, "Be careful, they're going to take advantage of you!"

I was the only boy in a middle income household with sisters. My parents divorced and remarried. Both households were in rough neighborhoods in Sacramento, California. Mom's house was in the thick of the hood; don't get caught outside alone or you'll likely get rolled. Verbal abuse was the norm; screaming about unhappiness everyday. But it was easy to get away with stuff, she and my stepdad both worked a lot and they were at AA meetings all the time. Dad's house was in east Sacramento; we walked through the ghetto to get to school. He and my stepmom both worked a lot, typically if he was home from work before bedtime we all knew somebody was getting an ass whoopin'. The fear of the belt from my earliest memories had me in chains.

Both my stepparents turned out to have great influence on my life. My stepmom taught me how to "be love". She was a tough no-nonsense woman, but she had a gentle touch on my soul. My stepdad taught me if I'm not going to do shit with my life then I needed to learn how to work. He let me do whatever I wanted Monday to Friday, but on the weekends I was his worker. We worked from sunup until late in the night with very few breaks in between.

The earliest I can remember earning money is at the age of 9 or 10 years old. I used to go to my grandma's apartment and help the maintenance guy do cleanup. He was paying me five dollars for whatever project he would have me do that day. I couldn't believe I was so lucky that someone paid me to get dirty.

At 14, I got a part-time job serving ice cream. At 15, I added a part-time job at a transmission shop. Right after my 16th birthday, I ran away from home. I could no longer accept the belt for my misbehavior. I saved every penny from my two part-time jobs, willing to do whatever it took not to go back to that life. I started selling 'weed' to make ends meet. Within a year, I was using drugs and gave up my childhood dreams to start living a life without chains.

Four days after my 17th birthday, I got in a gang fight with another student and was stabbed in the chest. Surviving that life-changing event would magically inject perspective into my life, giving me wisdom beyond my years. I realized that if I was going to do something with my life, I needed to get it done. Shortly after I got stabbed, my roommate was in a car accident that put him into a coma and put me and my group of troubled friends into a silence that we'd never seen coming. He was everybody's best friend. I was living on his grandma's couch and suddenly I was homeless. I had given up my secure couch, leaving me in a lost and scared spiral. I had no choice but to drop out of high school. Between my day job and dealing weed at night, I had become a working man. Although, somehow I felt blessed to be alive.

At 19, I landed a job at a motorcycle salvage yard that would change my life forever. Within two weeks I realized that I was working in a modern day California gold mine! Whenever I told people about my new career, they told me I had lost my mind. The only person supporting my decision was my grandfather; he told me he was proud of me. He said I had found an industry that needed really smart people and it will be easy for me to have great success because I'm a doer and a thinker. "Put your head down son and work like you've never worked before!" He encouraged me. After two years of grinding it out and creating my own opportunities, I was noticed by the owner.

At 22, I *made* my break. My manager called in sick and I didn't report it to the boss. Instead, I did his job and mine as well. He called in sick for almost the whole month. We were 10 days in when my boss asked me, "Where the hell is he? We're having a record month and he's nowhere to be seen." I had given up my sanity, came early, and stayed late for so many years just waiting for this moment when I could give up obscurity and get attention. I had done it again… I created my luck.

Over the next few years my boss was able to open three more yards. I'm a firm believer that before you can have a best guy, you need to be someone's best guy. I was given the title of general manager, but I really didn't know how to run multiple stores, I just knew how to grind and I could sell anything. The someday promise of being a partner had become a shining light — while I never truly trusted it, in some way it helped me to realize I was capable of doing bigger things. I was willing to give up anything to become a partner. Knowing that someone believed in me that much was raising my belief lid.

At 26, I got another break. My boss bought a yard that was three hours away in Fresno and he needed someone to run it. I wasn't even on his list; I was his moneymaker in Sacramento and he didn't want me to leave. Luckily, I used proximity long before I knew what the word meant as I had created a strong friendship with his business partner. I was able to establish enough influence to come up with the courage and the words to create my own opportunity. I gave up my chances and any hopes of being a partner in Sacramento but I was the lucky chosen one to go to build the Fresno facility.

At 28, I finished the Fresno project; I had built five buildings, poured 10 acres of concrete, and I was a partner in a business. Things were moving quickly and it felt like the sky was the limit. My dreams felt like they were coming to fruition. I locked in my commitment to Fresno and bought a home here, then decided to buy my partners out. I was scared but I did it anyway.

I quickly realized how much I don't know about business. I leaned hard into 'Robert Kiyosaki, Rich Dad, Poor Dad' series. I learned how to read financial statements and understand profit margins. The next several years went by just grinding away and learning how to transition from salesman to successful business owner. As the business survived every month, my confidence grew. Eventually I decided to buy the wrecking yard next door and expand. In order to do that, I realized I had to put my house up for sale.

In 2007 the housing market was spiraling downward out of control and it was a really bad time to sell. I listened to the great mentor, Art Williams, as he told me, "Sell it anyway!" I sold it, giving up my dream home for the expansion of my business. At 35 years old I was using what I had learned and began buying commercial property. I had reached beyond my limits and made something big happen again. I still had it!

Through the natural course of business my old partners evicted me out of the Fresno facility and my window to move into my new property added great stress to my life. Little did I know my momentum was about to come to an abrupt end.

I was now 37 and a broken mess. I was divorcing and I found myself in the middle of a big expensive lawsuit over my new commercial property. I had bought my next dream home and it, too, was slipping away. I had given up everything that felt normal to me. I felt like the only thing I had left was my business, and I would show up to work every day hoping that someone would take that off my hands.

As life went on and I approached my 40's, eventually I prevailed in the lawsuit, figured out that the marriage was built on a foundation of toxicity from the beginning, and that the big house… it wasn't meant to be. But something else *was* meant to be. A short while later, I met my dream woman; together we bought another house, blended our kids, and began our lives together.

In 2016 we sat on the couch in our beautiful new home, *Shark Tank* episodes and Marcus Lamonis from the TV show, *The Profit,* found their way into my life every night. The champion inside me was coming out of hibernation. My wife began seeing a man in me that she heard of but had never seen before. I happened to hear one of the investors on *Shark Tank,* Daymond John, talking about the '10X Rule.' I bought the book that day. Although I didn't have the discipline to read every day, I found the man who invented the '10X Rule;' Grant Cardone on YouTube™; my transition began.

"What do you need to give up?" These seven words began to haunt me; after listening to Uncle G on YouTube for about a year I started hearing him say, "What are you willing to give up?" over and over, on my drive to work, my drive home, I even started hearing it in my dreams, "What are you willing to give up?"

I had given up drugs in my 20's, except the one I thought won't hurt me — the sleepy drug — the one that's not addictive: weed. It was my dream killer and I was hiding behind it… until I woke up one day at 44 years old with those words in my head: "What do you need to give up?" and just like that I refused to give power to drugs anymore.

I just couldn't quit on my dreams anymore. After 27 years of smoking, I had enough. I wanted that laser focus so badly, but I couldn't see through the cloud of smoke; my vision was always blurry. I wanted to taste that success again. The little voice in my head told me that I could do it and I was sold! I had committed to massive success for my family, my business, and my community.

After a few months, my vision gained clarity and I began to see that my business had the potential to be the vehicle I would use to get my launch. Unlike previous times I had quit, this time the temptation was gone; something was different. I came to realize that I had only worked to my *full potential* during crisis situations in my life; otherwise I would work only to my *capability*. As these big thoughts took over my mind, I realized that my survival story was in its final chapter and my success story was beginning. As I began to study business again I found quickly that I now had the potential to be a great student and I was ready to learn!

We sold our house, bought another, and began fixing it up. Around the spring of 2019 I began hearing Uncle G ask me again, "What are you willing to give up?" Things were going so good I couldn't see what might be next. However, this time I was alert, waiting for the moment when I would realize the reason *why* I was hearing this.

In the summer of 2019, my young nephew came up missing. I was filled with turmoil and I started drinking heavily, not my typical style. And, I could still hear Uncle G; he had become the little voice in my head. After a few weeks of searching, my young nephew was found in the Sacramento River; he had drowned. RIP #22. After a few rough weeks of out-of-control drinking and being an asshole to the ones I love, I woke up and didn't want to drink anymore. It wasn't going to take me months or years to figure it out this time. I quit drinking to honor the relationships in my life and the commitment to live my potential.

In 2020 I began to invest in myself, changing my thinking and my language. I began to 10X my mindset. I committed to daily training for myself and my team. I started building what I learned to be human capital in my team members for the first time in 20 years of business. My dreams and ideas were coming to fruition.

Then, in the spring of 2020, everywhere I looked, the media had the world on its knees in the Covid crisis. As the world appeared to be falling apart around us, I had taken charge as the leader of my company. For me, drifting was not an option; I would need to become a strong leader if I wanted my business to survive. I put my head down and began drafting with the mentors in my life, sharing their messages. I began to coach and train people to achieve success beyond what we're accustomed to. I changed the schedule at work, paid overtime for mandatory daily team meetings, and we watched my mentors every morning via video training. I gave up listening to the outside world, completely blocked it out, just like when I listened to my grandfather as a young man. I had to give up my old way of thinking if we were going to survive.

My new way of thinking began to pay off, my business began to have record months, one after another. Investing in people was paying dividends; not just for me, but for them as well. Through the 10X ecosystem I would meet my next mentor Brandon Dawson, and it is through him that my thinking became transformational. He would quickly teach me that whatever I'm thinking is what I'm saying, and what I'm saying is what I'm doing, and what I'm doing is becoming my legacy. It's no longer about me, I would need to start giving people the opportunity of a lifetime if I wanted to achieve great things in life. It was time to give up my thinking of how to run a small business and start treating my business, my people, and my life like a *big* business.

As 2020 came to a close, my team had put together the best year that my company had ever had in business. My team is more inspired than any team I've ever worked with, making more money than they've ever made. We have followed a simple business motto: people build businesses, businesses don't build people. I listen to my team and help them develop and fulfill personal, professional, and financial goals. At the same time, the team is pushing the business to achieve its personal, professional, and financial goals. Building a big business is about people achieving great success through collaboration.

As I write these words, once again, we are wrapping up our best month ever. I have come to realize that things are never as good as they seem and they are never as bad as they seem. Trouble is always waiting ahead, so treat every experience as you would in a crisis situation. If I can do it, anyone can do it!

Commit to being accountable to yourself and your own journey. It is only through committing to giving up the things that you are most scared to let go of that you will find the great successes that life has to offer you. The most meaningful things in life are on the other side of fear. You will never be able to handle the problems of the next level if you can't figure out how to solve the problems where you're at. Solving bigger problems is how you add value to any situation in life. Learn how to intentionally work to your potential, not just to your capability. Ask yourself, what do you need to give up to reach *your* massive potential?

IGNITE ACTION STEPS

Write your goals down everyday. Don't miss a day.

Think way BIGGER than you're thinking. We as humans tend to think so small. In order to do big things, we have to start with thinking bigger.

Take responsibility for your actions. This is the only way to be in control of your destiny.

Stay uncomfortable. Comfort is the death of success. Be courageous!

Mike LeDoux – United States of America
Owner All American Truck and Auto, Inspirational Speaker
10X Growthcon Speaker 2021
www.559parts.com www.comeonnow.shop www.comeonnowmike.com
Clubhouse @comeonnowmike
⟳ *mike.ledoux*
🄵 *mike ledoux*
▶ *mike ledoux*
🄳 *@comeonnowmike*

IGNITE THE ENTREPRENEUR

BRYCE
MCKINLEY

Bryce McKinley

"Leaders, stop focusing on being in charge and start focusing on those in your charge!"

My intention is to encourage everyone. Anything is possible. I came from nothing, I built a massive organization, lost it all, and have been able to build it back up with little to no formal education. There's always light at the end of the tunnel, or when you're in a shadow, there's light somewhere casting that shadow. Like a sword being crafted by a master craftsman, sometimes you have to go through the fire to be sharpened for your calling. If you're reading my story, I hope you're inspired to just trust the process and keep pushing.

S.H.A.R.P.E.N.

I remember the moment vividly. The night was hot, the air was dense, my emotions were raw and ragged. I had used my gun before and never had it jammed, and it has never jammed since. But on that night, as I sat in the front seat of the car that had become my home, with my infant son sleeping in his car seat behind me, the gun I had pointed in my mouth jammed. Not once, not twice, but three times.

It was close to two in the morning and I had pulled out my gun to do the unthinkable. Parked on a busy street on the north side of McKinney, Texas, to make sure that someone would find my son in the morning, I had succumbed to my breaking point. The late-night hour had the streets eerily quiet which allowed me to perform my task. Nearby was a water tower with a patch of trees and woods behind it. For months I had been parking back behind the tower, away from the passing traffic so my son and I could sleep there undetected. We were homeless! My car had become our home, and concealed behind the imposing structure, we were never hassled or bothered there. I had attempted to stay in shelters, but my son, just a few months old, didn't do well in shelters so staying in my vehicle was easier. We had spent several months sleeping behind the water tower leading up to the night my gun jammed.

That fateful night in September, I had just gotten off the phone with my brother. We had been discussing starting a new business together. We were both feeling good, on a high note; we were positive about the opportunities that could come. But within 20 minutes of hanging up the phone, my mindset shifted back to my current and desperate reality; homeless, penniless, and in a brutal custody battle with my son's biological mother. Months of court battles and lawyer fees had burned through my savings and sunk me deep into feelings of giving up. Life had hit me hard, my world was crumbling, and everything going forward felt too difficult to overcome. With only 32 dollars left in my pocket, I used a tattered piece of paper to write a tearful letter to my son. I also wrote a letter to my mom, saying I was sorry and asking her forgiveness. Then, I parked my car on the busy street, knowing that somebody would find it, find my son, and find his mother's contact information in my letter. Like a robot on autopilot, I pulled out my gun, put it in my mouth, and as I pulled the trigger, it jammed.

A lot happens to a man in that moment; memories, priorities, purpose, regrets, anger, sorrow, and the fragmented feelings of God all come rushing in within seconds. With my life flashing before me, I was instantly reminded of my childhood. I grew up unlike most kids, in a very strict and cult-like religion. There were a lot of man-made doctrines and heavy persecution if things were not followed. Despite the strict disciplines, I did learn a great work ethic and high moral values. When I was 11, my parents separated and my mom moved out of the cult and into low-income housing in the projects. Like every kid my age, I got involved in gangs, drugs, and violence. Life was in disarray constantly and growing up fighting to survive was extremely difficult.

Between 11 and 17, I fathered a beautiful daughter yet got arrested and put in handcuffs more times than I can count. Not yet 18 and still considered a minor, I was fighting a hefty criminal case. I was facing multiple felony counts of manslaughter, drug trafficking, and conspiracy charges. It was not my finest hour and I knew my life and my future were on the line. Except, God had another plan for me. All but one misdemeanor was dismissed and I was acquitted. I got to walk out of the courtroom with time served and was released into my uncle's care. My uncle, unimpressed with my lifestyle, grabbed me by my ear and took me to live with him 100 miles away in Davenport, Iowa.

My uncle was a businessman and entrepreneur. He immediately had me changing my unfavorable habits by putting me to work. He taught me how to show care and attention to both myself and my potential, by detailing cars at his car dealership. There, working alongside him, I fell in love with the automotive industry. I saw how the cars created value, how the salesmen offered a service, and the customers bought what they wanted to fulfill a tangible need. A few months later, in the middle of a wintery blizzard, none of the other salesmen showed up for work. It was the middle of December, and there was no action at the dealership, and that's when my uncle said, "If you can sell a car today, I'll put you on the sales team next week." It was my chance to put into place all that I had learned and shift my life from where I was to where I wanted to be. That day, with only guts and gumption, I sold three cars! I was on fire! The next day, I went through the phone book, cold-called people, reached out to those who were scheduled to come in for oil changes ... and got them to book a *sales* appointment with me. One thing led to another and more often than not, that sales call converted them into buyers.

That is when I learned a powerful life-changing lesson of sales; selling is a service. I saw how mastering the art of conversation and sales — is a service! With that new entrepreneurial mindset, I became unstoppable. From age 18 to 21, I began dominating the market. In just two and a half years, I became the number one car salesman in the world! Yes the WORLD! Ford Motor Company™ recruited me out of my dealership with a multi-million dollar deal, and had me traveling to struggling dealerships and/or new dealerships where I implemented what is now known today as the 5-Star Blue Oval Certification. When you go and drive by a Ford dealership and you see FIVE-STAR certified, that's one of my training programs.

That success catapulted me to the top of my industry. I won several prestigious awards in the automotive sector and hold the record to this day of the most cars ever sold, non fleet, by a single salesman. Multiple other car companies gave me seven-figure contracts and before I knew it, I had all the 'toys' a guy could buy. I married a woman I had known all my life — my wife's mom had been my Sunday School teacher. We had a nontraditional relationship, it was open, because we didn't believe in anything conforming, confining, or following any rules. While technically we were only married on paper for a couple of years, we had known each other since we were kids.

Over the next five years, I grew my business while my wife grew her two businesses; a salon with two sites and a daycare with three sites, so essentially she had five brick-and-mortars within her two companies. We were enjoying life, traveling, overindulging, doing *everything* we wanted. I was 24 years old, spending like crazy; owning a $300,000 boat that I was driving once a year, just for the heck of it. Between the contracts I had and her businesses, we were doing close to 65 million dollars a year between the two of us. And, that's when everything came to a crashing halt.

My wife had a baby with another man. I didn't see it as a betrayal. We had an open relationship and I accepted that it had happened, but sadly the baby ended up becoming very ill. He was six months old and ended up in the hospital. The doctors mistakenly put a 'do not resuscitate' order on him; it was supposed to be on a different baby in the same room. The doctor panicked when our boy started asphyxiating on his vomit and didn't resuscitate him. Over the next two years, we went through countless legal depositions and lawsuits. It was emotionally and financially taxing and despite the loss my wife was going through, all I knew how to do was keep working. While my wife managed her stress and depression, I was a hard worker, but not a great husband.

When the baby passed, my wife struggled to cope with the loss. I just worked and worked to deal with the problems. Friday, June 13th, my wife drunk herself into a slow suicide and that day I got a call she too had passed! That was the moment I lost it. I just checked out. I mean, drugs, alcohol, and partying in excess. For a year and a half I slid down the proverbial rabbit hole. One hundred million dollars in contracts were lost; close to $80 million in cash, property, and assets swirled down the drain.

It took me a few years to recover and get back on my feet. In 2010, I sobered up and started returning to the corporate world. I got a contract with Tyco™ Corporation, which had offices in Denver, Dallas, San Diego, and Chicago. I ended up moving down to Dallas for a promising contract. Things were looking up and cash was coming in again.

I had met a girl in that period when I lost my mind boozing and drugging. A few months after I had moved, she found out that she was pregnant. Our son was born in November, and she moved to Dallas in January so we could try our hand at being a family. By the end of the month, I realized she had never actually sobered up. I came home one day and found her in the bed, passed out, and our baby, who was just a couple months old, was on the ground scream- ing and crying. There were pills and bottles everywhere. I picked up my son, went to a hotel, and that Monday I filed for custody. My last $100,000 in the bank went to fighting for custody of my boy. Due to the drama, and all the fighting in court, I ended up losing my contract. Down to just 32 dollars and no longer able to afford a hotel, my son and I found ourselves homeless. We started sleeping in my car. Everything was an emotional blur, and then came that moment by the water tower.

I remember fighting with the idea of what I was about to do both internally and externally. As I pulled the trigger not once, but three times, the gun jammed, and the bullet didn't come out! I remember thinking this is crazy! Like, WTF! Come on God, show up! My son was asleep in the back seat, so I got out of the car and I started screaming and yelling at the top of my lungs. I literally said, "F#&K YOU SHOW UP!" to God! I was so pissed off and furious at Him. Now, looking back on it, I see what God did for me; a true blessing. But, at the time, I was in an agonizing rage that God wouldn't let me succeed with my plan. My emotions felt like razors and my heart was gutted with grief. That was when I knew... I realized... I fully understood.... that I was on this earth for a reason! I *knew* that my life was important! I had a purpose for being here!

After the adrenaline had subsided and God's message was delivered, I got back into my car and pulled it into our hiding place behind the water tower. The heat of the night and evening events had caused my clothes to feel wet-like and stuck to my skin. I closed my eyes to calm my breathing and that's when I heard my son's voice speak to me. Even though he was a baby, sleeping undisturbed in the back, I heard him speak. I know babies don't talk at that age, but I heard his voice so loud and clear. It's the same voice that he uses today when he yells down the stairs, "Hey Dad, can I go outside and play?" In that terrible and life-altering moment, I heard his child-filled voice speaking directly to me. And that voice said, "Daddy, everything's gonna be okay."

I heard it clear as day, audibly, as if he was wide-awake and a confident young boy speaking lovingly and courageously to his father. Transfixed by his message, I turned around and saw my infant boy peacefully sound asleep. I can honestly say, I felt his presence; the caring child that would enrich my life and become my very best friend. He was right there with me in spirit and in strength. He reminded me of my worth and abilities. I knew instantly that giving him a beautiful life was a clear part of my purpose!

I settled into a slumber, still broke financially but no longer *broken*. I knew both God and my child were a magnificent force in my life and all 'the things' I was worried about didn't matter. His life and my life were all that did.

I awoke the next morning when a call came on my cell phone from Wells Fargo™ bank; saying I had some fraudulent activity on my account and I needed to come in to verify some transactions. I drove to the bank and sat down at the banker's desk with my son content, looking up at me from his car seat at my feet. The lady at the bank printed off a list of transactions and said that I needed to verify the last three. I looked down the list and I agreed I didn't recognize one specific deposit. She confirmed that was the one that prompted their inquiry. I asked who was it from? She pulled up the detailed report and gave me the name of the organization. It was a past client, a dealership I had worked for. I called them and it turned out they had missed an invoice from the last quarter and had wired money directly to my account. It was a 20,000-dollar delayed payment that instantly confirmed to me that God's hand was at work.

I went out to my car and sat there just crying, praying, being thankful, and showing gratitude to God. I had gone from a few dollars into my pocket to having all I needed to put my son and I back on our feet. It may be hard to believe but while sitting in my car, humbled by all that had happened, I got a phone call from an apartment complex that I had submitted an application to a few months before. They asked me if I was still looking for a place as they had something just open up. Within 24 hours, I had 20 grand in my account and a crappy one-bedroom apartment for my son and I to live in and call our own for at least a year. It was heaven.

Over the next few months, I started searching for a new business opportunity. My idea was to establish myself, then start pitching consulting, go through the hurdles of entrepreneurship, and create a business by solving a problem and providing a great service. I was determined to look at everything with an open mind, knowing that the right and perfect opportunity would arrive. I discovered some unique loopholes while dabbling in real estate, and that started with me calling homeowners to see if they wanted to sell their house at a discounted rate. I began wholesaling real estate, virtually because I didn't have the ability to drive all over Dallas with my son, so I did deals over the phone and via email. I conducted 23 transactions my first month, 37 transactions my second, and that's when I *knew* that I could build a new empire in real estate. I felt excited. I was inspired again and overwhelmed with joy because I had a small buffer in my bank account where I could dabble and play while perfecting my business experience and knowledge. And that's what I did. I dove right in and went to work.

In that moment when the gun jammed, I knew that I had something worth living for, I was called to be a father, a husband, and a leader — a leader who stops focusing on *being* in charge and starts focusing on those *in my charge*. Over the last nine years, I've rekindled my relationship with my daughter, remarried an amazing woman, and have been recognized as an international keynote speaker who has spoken with some of the greatest minds in the world, to the likes of Tai Lopez, Dr. Greg Ried, Les Brown, Dr. Eric Thomas, and Matt and Caleb Maddix just to name a few. They've hired me to tell my story, teach the sales techniques in my five-step process, and my seven steps to business that anyone can implement and get better results in their business!

I've learned to look at life knowing I can overcome anything and so can you! Regardless of our circumstances there is always a new or different perspective than the one that is holding you back. I truly believe that life is filled with explanation. If you live life as if there's another explanation, you can see other massive opportunities with all kinds of possibilities. There's always light at the end of the tunnel! Think about it this way, when you're in a shadow of life, there's always light, coming from somewhere. So keep pushing. Keep searching for the light. Trust the process. Let that fire inside of you *sharpen* your will. They now call me Coach Sharpen, so my friend, sharpen your skills and know that the best work you can do is the work that you do on you!

IGNITE ACTION STEPS

I believe that leaders are readers. Always be reading! If you're an entrepreneur, you're a leader. And if you're not reading, you're doing a disservice to yourself and others.

Stop focusing on being in charge and start focusing on those in your charge. You should be working to serve the people who look up to you and pour your skills into them.

It was Tim Ferriss who said, "If you win the morning, you win the day." Whether your day starts at 4 AM or 4 PM and you're working night shift, wake up a little earlier and spend some time with yourself. Put on your own oxygen mask first.

Whatever you do, just don't do nothing! The minute you stop is when your subconscious plays all the tapes, working against you! You don't have to be perfect, you should just strive for progress. Don't stop. Keep searching. Keep pushing. Keep going.

Bryce McKinley – United States of America
"Thought Leader"
CEO
EveryHouse, REI Results, REI Results Academy
EveryHouse.io   REIResultsAcademy.com
@CoachSharpen   @CoachSharpen
@ Bryce McKinley   @ Bryce McKinley

IGNITE THE ENTREPRENEUR

PAUL BATTAGLIA

PAUL BATTAGLIA

"Interest turns into passion through the process of mastery."

My wish is for you to enjoy the somewhat comical journey of a Jersey-born-middle-child-army-brat while opening up to the possibility that many of our PERCEIVED weaknesses are actually strengths, and will — over time — be the avenue through which you find your passion and purpose. I live an extraordinary life because I cultivated passion through a sustained focus on service to others.

WEAKNESS TO PASSION: A LIFETIME OF STRIVING

Imagine an Olympic-level gymnast who has perfected a ritual to 'get in the zone.' He is on the Olympic stage performing an elite routine, tuning out the judges, the cameras, and the crowd. Everything in his mind is silent as he surrenders to his decades of training, allowing his body to execute the routine without interference of the mind or ego. He is art in motion.

Now imagine Scarecrow from *The Wizard of Oz* performing the same gymnastics routine and you would have an accurate picture of me on the same stage: a fraction of the focus and absorbed in doubt. As a teenager, I displayed the perfect combination of army brat mixed with the quintessential middle child. I was naturally happy, however, I often felt frustrated and misunderstood. I would later discover that the root to my dissatisfaction was a lack of identity and passion, which I now understand is a function of follow-through. I loved 'doing' gymnastics, but I knew nothing about the process of discovering the inner greatness I was striving for. I was going through the motions, but I now know that action without passion is what left me feeling empty.

In 1984, I was 12 years old and relatively new to the sport of gymnastics. My self-taught backflip in the yard was sufficiently dangerous to earn me gymnastics lessons from my parents. I immediately took to the sport. Its physicality made my brain happy and I have stuck with it for 37 years. I had zero success with traditional ball sports. The patience and sportsmanship necessary to excel at soccer, basketball, and baseball eluded me. However, I enjoyed acrobatic movement and lacked a discernible sense of self-preservation, which helped as a gymnast. Gymnastics classes were the highlight of my week and within a year or two, I had secured a spot on the competitive gymnastics team at a local club. Being a gymnast had become my identity. Truth be told, it became a mask; a facade.

By the late 80s, I was competing 'seriously,' which meant skipping workouts only one or two times each week. I had no identity other than being a gymnast and in my heart I knew that I was not very good at the sport. With a false sense of pride, I shared my identity with everyone I met. I would tell people, "I'm a gymnast," which implied long hours in the gym (many of which I skipped), hard work, and sustained focus. I had not mastered or even scratched the surface when it came to learning these virtues. I was the opposite of a leader, an unlikely candidate to eventually own five gymnastics studios, employ hundreds of people, and shape thousands of lives. I lacked discipline, commitment, and hard work, which was odd considering my dad was incredibly hardworking. He's the greatest man I have ever met. He modeled dedication, integrity, and a strong work ethic. Despite my lack of follow-through, more of his values took root than my actions would have led one to believe.

By the time high school graduation rolled around in May 1990, I was ready for a change of scenery and moved from friendly slow-paced Texas to the cynical city streets of Massachusetts. I learned there is a whole new level of mischief available when you're living in a college house with equally undisciplined roommates, and I welcomed the chance to explore these new morally-questionable experiences. I got a job near the college house coaching for and alongside a gold medal Olympian. I was permitted to work out with the team and received direct coaching from world-class gymnasts and teachers. Along with my mother and father, these men should be awarded a plaque that reads "The Most Patient People on Earth."

The atmosphere in the gym was unusually warm and inclusive. The culture was about achieving as well as *fulfillment*, something with which I had very little experience. I didn't know it then, but my coaches were adding to the foundation laid by my parents, which over the next 20-plus years would become an identity of passionately serving others.

In the gym, I was surrounded by service-minded leaders who exuded integrity, hard work, follow-through, and dedication. The coaches selflessly and seemingly effortlessly served their athletes and the athletes' parents. They lived their lives artfully and elegantly, and I felt inspired working alongside them at the gym. I thrived there, where coaching and practicing gymnastics was a haven. It was almost too big of a contrast from my life at the college house. Although fun, my chemically-inspired extracurricular activities came at the expense of my emotional and spiritual well-being. I didn't like my roommates or my behavior at times. Mostly I hated the insecurity and weakness that showed up as blind conformity when I felt bullied by my roommates. Though I didn't know why, when I wasn't at the gym I felt increasingly sad.

At the gym, I modeled the great men who surrounded me. I stood tall, projected confidence, and enthusiastically served my students. I discovered an interest in being a great coach, but my mentors could sense a lack of congruence between what I said I wanted and how I acted. As an athlete, I resisted focus and hard work. However, as a coach, I had to model these unfamiliar behaviors to my students and my mentors knew better than to give me too much responsibility or put me in a position of leadership. The process of becoming a better coach was teaching me more than the joy I felt serving others; it was teaching me the skills necessary to succeed in life and business. For the first time, I was eager to grow and willing to work hard.

During that year in Massachusetts, my coaches and parents never gave up on me. They helped me survive poor choices and taught me valuable life lessons. After 10 months, at only 19 years old, I packed my two bags of belongings and newly-acquired bad habits and left to attend college in the southwest. These years were only slightly less volatile than the year before. My insecurities would eventually cost me friendships, the respect of men that to this day I admire, and my college scholarships.

Relocating in New Mexico, I once again met extraordinary individuals who graciously invested time and energy in me as a gymnast and a person. I was an elite athlete, on a Division 1 collegiate gymnastics team, and I loved it. Yet, I never felt part of the team. I admired the men on the team. They treated me with dignity and respect even when I didn't reciprocate. The coaches believed in me at such a high level that they gave me a gymnastics scholarship, which was a dream come true — and one that I felt undeserving of.

I started coaching in a gym owned by one of the most generous men I have ever met. In addition to sharing his knowledge and time, he exercised unworldly patience as my employer. He believed in me enough to give me a leadership role, helping me begin a lifelong journey of transformation. In turn, I shared his kindness and found myself growing increasingly invested in my athletes' development and my role in their success.

I projected myself as a passionate, hardworking collegiate athlete when in reality, I was cutting corners and feeling out of place. At the same time, my role as a coach was becoming a passion to the extent that I was choreographing workouts for my athletes instead of attending college classes. I cared deeply about my impact on my students and wanted to understand the psychological makeup of each athlete so I could help them avoid the mistakes I was making. I preached to my students about hard work, focus, sportsmanship, and follow-through... but had not yet committed to myself as a competitor in the same way.

I was making an effort to improve my follow-through, but when I was not working out or coaching, I continued to display the self-destructive behaviors that directly and indirectly sabotaged my goal of being a successful, nationally-recognized gymnast. At the peak of my career, I imploded. I called my coaches and quit the day before a regional competition, one which I was supposed to perform in five events for the team. By doing so, I forfeited both my gymnastics and academic scholarships.

That abrupt end to my gymnastics career left me disoriented. The identity I wanted so desperately was gone forever. I could no longer pretend to be a gymnast, and I didn't see myself as a high caliber, life-changing coach. I packed up a U-haul™ with my furniture — student-worn and destined to be thrown away within days of arriving in Missouri as it turned out — and left New Mexico humiliated and dejected. I had no college degree and no idea what to do next. The only thing I did know, with certainty, was that I would make coaching gymnastics my new identity.

In St. Louis, Missouri, the gyms had many coaches that did not have the technical knowledge I was accustomed to. Despite how undisciplined I was as an athlete, my performance as a coach had improved so dramatically that it was immediately evident to my peers that I was coaching to change lives. But even though I was pouring my soul into every hour of coaching, I was not enjoying it as much as I did in New Mexico. What was missing in the first few months of coaching in St. Louis? Passion for the business of transforming young talent and empowering kids who, like me, had doubt.

By 23, I felt Ignited by a strong desire to serve children by helping them cultivate confidence through the process of setting and hitting goals. I just didn't know how.

One night, I was drinking with a mentor, complaining about my job, and I kept saying something about how I could do it better. Over and over, I whined that same refrain until, tired of it, he said, "Talk is cheap."

His words were an explicit challenge. His comment hit me like nothing else. All the men I had admired who had challenged me to do better and be more were gone from my life. The words "talk is cheap" bounced around my brain and started wheels turning that hadn't been turned for a while. The idea he was implying was exciting and provoked me into action.

I opened a very small gym in a suburb of St. Louis that already had three thriving studios. Without any business experience, I made many mistakes the first dozen years, possibly setting the record for repeating the same mistakes over and over. However, my high-energy style of coaching and profound connections with students made the families continue to return month after month, year after year.

Eventually, my lack of business skills began to limit my ability to serve. Over time, my employees left for better paying careers in other fields. My equipment needed updating. My business plan was non-existent. I knew I had to become a better employer and businessman if I was going to continue. I decided to hold myself to the same high standard of constant growth I expected from my athletes. That is when I learned the difference between mindset and skill set — between *owner-operator* and *entrepreneur*.

I now believe that hard work is inevitable and can be a function of necessity or passion. Interest becomes passion through the journey of mastery, which I assure you involves hard work, long hours, and sustained focus. The difference between working hard out of necessity and doing so out of passion lies in enjoying the process and becoming a student of it. I always encouraged my students to make learning fun because when it stops being fun, their progress comes to a screeching halt.

I started taking business courses, enjoying the new information and challenges of implementing what I was learning. Being a great coach was only the first step in serving thousands of families. If the gym was to meet the children's needs at a higher level, it had to support full-time employees who loved serving others as much as I did, and it had to afford the latest technology being used in the sport. Obtaining better business skills was not an option — it was a necessity! For the company to grow, I had to grow.

My hunger for knowledge became the driving force behind cultivating the work ethic, focus, and follow-through I so desperately wanted to embody. I was coaching 50 hours per week and working another 15-plus hours on the business. I was obsessed with becoming a better person and coach. I took dozens of seminars, read hundreds of books, and humbly began asking for help.

I owe so much to all the athletic, business, and personal coaches in my life that taught me the formula for success. That means focus, perseverance, and follow-through. I owe even more to my father who modeled these virtues so consistently. I didn't cultivate them as much as I should have when I was young, but I am just grateful I was able to access them many years later. Their lessons inspire me to this day and fuel my passion for coaching and creating rewarding careers for extraordinary coaches.

Passion is the reserve tank in all of us that kicks in when we feel empty. Had I not improved myself, I would not have started the journey of mastering the art of relating to athletes, serving my customers, and meeting the needs of my employees. The more I improved, the better I felt about the athletes', coworkers', clients' and business' success. My interest turned to passion through the process of self-mastery.

Though it was not an elegant transformation, my weaknesses became my strengths. It was painful, but joyful also. I have watched thousands of children discover a strong self-esteem and powerful knowing that they can be-do-have anything. Most people have heard about the 10,000-hour rule; for some of us, it is more like 40,000 hours. At least, that is what it has taken me to transform from a wild and undisciplined teenager to an entrepreneur who exemplifies integrity and work ethic.

At 49, I am just getting started! The knowledge and entrepreneurial spirit acquired over the past 30 years is the foundation for what is coming and serves me in every area of my life. Both me and my business have grown. HI-NRG Gymnastics opened two new gyms, I became a published author, and healed a broken neck that happened on my birthday… all during a global pandemic. My hard-earned discipline and focus allowed me to triumph. I now know being an entrepreneur means being a leader who demonstrates integrity, perseverance, sustained focus, and passion.

By now you can guess what fuels growth, focus, and hard work: PASSION! In those times when you don't want to work and you're too tired to focus… when others might quit… passion kicks in and carries you. It is NOT necessary to love every minute of the journey. Many people preach passion as the primary vehicle to achievement and fulfillment, but I have learned it is only half of the equation — *self-mastery* is the missing piece. It is expertise which comes from thousands of hours of focus. Discover your areas of mastery and you unearth a passion that makes you a leader. Enjoy the journey to mastery… it is just beginning!

Ignite Action Steps

Passion must be fueled and this fuel is practice. The better we get at a skill, the more we enjoy it. At some time we all find mastery in something. What skills have you been cultivating for decades? Is it a physical skill like cooking, yoga, or caring for others? Is it an invisible skill such as compassionate listening or helping soothe those in emotional pain? Do you journal or write in a diary? What have you been practicing without knowing it? Cultivate that passion (those 10,000-plus hours) with sustained focus.

Paul Battaglia – United States of America
Owner High Energy Fitness, Hi-NRG Gymnastics, co-owner eJoy, LLC
hinrggymnastix.com

IGNITE THE ENTREPRENEUR

BRENDA
NEUBAUER

Brenda Neubauer

"Life has a way of throwing things at you but you have the choice to rise up and bring the best out of yourself."

I want you to feel that life sometimes throws you challenges that are gifts in disguise. What was something that I didn't ask for, that I would have ran away from had it come in any other form, that became something that fit like a glove in every way? I'm hoping that reading my experience will show how strong we all are despite being pushed to our limits. And, once we find those limits, we then can take a deep breath and discover the courage to be a better version of ourselves — there within lies our true potential.

The Gift I Never Wanted

Sometimes the very worst of events can become an absolute blessing in your life. When my husband was seriously injured in a car accident, not once but twice within a week's time, I had to completely reinvent myself. I had to embrace an entire new way of doing and living. Humans often take the easy way simply because it is human nature. What landed on my lap in a series of unfortunate events forced me to do something that went way beyond what I thought I was capable of to accomplish something pretty cool. I'm just so in awe of where I started and where I am now.

As a child, I was surrounded by strong women who set the example for all I would come to do. My grandma was widowed young with nine kids to raise on a farm. I hear her voice echo in my mind saying, "The bank can't take your farm if you keep paying even one dollar." I was in awe of her resolve and how she refused to give up. I knew that I was cut from the same resilient cloth, and that knowledge got me through the tough days.

It's funny how history repeats itself. I've been told that before I was born, my mom had a similar experience when my dad got sick, and she had to rise up and be the everything caregiver. My grandma babysat me a lot when I was small and she would tell me stories of when she was widowed with all her children and how she would handle life with no running water or heat, without a vehicle, sewing their clothes and washing them by hand. She lived with diabetes, broke both hips, and still made it to 95. On those days when giving up felt so real, I remembered the stories of my mom and grandma; how resourceful and resilient they both were and I admired them. I would take a deep breath and give it my best, even if all I had to give was a smile through gritted teeth. That courage against all odds and fears would keep me afloat through the scariest times that lay on my horizon.

Money in our family had always been just enough — just enough to live, but not really any extra. Everything had to be budgeted, and when you splurged it affected everything else. Working with money was the farthest thing from my mind, as I was very intimidated by numbers and finance. After flunking grade nine math, my belief became that I was no good with numbers, and from that point on, my view of my math abilities was in the toilet. I pursued more artsy things instead.

The first time I met my husband, I pretty much ignored him. I was 20 and he was 16, the friend of my friend's younger brother, and I had no idea how important he would come to be to me. At six-foot three-inches, he was a gentle giant with gorgeous brown eyes, a sharp wit, and a caring and generous heart. Over the next few years, his persistence and wit grew on me and we got married and ended up having four kids in six years.

Life was crazy, busy, fun, messy, loud, and amazing. Then, one frosty January morning, our life came crashing down. Gary left that morning to do his 35-minute commute to work as he did everyday when he was rear-ended in the morning rush by a mom who was late getting her teenagers to school. His doctor diagnosed him with whiplash, gave him a collar, and told him to rest at home and not to drive. Being the strong German that he is, he took that advice for a whole four days — then decided he'd had enough and headed back to work. The next thing we knew, he was in a second accident and lodged under a 4x4 truck. We realized in that moment that things had changed for good.

Gary's doctor was not pleased when we re-visited him regarding the second whiplash and concussion. His depth perception was gone, so he could no longer do things requiring hand-eye coordination. It all shut down at that point. Life went into a different phase. Our normal was no longer normal.

We limped through the next two-and-a-half years on a group disability pension that allowed us to sustain our new "not-so-normal" life. Gary's injuries required dark and quiet surroundings as he had the sensation that he was continually spinning and falling, paining him and making him nauseous. Our kids were two, four, six, and eight at the time of the accident. The stress of keeping four kids under wraps was some days more than I could handle. Right in the midst of all of Gary's challenges, we found out our four-year-old daughter had a speech delay and needed to have intense therapy. With two in school, the youngest two at home, and one with no speech — it was hard. Everything literally was left to me. Standing in my kitchen, I could feel the strength within me of my mother who worked nonstop to try to keep our family going, and of my grandmother, running the farm by herself simply because that was what was needed. And I was needed. All the errands, the never-ending doctor's appointments and therapy sessions, all the parent-teacher interviews, the grocery shopping, the parenting... it was all me. It was a hectic schedule. I dropped into bed each night, exhausted, and then got up each morning and did it all again.

Throughout the chaos, we continually looked at the silver lining of this cloud. We found joy every day. We found reasons to laugh and enjoy each other's company no matter the circumstances. Dad was home — he was altered, but home. Those couple of years raced by as we all adjusted to our new normal. Just when we had found a rhythm, we got a letter. The floor went out from under me as I read the words: "You have come to the end of the disability period, and this is the last check you will receive." I looked up from the letter to see Gary clutching the sides of the mattress; sweaty, anxious, and in pain — proof we weren't anywhere near "the end."

Then, my eyes caught a tiny lifeline at the bottom of the page: instructions on how to begin an appeal if the injury still kept you from working. I began the first appeal immediately, rounding up all the reports required, documenting the hundreds of appointments with neurologists, surgeons, physiotherapists, and psychoanalysts over the past 30 months. I was confident we had a case. When the response came back as "DENIED," I was shocked and shaken to the core. Even moreso, after we hired a lawyer for two more appeals, only to be DENIED again. My world was rocked in a way that I could not have anticipated. My lawyer delivered the grave news to me that I was up against a system that was not going to bend — because if they did, it would open the floodgates of appeals. That moment is as real and fresh in my mind as though it happened last week. I remember soaking in a tub of bubbles, thinking, "What on earth are we going to do now?"

My parents tried to alleviate some stress by offering to let us move in with them, but eight people in a three-bedroom house didn't exactly feel like a fix. Still, feeling we had no choice, we put our house up for sale, complete with a whirlwind fix up, cleanup, and staging process. But life had other plans, and after five weeks on the market, our house had not sparked any interest. We sunk into the realization that a quick fix to our situation was not happening.

I've come to realize that *life keeps moving even if you aren't.* We had racked up a fair amount of debt. I was paying groceries with credit cards, credit cards with other credit cards, gas, even our mortgage — it was getting scary pretty quick. I received our semi-annual mortgage statement among the bills and for the first time, I *really* looked at it. It appeared we only had 14 years left on our mortgage — we had accelerated our payments and now we had crossed over — paying more principal than interest for the first time! We were close to paying off our house, so I figured the bank might be able to help. I mustered up the courage to call the bank and spoke to a gal and explained that we had had a small snag and wanted to know what they could do to shrink our mortgage payment. I left out the part that I was paying my mortgage with my Visa™ as banks tend to frown on that! By the end of our conversation it was clear they were not going to help.

Again my world was crushing in on me. I started yelling at God, feeling very alone and very responsible. Our world was crumbling and I didn't see a way out. I am still amazed that when I speak of this experience with my kids, they were totally unaware of what was going on. Inside I was a wreck, but I knew I had to put on my big girl pants and figure it out.

It was then I heard an audible voice inside my head that said: "Trust me, I need you to say yes to everything that is coming your way, even if you don't feel comfortable or fully understand."

I felt the fear coursing through my veins transform into exhilaration; the sensation of my pounding heart taking on a whole new meaning. I took a deep breath and said "OK."

A few moments later, the phone rang. My kids were swirling around me and the house was filled with the same noise as always, but that sound of the phone ringing cut through. Whether I was conscious of it or not, some part of me had to have known as I picked up the receiver that fate was on the other side.

And no matter what it was, I knew that I had to say, "Yes."

I heard the voices of my husband's sister and brother-in-law. They always did the research in our family. When you went to buy a toaster, they would know if that was a good brand or not. They told me we needed to sit down with a financial company that had taught them something crucial before selling our house. They asked for my blessing to pass our number on to their broker. The "yes" I spoke would set in motion the change I never knew I needed.

The next day, the broker was at my door. She was eager to chat about the beautiful painting on my wall, but my life had no room for idle chatter. Gary and I sped her to the table, ready to just get on with it. After a 20-minute conversation, we were taught more about money and finance than we had ever learned before. It was a punch in the gut when I learned we had made mistakes along the way that cost us dearly when it came to retirement. The broker ended up shrinking our $1,200/month mortgage payment to $300; something our bank could have given us if I'd known how to ask. I realized at that moment that we aren't provided a financial education. Unless you're blessed with savvy parents, we will most likely make the same mistakes they did or worse. Then the light bulb went off in my head: I had to empower myself and my family through financial education.

Later I would look at this like it was a gift I didn't want. I felt it didn't suit me, was the wrong shape, color, and size, yet once I put it on — it fit perfectly. The broker explained there was a part-time training program with her firm, and Gary threw me under the bus by saying, "She's looking for a job," with no thought for how much the idea might terrify me. As all my fears about math rushed right to the surface, I remembered my grandmother's resilience, and decided to take a leap of faith. I knew the timing was right. My youngest child was headed to kindergarten, allowing me my first moments of solitude and silence to concentrate on what lay ahead. I started my business shaking in my boots; yet I remembered thinking 'no' was not an option, and I had to stay the course. It made me dig deep and get good at my craft fast. I was licensed in eight weeks and I went to work. It was hard, but oh so worth it. I faced fears I didn't even know I had, and finance ended up being something I loved and am really good at. When feelings of not being enough came flooding up, I would visualize myself already being successful. I launched into a whole world of self-development and created a vision board with a picture of the girl I imagined myself being... having it all together and ready to take on the world. I would focus on that vision knowing my family's future rose and fell with me. Despite my circumstances, I could control if I got up the next day. I could control whether I fell apart or made it work. Those are all choices, and we make them every day. Even on the days life got to me I still moved forward; always reflecting back to that picture on my vision board.

We stayed in our own home for my first year of business then my parents offered to sell us their house. We moved back into the house I had left at 17; to live beside the neighbors I had as a teenager. To come back in your 40s with four kids and a husband is a bit surreal. I took back my own bedroom, because taking your parents room is just creepy. It's a bit weird and wonderful to smell the same smells from your youth, hearing the same sounds waking up in the same room you remember as a kid! We have now lived here 16 years — and my kids have attended the same high school I did.

The strong women in my life started my journey, and they have been with me at every step since, reminding me we are all stronger than we think. I am so grateful for what these women taught me by example. Things keep moving, and knowing that it is going to change not only comforts me but cheers me up and cheers me on. Without this horrific experience I would not have challenged myself to become a better person. Life has a way of working things out for you if you are willing to hang on to the wild ride. You have to choose to overcome what's hard. If I would have chosen the "easy" route of finding a job — something that would have paid me a wage in exchange for easy, I would have needed three jobs to create enough income for us to survive. I would still be struggling today. I shudder to think where we would be. Instead I chose the harder path and to learn an industry I had no clue about. I decided to face my fears and get better at being "comfortable in my own skin," and as a result our life is much easier than I ever thought it could be. I bought into a better life for myself and my family, hung on with everything I had, and now we are excited about the future. Our attitude is *'bring it on!'*

I love what I do. I'm a financial broker and I truly enjoy it. Helping families navigate through life not knowing some basic financial principles is like trying to make a trip in a foreign country without a map or knowing the language. I know when I sit down with families the education I bring is life-changing. Through talking, finding out, and analyzing, I get to hear their stories. Stories of decisions and events and how life has kept happening and keeps going. I love delving into their stories and helping them come out on the other side, happy, whole, and ready to say "yes" to their lives.

Humans will take the easy way, every time, because it's human nature. What landed on my lap in a series of unfortunate events forced me to go way beyond what I thought I was capable of, to accomplish something pretty cool. I'm just so in awe of where I started and where I am now... I'm so aware of how much more we all are capable of doing. When I talk to people who are stuck in life, I tell them, "You have to give yourself more credit. You are capable of so much more. It's always your choice to reach a higher level. What are you going to say '*bring it on*' to?"

Ignite Action Steps

- You have to start where you are! Don't be afraid to look at your financial picture. List out your income and expenses. Read books, seek advice, and welcome the financial education that will help you achieve what you desire.

- I strongly encourage everyone to take some time to really assess where they're at and where they want to be in five, 10, 20 years. Write it down and work toward that.

- Having a plan of where you want to go is the first step to achieving it!

Brenda Neubauer – Canada
Senior Marketing Director
https://agents.wfgcanada.ca/bc/kelowna/brenda-neubauer

IGNITE THE ENTREPRENEUR

JOSE LUIS
CAMACHO

JOSE LUIS CAMACHO

"It is time to press on to your truth."

My desire for sharing this personal account of freedom is that you feel inspired to break free from the strongholds of your past that keep you from experiencing a great life. It is time to explore a most marvelous landscape: YOU! Whether it was words spoken to you, a person hurting you, or an event owning you, may my story give you energy to shatter untruths about the truly capable person you are.

YOU WERE SUPPOSED TO BE A BAND DIRECTOR

The cool air danced a gentle rhythm on our skin, a welcome departure from the usual scorpion sting of the southwest Texas heat. It was early fall 1996. My friends and I were caught up in our usual mix of fun and mischief: inventing games with nearby inanimate objects. This time, we were hopping into an empty 55-gallon bin atop a hillside, then kicking the barrel, propelling each other down a grassy knoll at dizzying speeds only until we'd crash into a brick wall! Onlookers that day, high school students from many different campuses across the state, at first looked at our work as unwelcome, attention-seeking tomfoolery. However, our cheers, laughter, and game were infectious, and won their hearts over to join us; resulting in long lines of adolescents waiting their turn to barrel roll.

That was our usual method to pass time at University Interscholastic League (UIL) competitions, whether waiting our turn to compete in events or having completed an event. UIL offered educational extracurricular competition in the areas of scholastics, athletics, and music. Our group of friends flexed for our school in each of these categories, often winning top places in many. In band competitions, I was a monster competitor, where my passion for music had me studying and crafting my drumming art form with disregard for anything else. In scholastics and athletics... not so much. Oh, I participated and made every attempt to dominate. I'd even pull some surprises and win a top spot from time to time. That was rare, however, and unlike my peers who were dominant competitors in their own respects, I mostly just did enough to win overall points for our school. Nevertheless, I was driven by school pride and committed to honoring my group of friends.

In my mind, I was an equal to my peers. One friend, however, did not seem to think so. He must have noticed the scholastic struggles I failed to acknowledge openly. He excelled in academia but struggled in music — quite the yin to my yang. Except the perfect circle was broken by inner envy; a secret assassin poised to end strong relationships between chums at the right moment. At the right statement.

"Hey Joe... you should stick with music, man. It's what you are really good at. I wouldn't mess with other things. Music is what you should do."

That came from Dylan, my childhood buddy that I spent countless hours with. Dylan, who I made laugh at my ridiculous disregard for school order by getting into situations that edged on being in trouble. Dylan, who beat me left and right in video games like Street Fighter II™. This dear friend to whom I would never make statements concerning his low musical skill was the one who ushered that statement into my plane of existence.

This hit me where it hurt, because my brother's legacy was that of a UIL mathematics genius. I was trying to fill his shoes at the time, and after my failed attempts, Dylan's statement moved in like a bad roommate. I tried to look cool and confident, but I'm sure the shock showed on my face. Was this meant to help or hurt me? I never had a chance to inquire; the statement landed, carved its way into my heart, and waited.

Your spoken word is the manifestation of your inner self, cloaked in timbre and tones of positivity or negativity and wrapped as a gift or hurled as a blade. Statements weave those words like measures of musical notes, carefully constructed with the sounds that convey our attitudes, our meaning, our truth. I was taught by my lovely, strong, and brilliant mother, Mary Esther, to be careful with the words we choose to speak, for they are powerful and can leave long-standing proof of how we helped or hurt.

I never knew if Dylan's statement was meant to help or hurt me. All I knew was that, once released, it left decades of doubt, challenge, and seeking of answers while pitting who I wanted to be against who I allowed myself to be.

The remainder of my time in high school saw more wins achieved in music to the tune of a full ride to University of Texas in Austin for a music education degree — along with enough financial rewards and scholarships to make a leprechaun grin. But upon graduation I could only think one thing: "What do I do now with my life?"

I was raised to believe life as a musician was a life that may not see big financial returns. I saw many great musicians whom I admired fall to divorce, bankruptcy, substance abuse, or poor paying lowly jobs as... 'band directors.' I conceived this notion through spoken words that filtered into my heart and brain and nestled in, but never greeted me until I was at university. I did not want the responsibility of *choosing* my path. Rather, I just wanted to keep making music and thriving in being a badass like I was in high school. I refused to imagine a life outside of making a living musically; it's all I thought I could do. I never believed I could create new skill sets or conjure up other abilities to create income.

When things are left unattended, they most certainly do not disappear, including problems. They may become silent, but trust me, they are still present and can become larger and more menacing when left alone. Statements formed by spoken words are no different. University is where my menace greeted me after all those years.

"Hello, Jose Luis. Remember me? The feeling of purpose assigned by another? You are meant to only produce musical fruit and nothing else. Nobody wants anything else from you but this. Don't kid yourself."

Defeated, I allowed that voice to penetrate deep. Evidence of my imposed reality spilled forth like a hose with tiny holes shooting out water: in my grades, my attendance, and my attitude toward ANYTHING not related to music. Who I chose to hang out with, where I went, what I opened my wallet for — if it was not music, I was not having it! All that seemed well and good, except I had my other roommate to contend with: fear; fear that I would not make it as a musician and wind up desperate for a low-paying job in a career I did not like with no marketable skills. I was not a flunky in school, mind you. I was in the top 10 percent of my large graduating class and in honors and accelerated programs in high school. None of this, however, felt genuine.

After falling behind in grades and attendance, I was placed on academic suspension. Being too proud to beg my family for financial help, I crawled back to my parents' home and took up a job I felt lucky to land: Assistant Band Director at a local school. That job, a favor from a friend, is where I met a United States Marine Corps (USMC) Band Recruiter whose intention was to recruit high schoolers into a career as a marine musician. His intent had nothing to do with me, but *my* intent was different. I inquired about what being a marine meant. He responded with the expected musical career mumbo jumbo, but I had zero interest in that path. I wanted nothing to do with music anymore. In my mind and heart, music had failed me. At least the marines could take care of me, pay me regardless of my circumstances, and provide for me where I did not have to do much but hold a rifle and blow stuff up. That was my plan. Join the marines and have a career outside of music. I went home and broke the news to my mother that night. She cried, unsure of my future.

"Mijo… what has happened to you? You were supposed to be a band director!"

Inside, I felt a flame of annoyance by her question, but I knew it was my moment and I had to follow my decision. I passed all the requirements for shipping out to the Marine Corps Recruit Depot in San Diego. Over the next months, I slowly forgot about being a musician. I became an attentive, dynamic, and organic machine that marveled at the new skills and abilities I obtained. That was very much in tune with learning a musical instrument… but I digress! Enough with music, I will become an awesome marine! For once in my life, I had 'Pax Romana,' a period of immense peace. I was far separated from those who had made statements that turned my life into confusion. I would be my own kingdom and rule as I saw fit!

"Recruit Camachooooo! Front and center!"

This was the cry from my drill instructor, a man I admired but hated for the pain he put me through in boot camp. I approached as instructed. He stared at me with disgust, then instructed me to follow him with purpose and haste. We arrived at a large building where I was directed to stand by a doorway and await further instructions. Nervousness set in as a taller, more senior marine appeared and ushered me into a massive room. At once, I felt a familiar shock, as I realized I was in the Depot Band Hall, home of the amazing Marine Band San Diego.

"Recruit Camacho, there are five immediate vacancies for marine percussionists in our Corps that need to be filled. Our database shows you have traditional collegiate schooling for percussion and an outstanding high school musical career. Son, you are invited to audition for one of these spots."

That I was even granted a choice of interest in boot camp was an achievement! But to go back to what I am SUPPOSED to be? I was both angry and oddly relieved. He explained that if I didn't audition, I would be stuck waiting for up to a year before I graduated as a marine. My choice was clear: return to music. I auditioned and made it.

After graduation, I was stationed with *Marine Corps Band New Orleans*. Music and I found a working relationship, one where I showcased my all and received numerous accolades for my skill. I married while in the Corps; together, we created the first of my three greatest life achievements: my first daughter. I was enjoying life and felt unstoppable. When I was not playing in the marine band, I was a recording artist, playing in clubs, or teaching students to drum. It was a great life!

Then those words came back.

"Joe! You were just supposed to be a band director!" The stinging statement delivered that time by my wife was wrapped in disgust for the busy life I created with music. Immediately, I felt embarrassed, incapable, ashamed, and responsible for destroying a good life. My old roommate, *fear*, returned.

I got out of the marines and moved my family to my wife's town to try my hand at civilian life. I took up a job at my local regional health center as a janitor, determined to have some income. Sadly, we divorced, but I remained in this small town for my daughter; the only light I had left in my dark reality. I was broken down. "Music failed me again," was all I could say to myself. I lost 80 pounds of weight and cried every ounce of water I had in me. I reached out to my God for answers, though I felt I had nothing to offer in return — to Him or anyone.

I remember being in my Oldsmobile™ Cutlass Supreme in a trough of roadway that never receives radio or satellite signal: a void like me. I screamed out for answers to my empty life! The response came. Out of nowhere, the regional Christian channel faded in with an eerie yet welcome analog radio scratch. The words, as if sung by an angel, sounded from my cheap, broken car speakers: "In Jesus Name… we press on!" This was a chorus from a song I would sing at church. After the chorus, the music and analog noise faded and disappeared, bringing back the void. I sat in stunned silence, my jaw wide open and the hair standing up on my arms. I heard the message — a loud and clear call to action.

Press on. From what? I spent the next year trying to discover what that meant. I couldn't deny the divine intervention, nor will I ever. Clarity came to me in a few pages from a self-help book. In a guided activity, I catalogued events, moments, and statements that I felt did not support who I wanted to be or how I wanted to feel. I entered the one statement I knew that cloaked itself in three shrouds over the years and was delivered by people I loved: "You were supposed to be a band director."

It hit me like a ton of bricks. Many tears flowed soon after I realized I had allowed this statement to define me. I decided that day to press on and disallow the power it had all these years. With great fanfare and celebration, I accepted my new voice and desire to change. I was confident to do greater things for my life and for those I love.

I served in the healthcare industry for 17 years, climbing the ranks from janitor to Information Technology Director. I took a risk and left my secure job in order to explore my entrepreneurial spirit through starting and leading several corporations in service industries that are growing and serving our communities in southern Colorado. I allowed myself to be bold and do public speaking at conferences and media platforms such as BEGrowthDriven.com™! I even decided to become an author of empowerment stories through Ignite! The yummy icing on top of this all? I still do musical things! I record, I play, I write, and I teach music. These are things I never thought were possible. Choosing to press on, to trust myself, and celebrate my accomplishments made the difference.

As I reflect back, I realize those individuals never meant to hurt me. The statements came out of fear, or concern, or retort to a moment in our lives, yes, but they weren't meant to change the tone of my life. *I did that.* I *allowed* that. I never challenged the statement directly, nor in the revisions to follow. I allowed that statement to command my life, to dictate who I thought I was supposed to be. I cried for hours over this revelation. *I had the power* — all these years! I could have delegated that statement and the fear I'd associated with it to do things *besides* rule my core.

Today, I live a purpose-driven and authentic life, one where I do things that aren't musically centered, but have the power of musical creativity to get them accomplished. I lead my beautiful family of three daughters, Christiana Ramona, Nickeya Cortana, and Micaela Amoriel, along with my gorgeous wife, Michelle. I lead several businesses in varying industries that are not of musical origin. I choose to press on from the false image of reality I created in my past so I can enjoy an authentic life today. I am free to explore new possibilities in markets I never thought I could play in.

Let my experience Ignite you to press on from the statements you might harbor and unnecessarily cultivate from your own belief that you are not capable of being anything but what others believe you to be. *You* are a being capable of creating wonderful outcomes and across multiple landscapes if *you* choose to claim your belief in yourself. It takes more work to carry unresolved baggage than it does to meet it face on and resolve it. It is time to press on to *your* truth.

IGNITE ACTION STEPS

Take some time away from distractions of the day or night, and list moments, events, or statements that you feel do not provide a purposeful and positive picture of who you want to be.

Take that reflection and acknowledge that those things happened and may continue to throughout your life. Delegate those feelings away from where you are headed in the future.

Accept that these did happen in your life or continue to happen, and that you are ready to press on from the negativity and untruths they have created about you.

Pressing on is an action. Act on choosing to press on and instead fill your thoughts with what is true; you are capable of many things. Do this as a daily commitment, and you will see how untruths step out of the way, revealing what is 'truth' for you.

Love yourself each day, claiming your new creative passions.

For my Daddy, Jose Moreno Camacho, and my Sis, Marisol Camacho.
Your love lives on, eternally.

Jose Luis Camacho – United States of America
Husband & Daddy,
CEO of AshcaTek LLC
CEO of American Log Home Blasting, LLC
joseluiscamacho.com
@joecamacho_colorado

IGNITE THE ENTREPRENEUR

CYNTHIA CAUGHIE

CYNTHIA CAUGHIE

"You can do hard things."

I want you to know one thing above all else: You can do hard things. Believe in the power you have inside of you. Be proactive with your growth instead of reactive with your life, and let that inspire you to be better; to seek something else. Live your life two steps ahead instead of two steps behind. Believe in yourself.

YOU ARE YOUR OWN SUPERPOWER

Today was a big day. It was the day I had waited for and dreamt about for so many years. It seemed like a day of unknowns, excitement, and pride all in one. It was thrilling and scary, but I wasn't nervous. I was getting everything I had worked so hard for. My lifelong dream of becoming a business owner had come true. I was going to become the official owner of Homerun Pizza TODAY!

It was a turning point for me. I had believed in myself and this dream for so long and today was the day I knew all I had gone through — all the struggles, the sacrifice, the joy — was with absolute certainty what I was supposed to be doing with my life. Looking around the dining room, I saw so many amazing smiling and laughing faces touched with joy. There was a subtle hum of happiness, the sweet smell of fresh pizza dough, and a hint of spice in the pepperoni overlaid with the sweetest smell of BBQ from the special pork sliders we all enjoyed. Music echoed through the corridors and the karaoke vibe of everyone singing along invoked the joy of happiness in this place.

Homerun Pizza was not just any other place where you eat dinner. Every single person who sat in that restaurant meant something to me. They were there for the journey. These people had supported me for years and for them to be here now meant the world to me. My family, who had been so great watching the girls as I worked, were there. My husband's smiling face cheering me on filled me with gratitude for how he had taken over parenting duties so I could grow and become the woman who brought me to this point. I could see my best friends who had said, "Yes, you can!" The 'regulars' I knew by name and I had become a part of their lives. So many relationships I had made from all of those who cared, and I cared for them. This day was for not only myself but for all those who enjoyed the spirit of Homerun Pizza.

To know that four days a week for 13 years, I had enjoyed, nurtured, and cultivated relationships with these amazing people; and that brought me to this point in life… WOW! I just couldn't comprehend the overwhelming sense of accomplishment and pride I had. The energy in the room and the praise from others for my transition from serving for 13 years at this very place to *owning* it was glorified and humbling. I heard, "I'm so proud of you!" so many times that night from so many people. It was life-changing. Stepping back to enjoy this celebratory scene, I had visions of my journey of becoming a restaurateur. Some of my favorite moments leading up to this surreal night came racing back to me.

The journey to get to where I was had been 13 years in the making. I first set foot in the restaurant when I was a young 28-year-old, fresh off a girls' night of partying in the city, just three months after I had my first daughter. I walked into the restaurant at 8 o'clock in the morning, wrapped my apron around my waist, and started my first day on the job. I had worked for the owner Greg before at one of his other restaurants. Greg had three partners and he invited me to come check out his new place, Homerun Pizza, in the small community of Larkfield, California. He was one of the original groups of guys who started the restaurant from the ground up, and they were fun and crazy! The three of them were always easygoing and had an 'it's just pizza and beer' mentality.

Three of the partners got out of the business and then we had new owners. Going from what had been a casual and comfortable working atmosphere to a group who didn't have a good handle on how to run a restaurant and were just barely making ends meet was a challenge. By then I had moved into night shifts and worked even longer hours. This group of owners managed the restaurant as a second job, not knowing what it took to run a restaurant, but they loved it for it's potential. We all did our best, but it wasn't quite working and staffing issues meant we were often slow in service or food. I remember countless nights running around to all our beloved customers and giving them a 'homerun half' on their drink (which is what I like to call the top half), always trying to make customers laugh with a smile and a hug!

When the owners couldn't handle it any longer and I couldn't be the only one responsible for keeping it afloat, the restaurant limped along. I felt at times that I was the only one working to keep the light on and doors open for years. During those hard times, one of those owners said to me, "You are the best thing going for this place." It made me think how much I loved Homerun Pizza and always had. I loved that restaurant so much that I would daydream about trying to buy it. But by that time, I had three small children, my husband was out of work, and I lived in what I called a 'shack!' How could I ever buy the place? It was a pipe dream. You know the ones that never really come true? They just stay underground. In my heart of hearts, I always believed that it would someday be mine, but with all of those things stacked against me, it was hard to imagine how.

We continued that way for months then the dreaded day came when they decided to sell it. It hurt to hear the news because I didn't know what was going to happen, but I still loved the place and wanted to be there. There was a glimmer of hope that maybe I could scoop it up from them as they were selling it cheap. I entertained the idea that my pipe dream could become a reality, but it stayed a dream when they confided in me they had found new owners, a local couple. Del had grown up in this area and he and his wife Salana were buying the restaurant. My heart dropped. Would they change it? Would they keep me on as a server? It was a hard transition because my heart had wanted that entrepreneurial dream. It hurt that I couldn't find a way to come up with some money to purchase it.

Even though I didn't get it, the dream wasn't gone. I just believed that it wasn't my time to purchase it. I didn't know it then, but these owners would be the best thing that walked into my life. They had been customers for years and I had served them often. Homerun Pizza was their Sunday night spot on the weekends with their blended family. They loved coming in for a custom pizza that took Salana five minutes to order because she was very specific — we still laugh about it now. By the time they bought the place, I knew her order without her telling me. That's what I did, who I was, how people knew me, and why they loved me.

The day came when they no longer stepped through the door as customers but as owners. The transition was a bit rocky in my head because of the lingering bitterness of not getting to buy the restaurant. In all honesty it didn't take me long to get over it because I told myself with three young daughters and me not being in a financial place to secure the restaurant, it just simply wasn't the right time. I learned quickly Del was a doer! We got a new computer system, which we never had with previous owners. He hired a new manager/day server to really help clean and organize things. He was a businessman not a restaurant owner. He took the necessary steps to make things run smoothly on a budget while he cut the fat and turned it around in two short years, and I learned so much just by watching him.

After they had been owners of the restaurant for a year or so, we became very very close friends. I mean so good we would spend birthdays and go to the lake together. As time passed we got closer and closer. They were amazing friends and still are. We were out one night with another couple. Salana was telling the story of their purchasing Homerun Pizza and related that they had asked the sellers, "Does she come with the restaurant?" Unbeknownst to me, this couple was changing my life.

Four years into their ownership, I remember having a conversation with one of the other servers, Wendy, who worked with me at the time. I remember it vividly. It was the end of our serving shift and we were chatting at the bar 'having a glass' while closing. It was late and we were doing the girl chat catchup when she asked me, "So when are you going to buy this place?"

I literally stopped, frozen in place, the rag in my hand paused mid-swipe in cleaning off the bar. While we are besties now, at the time we didn't know each other that well and having her acknowledge out loud what I believed inside was astonishing. It was something I had thought about and envisioned for so long that it was as if, in my mind, Homerun Pizza was already mine. Except apparently it wasn't just in my mind since Wendy had picked up on it also.

"WHAT?! You see me as the owner of this place? I thought that was only something I saw in my own mind." Well that opened the floodgates and we had another glass of wine talking about how, "if I could, I would" and "let's be partners." That night, the true vision was cast and I could see myself smiling, laughing, and enjoying the community and friends of Homerun Pizza *without* the apron on! What a concept! I could be the one to create and inspire the warm and caring people that came into our restaurant. My vision was clear, but there wasn't a path. We finished up our wine and let the dream fade for a while as we went home to our little ones to nurture and care for them, but that night had reignited my belief that Homerun Pizza would be mine one day.

And then, the day of my birthday, Sonoma County caught fire. October 9th, 2017, the Tubbs Fire, the biggest forest fire in history, burned over 5,200 homes and took absolutely everything we had. It took the tough stuff that can never be replaced: the girls' baby videos and pictures, the favorite jean jacket of my grandpa who passed away, the one he wore in the vineyard for years while he worked in it. I loved that jacket! Salana was the first person who called me and told me to get out of the house when the fire came through. We escaped the rolling flames, 80 mile an hour winds, and smoke so thick you couldn't see 10 feet in front of you. It was a very scary and hectic time not knowing where to go or what was next.

And then people started reporting that the restaurant was also lost. I couldn't believe it. I *wouldn't* believe it. Once we confirmed that our house was gone, I couldn't imagine losing the restaurant as well. Del and Salana had also lost their home and we became inseparable from that moment for the next year and a half. For all of us, everything had changed. That event changed my life dramatically in ways I could never have imagined. Finally it was confirmed by a regular that the restaurant along with the complex it was in had all been spared by the flames by just under half a mile.

It would be one week before we could reopen the restaurant. The day we reopened, it could have been anyone's night to serve, but it was *my* night to serve. I was always deemed the 'Homerun Pizza Girl' — it was my place. I knew without a doubt that I should have been the one to welcome everyone back in the community with open arms. Homerun Pizza has been a staple to the community for 12 years. We needed to pull together and show our friends and customers that we could make it through this devastating time. Del and Salana pulled the back of the house together and I pulled the front of the house together. I welcomed our customers in with a beer and a hug! It was so important to be all together; in an even bigger and more impactful way than ever before. I lost my house, but I was so blessed to have my family and my home-away-from-home, Homerun Pizza family, to get me through this time to rebuild not just my life but my faith in the community.

Del and Salana were into both business and self-development and introduced me to many new ideas over the years. There is a quote I still use to this day that Salana gave me: "What if everything you're going through right now is preparing you for a dream bigger than you can imagine?" I realized that my life *was* bigger and I had changed. My thought process was different. My heart was different. I took more risks. I didn't care about material things. I was thankful for all l had. But more than that, I was determined. I would make the best of this situation. I would help others through this devastating time. What doesn't kill you makes you stronger. I wanted to make a difference.

Eight months later, after all that happened in our lives, Del and Salana decided the time had come where they wanted out of the restaurant. They wanted to move on to the next chapter of their lives. I remember it as clear as day, we were standing in the kitchen on Coveline Street where we all lived together. Yes, after the fire, our two families of seven all moved in together to support each as we rebuilt our lives. Del said, "I've thought a lot about it and I'm going to sell the restaurant." There was silence for what seemed like forever as my thoughts raced and my heart dropped. How could he do this? We had been through so much together. Why? I mean come on, I can't take much more! It was like a gut punch. In his next breath, he looked right at me and asked, "Do you want it?"

The words, "Of course I want it!" flew out of my mouth. Then my brain engaged, shit how am I going to do this? Financially I can't. I don't have a home. My family is traumatized from the fire. WTH. Why now?!? WHY? Still in complete shock, I calmly said, "Let me go ask the bank."

If not now, then when? I had to go ask the bank, because that was the only way I was going to get it. And, if I didn't at least try, then the answer would have been no. It was the craziest feeling to know I might be in a place where I could have my dream come true. What if they said yes?! I just kept telling myself to believe this was going to happen. This is your time. You are ready.

YES! Yes, was the answer from the bank! I had wanted and had dreamt about this for so long. Yes, I could have the loan for my very own restaurant. Not just any restaurant, *my* restaurant! Homerun Pizza, where everyone knew my name. The sheer joy of what had just happened had not sunk in. I was in awe and disbelief, yet I knew I could do it at the same time. WOW! This is it. I'm going to be a restaurant owner... Holy shit!

On my first day as owner, Salana walked in, sunglasses on from too many tears of joy, and made a beeline to me for a hug. Our friendship journey was one of joy, love, laughter, resilience, comfort, and so much fun. This was a big day of accomplishments and perseverance; for both of us! She was beyond proud of me and couldn't get the waterworks to stop! I was honored and grateful that they trusted me carrying on the legacy. Del had passed the baseball bat to me. Our next page was about to turn and it was scarier than the Tubbs fire we had all survived.

Today, it is all mine, the laughter, the fun, the long nights, the debt, the profit, It's ALL mine! Gulp! Holy shit! It is ALL mine! What was I doing? How did this happen and what the hell am I going to do now? While all those thoughts did run through my mind, I was comforted by the fact I had me! The one who had done it for so many years without the title or the profit. The blood, sweat, and tears, the long nights, the missed dinners at home with the girls. This is when my belief in myself grew to the level of never turning back. I could do anything I set my mind to. The 'can-do' attitude and my positive personality would create more opportunity than I could ever imagine and this is just the beginning. It was the true Ignite moment of my entrepreneur story.

You can have this too — the power that is in you. You are literally one person away from the next chapter in your life. Every experience in your life is designed for you to take in and learn from. Be proactive with your growth and not reactive with your life. Stop long enough to see what is ahead of you. You have all the power inside; it's all in how you look at it. Believe that you can do it. Believe in yourself. You are your own superhero.

IGNITE ACTION STEPS

The best investment you can make is in yourself. Grow every day. Learn something new. Read a book. Don't just be stagnant in life; that's not living, that's just being. Live! Grow. Believe in every possibility. Every day you learn, every day you get better.

Cynthia Caughie – United States of America
Entrepreneur, Mom, Owner Homerun Pizza, Realtor
www.homerunpizzalarkfield.com
www.cynthiacaughie.exprealty.com
@CynthiaCaughie
@CynthiaCaughie
LI Cynthia Caughie
@Homerunpizzalarkfield

IGNITE the ENTREPRENEUR

MIKKO JARRAH

Mikko Jarrah

"Giving up is not an option!"

I believe life is for thriving, not just surviving. The best way I have found to thrive and live my happiest life is by becoming an entrepreneur. I want to give back as much value to all fellow entrepreneurs as I possibly can. I want to offer you hope and belief in yourself so you can always keep moving forward, even in your darkest moments. I'm grateful to play a part in supporting you in overcoming your biggest entrepreneurial challenges so you can thrive beyond your imagination.

From Bankrupt to Totally Free

When I was six years old, my uncle asked me, "Mikko, what do you want to be when you grow up?"

"I wanna be a businessman," I responded.

For as long as I can remember, I have wanted to be a successful businessman. I'm forever thankful to my dad for planting an entrepreneurial seed in me from a very young age. Yet despite the strong examples in my life and my dreams of being a businessman, my road to being a thriving entrepreneur has had quite a few twists and turns. At several points, I almost threw the towel into the ring altogether.

I have been a serial entrepreneur for most of my adult life and have been a shareholder in approximately 30 companies. I have witnessed the ups and downs of many ventures in a variety of business sectors over the years. This period of my life has taught me more than any school ever could.

I grew up around money. I spent my childhood in an unusual environment in Dubai, in the United Arab Emirates. I went to a private school and I had very affluent classmates. Every year when Dubai got too hot, we would spend our summer in Finland. It was great to have such a big family in Finland and a safe neighborhood with lots of fun friends living on my block. I felt like I had two totally different lives and I was privileged to experience the best of both worlds.

During my childhood, my father worked hard to create the best possible life for his family. I am grateful to him for the luxurious life he provided us with in Dubai. The downside was that he and I didn't bond that deeply on a father-son level. Of course I loved him, but I also struggled to connect with him because of his frequent absences and strong personality when he was home. My favorite memories are from when he took me to see the Dubai International car rally once a year. The local champion was his friend and we got to hang out at his pit stop together. We really enjoyed the speed and adrenaline of the event.

Looking back now, I realize that my father set a complicated example for me. He funded our lifestyle through his successful business dealings, but his work took him away from me and he rarely enjoyed the wonderful family moments that he was financing.

In school, I never found a subject I was good in or passionate about, so I ended up being a very average student barely passing most of my subjects. I became bored very quickly. I wanted to try all the different sports, but nothing excited me enough that I wanted to consistently practice it and actually become good at it. By nature, I'm an 'ALL IN' or 'ALL OUT' type of guy. If I get excited by something, I tend to give it everything I have; but if something doesn't interest me that much, I'm too lazy to put in the effort.

After this rather carefree lifestyle in Dubai, my parents got divorced when I was 16, so my mother, sisters, and I decided to move back to Finland. We had experienced a good life in Dubai, yet a part of me felt relieved that I was no longer under the scrutiny of my father and that life had become more flexible.

At first, I felt a freedom I had never experienced before. It all seemed so fun and carefree. I spent most of my high school years hooked on the game Counter-Strike™ and getting 'high' with friends, even on school days. I made a lot of cool connections and girls took more interest in me. My business dealings were limited to buying and selling cigarettes, which gave me an entrepreneurial thrill, but for the most part, my childhood dreams of becoming a successful businessman had taken a back seat to my social life.

In my 20s, I lost my motivation to study completely and went all in by partying hard on the weekends to escape reality even further. I have never been very interested in how things work in theory and I was unable to find any practical courses in school about how to be successful in life. Isn't that funny that school doesn't teach you how to be successful?

Thankfully, after feeling like a loser and becoming a college dropout, I was introduced to my first business at the age of 21, in the direct sales industry. I honestly don't know how I ended up on my friend's prospect list, but luckily he believed in me more than I believed in myself and my dreams of becoming an entrepreneur were sparked. When I was first shown the concept of passive income, I thought to myself, "Now I can become a businessman like my father, but I can have time, money, *and* freedom." This felt great. I was also introduced to the world of personal development and started studying legends like Napoleon Hill, Dale Carnegie, and Jim Rohn. This led me to understand the concepts of *you can if you think you can* and *where you put your focus, it becomes stronger.*

After a few years of struggle, jumping from one company to the next, I finally started having some success. After reading many self-help books, I learned that you can only reach success through failure. Because I was impatient, at 24, I decided that I wanted to fail *faster.* I started 10 new companies with my closest friends from the direct sales industry.

We were so excited about the future that we couldn't sleep. We worked flat out during the days and at night we used to hang out together until 3 or 4 AM at local gas station cafés reading *Robb Report* and other lifestyle magazines. Together, we used to visualize our perfect day and our future life, and it felt incredible. Everything looked good for a few years. Even though we weren't making much money from most of the ventures, we certainly had a lot of fun and learned an incredible number of new skills.

Things started going rapidly wrong when the global financial crash happened in 2008.

At the time, we were building online auction houses in Spain and the United Kingdom, and we had several businesses running in Finland — from an advertising agency to a telecom retail chain, and from a human resources company to a hot dog franchise concept. We were able to juggle all these balls in the air until 2009, but that's when we couldn't hold them all anymore.

In early 2010, I suddenly found myself going through two bankruptcies in Finland and had hundreds of thousands in loans fall on my shoulders. The reason I had gotten into this mess was because my biggest weakness was a lack of patience and focus.

I have to admit that for the next couple of years I went through life like a living zombie. I remember calling collectors almost weekly and pleading with them not to seize my house and car. I lost the car, but was able to save the house. I kept questioning whether I had what it took to be a successful entrepreneur and wondered whether I should give up my dream and go work in sales.

Worst of all, because of the burnout caused by the bankruptcy, I had totally neglected my relationship with my fiancée. We ended up separating for six months during my darkest moments. I thought that I had lost my true love and it felt as though I was living in hell. That was definitely the lowest point for me.

I remember crying in the shower countless times, frustrated by how big of a mountain I had to climb. Whenever I thought about all the loans and collectors, reality and anxiety struck me hard and I felt all my energy and hope disappear. I used to spend up to an hour in the shower crouched with my back to the wall just getting myself together. There were many months where I didn't see any light at the end of the tunnel, which led to many sleepless nights and even more anxiety.

I'm forever grateful for all the support and belief that my mentors gave me. They helped me turn my demoralizing questions into empowering ones like, "How can I grow and learn from this?" "How can I shift this around and turn this into my biggest victory?" "What have I had the most success and fun doing in the past?" "What do I really feel passionate about?"

Thanks to all the years of personal development, I had instilled the statement "GIVING UP IS NOT AN OPTION" into my subconscious mind. Something inside me kept telling me that great things will come out of this, one way or another. I made a committed decision to turn the situation around and come out on the other side as a winner. That decision was a game changer. It formed the foundation of my successful businesses going forward. Even though it certainly didn't feel like it back then, my bankruptcies were the best thing that ever happened to me. They showed me my weaknesses — impatience and lack of focus — and taught me that I have the tenacious and brave mindset that it takes to be a successful entrepreneur. I now understand firsthand why people always say you can't be a real entrepreneur until you've gone through several bankruptcies. Bankruptcies test whether an entrepreneur has what it takes to keep moving forward.

When I realized the course I wanted to be on, I then decided for once in my life to follow one path until successful, and I promised myself that I wouldn't look left or right before I had paid off all my loans and had a big profit in my account. I knew this would take a lot of effort, yet I felt unstoppable.

Shortly after, I attended a seminar in Helsinki by Joseph McLendon III, which was transformational. We did a 'Perfect Day' exercise visualizing and journaling about what our perfect day looked like six months from now. We pictured it very vividly, activating all our senses and really tapping into the wonderful emotions as the future played out in our minds. We then wrote ourselves a postcard about the main achievements in our perfect day and left it with the organizer. I was more rejuvenated than I had been in a long time and was ready to hit the ground running.

Somehow I managed to turn my dire financial situation into a hunger. I kept pressing play on all my best personal development materials every day to stay inspired and motivated. I got hold of CDs (yes, this was still the time before Audible) and books from all the incredible leaders in the industry. I read everything I could find from legends like Jim Rohn, Randy Gage, and Tom "Big Al" Schreiter. I listened through Jim Rohn's *Building Your Network Marketing Business* CD so many times that it was full of scratches and it wouldn't play on any device any longer.

I also found mentors through the direct sales industry who had been in a similar situation and had climbed out. What I love about our industry, despite all its flaws, is the caring community and WIN-WIN philosophy that is embedded into the culture of ethical companies. Some of my colleagues who had also gone through financial turmoil in the past poured belief and love into me when I lacked it the most.

Thankfully, I understood when I needed to raise my hand and ask for help because I did find myself feeling paralyzed when I had to call up collectors about not being able to make the next payments. One of my mentors was able to get me running again by giving me a challenge: "Let's make a plan with the collector. Then, decide to not think about your payments for two weeks and we work full-out during that period, doubling the amount of money you have in the bank so you can start making your payments again." I decided to go for it and just do my best to fill my calendar so I wouldn't have time to think. I had two great weeks, then made new plans with my collectors, deciding to go for a month with maximum effort and minimum amount of worrying.

I kept telling myself that we are given as much heat as we can handle and the bigger the dip, the bigger the expansion and growth out of it! My fiancé Anita and I also decided to go into therapy both individually and together. We wanted to work through and talk about all the reasons that caused us to lose each other on the journey. We learned about different love languages and how important it is to communicate; and what it means when you seek first to understand, then to be understood. Somehow, we pulled through and decided to give our relationship another go. It was the best thing we ever did. I was learning to be a successful entrepreneur *and* a loving partner.

I'm so grateful that this path gave me hope of a better future — one where I could see myself with the freedom I desired as an entrepreneur. It gave me the courage to dream again.

Six months later, I went to the mailbox with my morning coffee in my hand like every morning. Instead of finding letters from creditors in the mailbox that morning, there was my postcard. Tears of joy started rolling down my cheeks as I read through the postcard and saw how everything I had written down had come to fruition. I was thriving again, growing faster than ever before, and it was the best feeling of my life.

Today, I am happy to say that I have built an incredible business and traveled around the world together with my wife and our two amazing boys. The last 10 years have been in many ways the most challenging, but at the same time the most rewarding in all possible ways. The best part in owning my business is that now I have time, money, and freedom to be a present father for my children — the thing I missed, growing up. After years of hard but rewarding work, my bankruptcy has turned into freedom and I am more excited for the future than ever before.

One of the biggest tips I can share is that the key to not giving up is to always keep learning and growing. Growth can be painful and messy, but it can also lead to the biggest happiness boosters. Remember that it normally gets worse before it gets better. When you feel like you're trying too hard and there is no result, release the pressure and let go of the outcome. As a wise man once said, "The secret of success is flowing, not forcing." Focus on going within and surrender to the process. Everything is simple when you break it down. So keep it simple, and keep moving forward! On the other side of that 'discomfort' zone awaits bliss.

Even after 17 years, I feel I'm just getting started in my incredible entre-preneurial journey. The best part is that we never graduate from this school. Keep believing in yourself. Surround yourself with like-minded people. The results will follow. The main thing is that you keep going toward your goal. Never give up!

IGNITE ACTION STEPS

- Write your perfect day down in your journal and read it to yourself a few times every week.

- Create a vision board together with your family of things that you want to do, become, or have. Make it fun. In my opinion, the most powerful vision boards are ones that you create with your family using lifestyle magazines, cutting and gluing the old-fashioned way.

- Take time every morning to meditate, do breath work, and exercise. I recommend doing all three before turning your phone on and logging into social media. It only takes one hour, but you will be set for the rest of the day.

- Ask these empowering questions: "How can I grow and learn from this?" "How can I shift this around and turn this into my biggest victory?" "What have I had the most success and fun doing in the past?" "What do I feel passionate about?" Suddenly today's problem seems tiny when you zoom out and make sure that you are focusing on the most important thing every day.

Mikko Jarrah – Finland
Entrepreneur, Investor, Health and Wealth Creator,
Speaker, Mentor, Influencer
https://mikkojarrah.com

IGNITE THE ENTREPRENEUR

KAREN
RUDOLF

KAREN RUDOLF

*"When you change the way you look at things, the
way you look at things changes!"*

**My wish is that, when you read my story, you find your own personal
Wonder Woman® within, reflecting back to the world the gift that you are
and always have been. May you realize that you have the strength and
ability to create your own 'Best Life's Story' outcome.**

DISCOVERING MAGNIFICENCE WITHIN

The day of my very first client appointment, I was scared shitless. What
was I doing? Who was I to start mentoring others? Everything I had thought I
wanted to do was not quite turning out the way I had envisioned. My idea of
being a business *for* women was coming face-to-face with the reality of who,
it turned out, was interested in what I was offering... and my first client was
a man. As I prepared for this man to arrive, straightening the pens on my desk
and wiping a cloth across the table, I told myself, "You got this," and stepped
into what I knew I could do: I could make a connection with others. It was my
gift. It had been ever since I was a child.

When I was a little, I believed that I would live forever. I believed the lady
slippers in our garden could carry me away to some peaceful, magical fairy-
land where no fighting or hitting were allowed. The woods at the end of the
block became my escape. I would take my Barbie™ dolls there and, under the
shelter of a bush, practice 'healing' them. Even back then, I knew what I was

destined to do: to heal. I mostly wanted to heal plants, loving those moments when I would see dying plants start to flourish under my tender care, but my father wanted me to heal people. I became a nurse to please him.

As an adult, I carried with me the belief that I'd get married, have a perfect princely husband, a perfect family, a perfect life. Ideal at best! Well, my life looked nothing like that. What a letdown! I had huge expectations I strived to meet — talk about self-imposed unachievable goals for my husband, my family, and more importantly, myself! It was a formula destined to fail.

I grew up with a curious mind. I loved puzzles and asked lots of questions. It was a natural thing that came effortlessly and brought me so much satisfaction. Only, the adults around me didn't see it that way and I was often told, "You ask too many questions, go play!" The message was clear: Kids were to be seen, not heard. I wasn't allowed to express myself freely, which translated to 'stupid' and 'not enough.'

Being an adult consisted of cyclical days filled with overwhelm and madness with the stresses of cooking, cleaning, caring for our horses, and driving our usual six hours of carpooling each day. One particular day, coming home after another busy day of driving our three daughters here and there to lessons, I was getting off the highway at the Lake Mary exit in Orlando, Florida, when a woman's voice came onto my playlist. She said quite strongly something to the effect of, when we pray for strength, the Universe gives us more challenges. I heard this as, "You need to be clearer in your thinking."

Who was this woman anyway? I never recalled downloading her podcasts, yet there she was on my iPhone speaking like she knew me well. For years, I'd been praying, "Please God, give me the strength to…" and I would fill in the blanks with whatever struggle I was facing that day, small or big, asking over and over until… "Please God, more strength," felt like all I could say. It seemed to be my mantra. That day in the car, something shifted. For the first time, I asked, "What should I be praying for if not strength?"

Later that day, I looked up the word *strength* in the dictionary. *Strength (noun). 1: The quality or state of being strong. 2: Mental power, force, or vigor. 3: Moral power, firmness, or courage.* I'd been wishing for something bigger and better to keep me from falling apart. I'd been praying all wrong. I discovered that words had a vibrational energy and the dictionary quickly became my friend, showing me I had the ability to change my thoughts.

Feeling beyond stressed and at the end of my rope, I made a point each Wednesday to create a 'Me Day' to power walk on the beach and have conversations with God. I'd drop the girls at school and head to the beach, walking all the way to the pier at the far end, alert for small treasures and hidden signs in the shells and sights along the way. I would pause at the pier to breathe, letting the tranquility soak into my bones. I really learned to breathe at the beach. It was liberating! I tried hard not to listen to my husband complain each week about how *selfish* I had become; how I was neglecting my wifely responsibilities. Yet if I hadn't gone, my daughters would complain of my bitchy attitude and request I go. I began to see patterns unfolding in my world.

Having been a doormat and people pleaser my whole life, I couldn't look others in the eye (let alone myself) out of the shame and guilt I felt around my 'not enoughness.' One day, listening to my husband's rambling, my courage bubbled up and I blurted, "Stop! If I fall apart, this whole FAMILY falls apart." He stood there dumbfounded. I had been telling myself for so long that life would change, that my marriage would get better, but I knew then that it was over, though it would take a few years before the divorce would become final. I wasn't certain where my newfound strength came from. I didn't recognize this person, yet felt relieved she had turned up. I'd look forward to my Wednesday trips to the beach where I nurtured her and helped her breathe in the ocean air. I began discovering and acknowledging my growing strengths and took notes! Finding balance and slivers of self-love was my new life preserver.

A couple of years before my divorce, while tending to my daughter's bathing suit alterations, we heard BOOM! The sound of lightning hitting its target. The hairs on the back of my neck stood up. My thoughts went to the barn three miles away where our horse Scamper was stabled. I turned and faced in the direction of the barn. I stood planted on the spot as my chest tightened with that gripping feeling of being 'off.' Soon after, the phone rang. "Scamper was struck by lightning. He has died." My ears heard the message, but I wasn't listening. I already knew. I collapsed into the chair, this unbearable tightness overcoming me. It was as if I was sinking into total darkness.

My daughter's blue eyes looked at me with concern. "Mommy?" I began crying. I was devastated. Scamper was my one true savior and friend; my 'go-to.' If that horse could talk, I'd be in really deep shit — I told him everything. He seemed to know when to nuzzle me, as if he understood my pain. I lost a piece of my heart that day.

With Scamper's death, I knew my life was about to change. I began praying for freedom, though I had no idea what that would mean for someone like me. It wasn't about getting out of my marriage; it was about personal freedom. The day I left the courthouse having signed the final divorce decree, I felt alone and scared. I had spent three stressful years of not knowing what was next.

204 / KAREN RUDOLF

During the entire legal battle, I was raising our three small children, alone. It was grueling.

Straight from the courthouse, teary-eyed and in need of hay for my other horses, I pulled up to the local feed store's loading dock and heard a POP! "Dear God, now what?" Dang! Flat tire! I ran over what looked like a license plate and tossed it into the back of my truck while I was on the phone with the repair service. With the tire repaired, I headed home to unload the hay. I began brushing out the debris and my eye caught the license plate. I reached in and turned it over. It read 'Freedom.' A chill ran through me. Messages from the Universe! My tears from earlier returned. Dear God, I'm not certain this was the freedom I had in mind.

Our daughters were court-ordered to go to see their dad after eight months of him disappearing from our lives, and they were scared. Their little tears and outstretched hands pleading, "Don't make us go, don't leave us, Mommy," were heart-wrenching. As I drove home, I was actually contemplating ways of ending it all; drawing a bath with candles, wine, and music and perhaps drowning myself in my pity party. I had been hiding behind my daughters for a long time in my abusive marriage, as I hadn't any idea of who I was supposed to be other than 'Mom.' I was deep in thought when my best friend called and insisted I not be alone. She asked me to come to her house. Had she been reading my mind? Funny how I started noticing those little synchronicities that were occurring in my life. Had she been collaborating with the Universe?

At her house, she asked, "What are your dreams now that you're on your own?" My dreams? I had absolutely no idea. Boy, I felt naive. I drove straight home, pulled out my dictionary, found the word *dream*. The words refused to make sense, my brain unable to process the idea of having a dream. I stood there lost in a sense of surreality and cried tears of inadequacy. That very night, I began identifying my strengths by using mind-mapping to clarify all my skill sets, something I'd done for years with my daughters for homework help. Should I go back to nursing? Dang, let that license expire when I raised my children. Six hours carpooling daily… taxi driver? Not very fulfilling. I continued to brain dump for hours until the common threads began unfolding hidden self-worth and self-esteem. It wasn't that I didn't have any skills; I just hadn't acknowledged them! And not only did I have skills, I had skills that could help other people! I decided to start my own business venture using all my skills to support other women's inner wisdom such that they will be free to live their best lives financially and relationally while finding optimal health and personal freedom. In short, I decided to start the business I had so desperately needed myself.

To my surprise, God wasn't done making sure I heard the full message and it came with yet another great big Boom! Truman, our second horse, was also struck by lightning, though against all odds, he survived it. When the second call came, I stood there dumbfounded. Impossible! What were the chances?! There must be a mistake!

When the vet arrived and told me to put him down, citing expense and low odds of recovery, I recall closing my eyes and taking a long deep breath. When I opened my eyes, I looked the vet straight in the eyes and declared, "*No*. Truman *will* survive, and thrive, and we will be catalysts for change!" The vet wore a stunned expression. I probably would've looked at myself with astonishment as well. Where the heck had that come from? I was certainly learning to be bold!

Right after Truman came home and we began his long arduous recovery process, my mother, who was two and a half hours away, became incoherent and was slurring her words. My inner nursing alarm went off in my head! Growing up, my mother appeared as a hypochondriac which frustrated me no end. She came across as self-centered and needy. I'd be in the midst of scrambling about my day and she'd be rambling about her latest art pieces. When she stopped calling, I worried and called her. She was incoherent. I raced to her apartment and found her on the floor.

In that moment, I saw a different person. Not just my mother, I saw a little girl in an adult body whose only desire was to be seen and heard. A lonely little girl who wanted acknowledgement and wanted to be loved. Now who had been needy and selfish? Me! I have learned we are always mirrors of what we see in others. I was angered at myself for not being present enough to understand her pain sooner. How many others were going through similar situations? I declared, "*The buck stops here!*" Between my mother and the lightning strikes, I WOULD survive and I *will be* a Catalyst for Change. I was clear — I am here to create a ripple in the world raising awareness for 'W'Holistic Health and Well-being. Out of these experiences arose Tranquil SOULutions, and I began to let my newly discovered gifts flow.

My Spiritual Mentor, who was such a huge part of my growth and knew me well, asked once why I had never looked up the meaning of 'lightning strike.' Knowing everything was energy, I did have a clear understanding of my not wanting the responsibility that came along with the knowledge. I finally looked it up and it represented being a 'light in the world.' I've since owned it fully.

Ever since that day, I began diving into the study of human nature, quantum physics, and neuroscience. It was no longer about me - Self-expansion was key! Wayne Dyer's quote crossed my path around this time: "If you change the way you look at things, the things you look at change." My brain heard it as, 'When you change the way you look at things the *way* you look at things changes.' In that context, I began my global journey. I found myself in China, Canada, and South Africa, creating ripples wherever I went and manifesting my own internal ripple at the same time. No matter where I was in the world or with whom I spoke, I realized that the more I changed my thoughts — my way of being — the more those around me changed. I came to realize that we all have the same fears, thoughts, and many similar beliefs. And the same heart for love.

I began seeing patterns that many hadn't seen in themselves — something else to add to my growing list of gifts and strengths. It felt good to notice and feel again! The more I grew, the more I felt the sense of personal freedom, similar to the way I felt on my kayak — struggling upstream was much easier when I pulled up the oars and relaxed, surrendering to the flow.

Shifting my perceptions around those experiences allowed me to create my business. I love supporting women as they discover their authentic nature and find their Best Life Now! Choosing to change the way I looked at things let me acknowledge my inner child, the Wonder Woman who was living inside myself. The more she came out to play, the broader my journey unfolded and the more I was able to serve.

As I look back upon my journey, I realize today that everything is in Divine order. I believe that the Universe is always giving us messages in signs and symbols. The lightning strikes have helped me look at others through a different lens and I now see power, beauty, grace, and ease *everywhere*. Everything is for our highest good, no matter how uncomfortable it feels in the moment, and finding gratitude for the awarenesses coming from those experiences helped me shift my consciousness around the events that transpired. With the right mindset, we will get through it. Choose to see the good and learn from it; there is always a silver lining.

IGNITE ACTION STEPS

My Action Formula

What if you focus on just a few things that would profoundly affect the way you impact the world? Start with a desire to create a ripple and declare it out loud. I wanted to support others, therefore I created a book called, *5 Ways to Create a Ripple,* which are the very same action steps you can take to live your best life.

1: Identify your Strengths.

Become fully aware of your gifts, talents, strengths, and who you are for others.

2: Collaborate.

Go beyond connecting. Create synergy and invent new possibilities through intentional conversations with others.

3: Take Action.

Taking an okay action step beats not taking the perfect action step every time. Life is too short to hesitate.

4: Trust yourself to be Bold.

Listen to your inner guidance. The journey toward having your 'Dream Come True Life' begins with the first step.

5: Let Your Gifts Flow.

Be generous. Flow and fear cannot occupy the same space at the same time. As you open up and share yourself, the Universe has the opportunity to contribute back to you. Flow is about giving *and* receiving.

Most importantly, have fun. Look for the silver lining in all of your experiences. Know that you have been brought to them all for a reason! They are a gift to explore and you can create success from every setback. Find the joy in the journey!

Karen Rudolf – United States of America
Heart Based Breakthrough Coach
Www.TranquilSOULutions.com

IGNITE THE ENTREPRENEUR

JONATHAN
DOMSKY

JONATHAN DOMSKY

*"The most important choice we make in life isn't who we
choose for a partner or what we do for a living — it's how we
respond to life after those big decisions have been made."*

**Is your life devoted to the work that makes your heart sing? Are your
life and business easy, meaningful, and joyous? My wish is that this story
inspires you to ask what you need to learn, who you need to be, and what
action you need to take.**

HOW LISTENING TO MY HEART SING CAUSED AN AVALANCHE

If you had ever asked me, "Are you passionate about *Kidorable*?" I would
have said, "Yes." I love this company that I co-founded when I was 24 years
old. It has shaped the course of my life, making me an entrepreneur, with all
the freedom and abundance that comes with it.

But if you had asked me, "Does selling fun, practical, unique children's
accessories make your heart sing?" I would have to say "No."

I enjoyed everything I did at Kidorable. I had learned how to be a skillful
manager. I had learned to be a confident leader and efficient administrator. I
was good at it. But it did not make my eyes shine and my heart sing.

The highlight of my week at Kidorable was the 10 or so hours I spent in
meetings. I love meetings. I promised my team that our meetings would be
the most impactful time they spent all week — the place where problems are

solved and I could remove obstacles. It's where I could teach and help people grow to be their best. It's where I could untangle the clutter causing all their stress and anxiety and help them see a clear path to become who they most want to be at work. And it wasn't just at work — I did this with everyone I knew.

Sometimes I would see a look of desperation on my colleagues' faces and mercifully adjourn. I know my love of meetings is a tad unusual, but I could meet with staff for hours without any feelings of fatigue or boredom.

Off and on over the years, I explored the idea of being a coach. I lead three forums, monthly gatherings of about 10 fellow entrepreneurs who get together for friendship, lifelong learning, and peer support. I loved running my three forums and would coach any presentation I could. On a retreat one year, I even presented to my forum-mates on being a coach, 'putting it out into the world.' I had a fantasy that this one small step would make clients magically appear in front of me. But as I didn't take any action to actually make it happen, no clients appeared.

After a couple decades, Kidorable was highly optimized. I only worked in the business a couple hours a day. I worked from home, coming into the office once a week for a day of face-to-face meetings.

I tried to express my entrepreneurial energies in other ventures, and like Kidorable, I was good at running my remodeling, staging, and real estate companies. I was conventionally successful, with the freedom and abundance to do what I wanted to do — but none of these things made my heart sing.

Until one seemingly ordinary day, the 31st of January, 23 years into my entrepreneurial journey.

This particular Friday is a crisp, winter afternoon like any other. I take my well-trod walk from my home to Lake Michigan, then up to the Northwestern University campus to clear my head and process the week. As I mentally tie up loose ends, my feet follow the familiar route seemingly of their own volition. Like the hundreds of other days I've walked this path, I let go of my thoughts, look up at the sky, and I notice how this moment is unique, that this combination of light and clouds is different than any that has ever been. I notice the simple beauty of the bare winter branches. I feel present and out of my head.

The lake is different every day, some days choppy, other days smooth as glass. Today, as soon as the lake comes into view, I feel the pancake-flat ground shift beneath my feet. It is a strange combination of both a physical and a dissociative experience. It wasn't so much that the ground was shifting beneath me, but that my soul's foundation was shifting.

I disconnected from the work I had previously devoted my life to, and felt very unsteady. I was riding an avalanche. I felt waves of feeling lost, unsure, excited, exhilarated, and scared. These feelings lasted for several minutes. Untethered and unmoored, I had nothing solid to hold on to. It was an emotional upheaval of deep uncertainty.

Help! In a flash of inspiration, I felt in my bones that my life had to take a different course. And I knew right then and there, despite two decades of owning a successful business, my calling had arrived. It was no longer 'good enough' to just do something I was 'good' at. Work had lost its challenge. I love to listen and solve people's problems — to help others understand themselves in a way they never had before. And I was ready to share my true gifts with the world on a much larger scale. Kidorable was a wonderful platform for me to become who I am, but I know I am more than that. I was born to be a coach.

After a few minutes, there was still the shock of no longer feeling that I had anything solid to hold onto, but the ground had stopped shaking. I was able to regain my spiritual footing and start thinking, "So, now what?"

I am a personal growth athlete. I've read thousands of books and attended dozens of programs. Everything I had learned up to now had prepared me for this moment. I was no longer willing to accept devoting my life to work that does not make my heart sing.

For years, my wife and partner in Kidorable had been on her own parallel journey. She had been longing to take on more responsibility in the day-to-day operations of the company. I came home from my walk, filled with resolve and quiet determination — sure that despite all the unknowns, there was one very clear next step. We discussed a plan for her to be president of the company, and for me to transition to be a full-time coach.

I wanted to wake up each morning alive with passion and purpose — to devote myself to what truly matters to me. I love to learn. I'm good at teaching. The world needs more people doing what they love. And I knew at my core that I have something special to offer that people would be willing to pay for. I realized that day that my Life Purpose is to untangle the clutter in our business and personal lives to help entrepreneurial leaders solve their most stubborn challenges.

But how do I start? I had been toying with this idea for four years. I know how to coach my friends. But how do I find paying clients?

This time I was not going to just 'put my vision into the world' and hope for the best. Each morning I started saying to myself, *"I declare the possibility that I am a master coach and entrepreneur with a unique perspective on business and relationships who shares my gifts with the world. I am someone who acts — who comes up with ideas and tries them. I am not afraid to fail, and fail again, until I find a joyful solution that works."*

Then, I would look at my present situation, compare it to my vision of my beautiful future, and ask, "What do I need to learn? Who do I need to be? What action do I need to take?"

I started calling the 60 successful entrepreneurs who know me best, telling them my story, and asking if there was anyone in their circle who had come to accept things in their life and business that they would never have consciously chosen. I sought people who wanted to change, but didn't know how to make that change happen themselves.

That was enough to get Untangled Coaching off the ground. It was good. But it wasn't enough for a master coach who acts, who comes up with ideas and tries them, who is not afraid to fail, and fail again, until I find a joyful solution that works.

I thought of the best coaches I know — sages who can meet someone they've never seen before and in less than an hour completely change their outlook on life. To be that kind of coach, I needed a new declaration to inspire me to action. So I started saying this to myself each morning:

> *I declare the possibility that I radiate a palpable wisdom, compassion, and all-embracing acceptance of people just the way they are, so that they feel safe enough to approach me, engage, and do the work. That I untangle the clutter obscuring their best, most authentic Self, so they see a clear path to become who they most want to be.*

This is who I am at my best. But I aspire to be this way all the time and an order of magnitude more. So, again I asked, "What do I need to learn? Who do I need to be? What action do I need to take?"

To be this best version of myself, I need more than just the vast array of tools and mindsets I've collected — I need a coaching framework that I could apply to any situation. I researched. I reviewed all the tools I had learned. I wrestled with dozens of pages of notes, asking each day how they all fit together.

I came to understand that in the end, everything I do, all my tools, are in service of one thing. I now approach everything I see with this intention — no matter the challenge, what is the path to make life and business more easy, meaningful, and joyous? Coaching framework accomplished.

I knew I could be compassionate and accepting of people I already know and love. But I needed to learn to grow my compassion to make strangers feel those emotions from me.

Years ago, I was diagnosed with Lyme disease. Part of the treatment was daily hour-long IV infusions. They hooked us up, four to a room. One of my fellow patients was a man with severe developmental disabilities. He had the mind of a small child and made constant nonsensical chatter. I remember feeling pleased about myself that I was able to ignore him and read my book without being annoyed by him like many of the other people in the room.

One day the IV needle hurt more than usual, and he grew increasingly agitated. The woman next to me soothed him. She knew his name. She got up and caressed his arm, making him feel safe. I left the treatment that day thinking the milk of human kindness was somehow lacking in me.

The gap between who I was at that moment, and who I aspired to be, demanded another transformation. I once again declared the possibility that I radiate a palpable wisdom, compassion, and all-embracing acceptance of people just the way they are…

Again, I read and researched. It turns out Buddhists have been teaching compassion for over 2,000 years. Now, everyday I do a remarkable compassion meditation. In my mind's eye I focus on a person I want to feel more compassion for. I name their pain and breathe it in, taking it into my body where it is transformed. Then I breathe out its opposite into the world.

I breathe in their resentment. I breathe out loving acceptance.

I breathe in their anxiety. I breathe out calm presence.

I do this every morning for myself, my family, and everyone I'm expecting to engage with that day. I feel my heart has grown three sizes. Were I back in that IV treatment room, I know I would now pass the compassion test.

I also realized that to get my message out, I needed to learn to be a more compelling speaker. So again I read and researched. I hired a speaking coach. And now I speak and lead transformational workshops every single month.

Bending reality to your will is to be expected when you have a clear vision for your future. Compare that vision to your current situation, then take action to bridge the gap. And that's exactly what happened to me. But there was another wonderful and unexpected side effect.

Most of what I teach I have known for many years. But there is a difference between knowledge and knowing. If you want to learn to ride a bicycle, I can give you a book to read on the physics of how bicycles work. But that won't help you actually learn to ride one.

I use all my tools on myself. After months of teaching the tools and frames that lead to a life and business that are easy, meaningful, and joyous, sometimes repeating the same wisdom to different clients three or four times a week, I have been able to internalize this mindset in a way that is now effortless. It radiates from my body, and I have experienced an unbroken period of enhanced well-being. By teaching others to live their best, most authentic life, I finally learned how to do it myself.

As entrepreneurs, we're taught that not many people care what we do. Everyone knows WHAT they do. We're told that the HOW, our core values, and what distinguishes our company from everyone else, is what makes us special, and that our WHY, the deep reason we do whatever we do, is what motivates people to engage and connect.

I think that makes perfect sense for a company and a product. But I believe that when it comes to actually living your life, your WHY only points in the right direction. When it comes to living a deeply rewarding life, start with WHAT, the stuff that makes up our hours and days. Shouldn't your WHAT make your heart sing?

It took a single, ordinary day to trigger the avalanche I'd been riding since that Friday, January 31. You can't make an avalanche happen in your life. There's nothing I can say to you to magically spark your reinvention.

Find the union of what you love, what you are good at, what the world needs, and what you can be paid for. When you have a clear vision of your best future self — that's how to set the conditions for an avalanche to occur.

Be present and listen for the ground shifting beneath your feet. Embrace the part of you shouting to see the light of day for the first time. Have courage to take the first step of your new journey. And... when the avalanche begins, be ready for the ride of your life!

IGNITE ACTION STEPS

Bending reality to your will is to be expected when you have a clear vision for your future. Compare that vision to your current situation, then take action to bridge the gap.

Your vision is the best version of your future self.

Ask yourself: Who do you aspire to be? What are your future self's best qualities? What does your future self do? What has your future self accomplished?

Now write a declaration that inspires you to action. Always start your vision with 'I declare the possibility that…' This isn't 'current' reality… yet! Don't discourage yourself by saying something that isn't yet true. This isn't who you are now. This is who you will be in the future.

Every day, recite your declaration. Then notice the gap between that future best self and your current circumstances, the gap between who you are being now, and who you are as your future best self.

Each day, take appropriate action to bridge that gap, bringing current reality closer to your vision, one action at a time.

One person I led on this exercise declared the possibility that he was on the path to sainthood. Imagine the action that propelled him to take. Imagine yourself making such a declaration and the actions that would propel you to take.

Before long, the best version of your future self will be who you are right now.

Jonathan Domsky – United States of America
Founder
Untangled Coaching for Business & Personal Growth with Jonathan
Domsky (untangled-coaching.com)
jonathan.domsky
jonathan-domsky
Jonathan@Untangled-Coaching.com

IGNITE THE ENTREPRENEUR

PARNELL
JAMES QUINN

PARNELL JAMES QUINN

"Just because it is simple doesn't mean it is easy."

This short story will hopefully help you see a few of the secrets required for reaching your heart's desire. Seeing your future on paper and focusing on it, on a daily basis, will be most helpful. Daily planning of the work you need to do everyday is a must. There will be tough days and days you will need to pivot around obstacles and setbacks, but these are the days you must get up and go after it! Plan and think before you take the next step or make the next courageous move.

THE ENTREPRENEURIAL ARSONIST

As my foot hit the moving pavement, I was instantly sober. The 65 mph speed limit sign, the white line, the green mile marker, the back of the minivan — all flashed past me. Reflexes took over, as I went flying ass-over-elbows and dirt kicked up into my mouth and eyes. I could feel every rock, prick of sagebrush, and grass as I tumbled, stopping short of the barbed wire fence. The voice in my head was laughing and shouting, "GET UP!" My soon-to-be ex-wife was probably still screaming at me from the driver's seat of the minivan, but I didn't care. Escaping from the insanity of the life she wanted was worth the consequences of jumping from a moving vehicle. For the next 12 hours I walked endlessly in the dark across the familiar landscape, the mountains and valleys I'd grown up in; unintentionally avoiding the search party that had been trying to find me to force me back into their superficial 'cult' of 'Stepford hell.'

I made my way to the local golf course the next morning so as to not miss the shotgun start of the community's annual tournament, knowing I'd be taking a lot of grief from everyone that was there. Arriving at the golf course, my smile spread when I saw Megan, the person who made my dull life brighter. I knew she would give me shit and joke about the scandal I'd just created: "Did you hear what Parnell did last night?" My ill-considered leap could have been the end — I could have been seriously injured, dismembered, or dead — but that was the moment my life started. And, it wasn't the first time I tried something reckless in an effort to make a change.

At 11 years old, my mom saw me walking across the backyard with a jug of gasoline. She asked, "Parnell what are you doing?" I told her I was going to pour it into the neighbor's pool and set them on fire. My purpose was to get vengeance for what the adults had just done to me and I think my mom knew I was hot with rage. I do not remember much after that as my mom and dad never said anything about it or made it a big deal — because in those days, being molested (by another adult that lived next door) was a taboo topic to discuss. There was no counseling, and no over victimization. A few weeks later, the neighbors moved as we were getting ready to go back to school. The months that followed are a black hole in my memories. The next thing I remember was going up to the mountains for Christmas break. My parents asked how my siblings and I liked the house we were staying in, and we all gave our approval. Good thing. The moving truck pulled up that afternoon and we were at our new home. It was a strange time to move with five children and for the longest time the story in my head was that we moved because of what happened to me.

We moved to the mountains of Grand County, Colorado. The school, 7th through 12th grade, had a total student body of 178. Most of the kids had lived in Grand County their whole lives. We were outsiders and the bullying started on the first bus ride home from school. A coach saw me come out of the locker room one day with a bruised belly and wet hair from a toilet-dunked 'swirly' the roughneck kids had inflicted on me. He told me if I wanted all this to stop I should go out for wrestling. I joined the wrestling team because I wanted to defend myself. What I ended up getting out of sports was so much more. Four different men, coached me and taught me you cannot win if you do not get backup, pain is only in the brain, and you can lift more, run faster, and be the best, if you work hard. A lot of lessons are learned in sports: teamwork, pushing past your mental and physical limits, and why devoted coaches and teammates are so important. To this day, I am thankful for outstanding coaches.

The hard work I applied to sports, I also applied to helping my mom keep her dream of running our restaurant and nightclub —The Stampede, afloat. It was a party every night. "A 12-hour workday is only half a day," I would say. I'd get to the restaurant by 5 AM, prep for breakfast and lunch, and set up for a couple hundred people for each service. Then I'd be cooking. It was always so hot near the grill. I was constantly grabbing for water and things moved so quickly. You barely had time to read all the tickets that were coming in and just hoped you were making the right meal. Seven waitresses would be screaming at me through the window, "When is my order going to be ready?!" The stress of trying to keep everyone in the restaurant happy was overwhelming most days. I'd get a small break around 3:30 PM and then it was time to prep for dinner. I'd pull out a couple hundred pounds of meat — hamburger, ribs, prime rib — and make five gallons of baked beans for the night, while endlessly slicing tomatoes, onions, and garnishes for salads. At 9 PM dinner service was over and then it was a quick run to the mop sink to 'freshen up' by splashing water all over myself before a quick change of clothes. Then I'd run to the DJ booth and start spinning records. Our little ski town's music taste ran the gamut — from classic country to rap music and then whatever pop music was popular at the time. My job was to keep people on the dance floor for three or four dances just to get them thirsty enough to buy another drink. The endless requests of the 'one-hit wonders' hurt my brain trying to remember all the different album covers. At 1:30 AM I'd yell 'last call' and by the time we got everyone out of the bar, I was back in the kitchen getting things cleaned up to start again the next day. I was like a machine. Day in and day out for five years, this was my life.

When my mom lost The Stampede, it was the first time it occurred to me that I wasn't living *my* life. After working for my mom, I jumped into my dad's real estate business to help him and my older brother. It was what I was expected to do next. It was around this same time that I got married and started a family. These decisions were not thought-out. I was just going where I was needed. I got married because I was supposed to. I went from living my mom's dream, to living my dad's, to living my wife's expectations, and being led by others' fears and doubts at the sacrifice of my dreams. It was a life sentence, not a life, and sooner or later my light would go out or everything would burn down. When you get yourself into a bad partnership, a bad business deal, or step out of a moving car, then you better have some strength to get yourself through what comes next. I tell my kids, "If you are going to be dumb, you better be strong."

Once I finally left my house and marriage, it was back to what I knew — work your ass off and do all you can. I'd leap up at 2 AM, jumping in the truck to plow snow or shoveling icy roofs three to four stories off the ground, logging, deconstructing homes that were damaged by fire or flood, and washing dishes at three different restaurants all while putting real estate deals together during the breaks of the day. After the divorce and ensuing bankruptcy was over, from my burnt down life I knew I would have to rise from the ashes and turn my next vision into a reality.

I describe myself as a 'recovering Catholic' due to the events of the first quarter of my life. Fortunately, a little bit of remaining faith (plus those years listening to my coaches and working hard) worked in my favor because the universe brought Megan into my life. The second day at the golf tournament, as Megan and I got into the carts, she didn't care about what happened the night before. She laughed and looked at me with a big smile and said, "Those fuckers woke me up three times looking for you!" I knew the search party of artificial friends was trying to catch me somewhere I shouldn't be, so they could hold something over me. And at that moment, joking with Megan, felt like a knife sliding down a champagne bottle and popping off the cork, as a sense of freedom surged through me; my 'Cheshire Grin' was back. She was my person. It wasn't perfect timing. Things were not easy. Not everything went as planned and we certainly didn't do everything right, but Megan and I had each other's backs and we were both all in.

We learned a lot of lessons first few years. In the 4th year we brokered a small hotel deal and had a little bit of extra money for the first time in our life together. As we were starting our business, we needed to invest every penny back into it. A home came on the market that had been abandoned midwinter. All the pipes were frozen and the walls were full of mold, however it had a garage with a large wide-open second level. Putting my ego aside, I asked to borrow money from my friend's parents and, no questions asked, they gave us the loan. You would not call this a dream home. Fixing the front house so we could rent it took all of our money, but having a home that paid for itself was the beginning of the vision for our business to come; The Simple Life.

The Simple Life Real Estate Company was created in 2011. Megan and I started selling more and more homes each year and were able to leave the various other jobs we had. Around 2016 we had decided to hire a coach to improve our real estate business. The 'guru' had nothing original to say. The people we met at the live seminars, however, were different. They shared their very best strategies and procedures for success. Yet, with all their help, something was missing. We knew how to put a deal together and get it to close. We knew outworking our competition would help us be successful. Our profits had been growing year after year, but then it just stopped. No matter how many hours we put in, no matter how much marketing we did, we could not grow. We were living the 'E-Myth,' the classic entrepreneurial mistake referred to by author Michael E. Gerber — *all work and no strategy, and no clear vision.* We started hiring sales agents. They took out the overflow of buyers so we could get more sales per year, but that only lasted for a short time. We had deals but there was no one to manage the office or make sure all the side work was done. Megan and I were working 16-plus-hour days seven days a week, and the agents were working less than half a day and making great money.

What were we missing? What did we not know that we should know? We had list upon list and procedure upon procedure for everything that needed to be done in an office. Other teams with the same coaching were hitting record sales in a year and making millions. We hired sales agents, administrative people, and marketing consultants. We were still working 16-plus hour days, seven days a week. And the profits were decreasing. We implemented everything we knew, yet we could not get the business off the ground.

One day Megan said, "I want to go to a mastermind with Grant Cardone, but it's $10,000 for two days." My stomach dropped. *How can we afford this? How is this going to be different?* Then the voice in my head said, "Let her go, we can always make more money." Megan couldn't see my hesitancy, but I'm sure she felt it. I put a smile on my face and said, "That's awesome. You should go!"

During the first day, Megan met the Cardone Ventures team. She said it felt like being around family. Full of energy and excitement, she texted me, "This is where we fit." Dr. Ashlee Edwards was the first to welcome Megan, and Buck Wise took the time to introduce himself and talked to Megan, making it clear it mattered that she was there. As Megan was being inspired by Grant and the multi-million dollar business owners in the mastermind, I was upstairs in the hotel room in full drive mode, cranking out deals knowing that the grass in my yard is green because of my sheer willpower. I was invited to lunch on the second day. As Megan and I were sitting at a table in the back of the room eating lunch, Buck came over to our table and I knew a sales pitch was coming. As he sat down and started talking, he showed more interest in us which made me feel like he really cared. Megan was right, this felt more like family. He took the time to ask us about our business and we shared stories about our past. He asked about the biggest problems we were having in our office, and then he listened. He suggested we come to a 10X360. He told us the price and once again my stomach dropped. Megan looked over at me and smiled with bright eyes and said, "We should do it."

Trusting her, I agreed to go to the 10X360. Prolific coaches taught us the keys to business success in easy to remember 'groups of three.' I felt like I got slapped in the face and everything we didn't know was laid out in front of us. I learned a lot. You need to believe in what you want and can accomplish. You need to know how to be a good leader and how to *draft* behind others. You have to be willing to compare yourself to people and understand what they do versus what you do and let go of your ego. Then you can make changes happen. Within three months we were breaking our sales' records and had reached the million-dollar mark in gross commissions. I felt empowered and vindicated. Megan and I were creating a future for ourselves, and for the members of our team; who believe in our vision for the company. Our profits for the first time were over 20 percent. We had found the right mentors to help us make our vision a reality.

Just because it is simple doesn't mean it is easy. We are still working six to seven days a week, starting before the sun is up and finishing well after the sun goes down. Being inspired by our team and watching what we implement come to life, we are excited for each day. Now knowing that being effective and intentional is the difference that separates the average from the great, we are moving fast and in the right direction. Megan and I now shared a vision, after having not realized we were pulling in opposite directions for so long. Clarity of your vision is the most fundamental part of your foundation for life and success in business.

We attend as many webinars and live seminars as we can with our new extended family because as Jim Rohn said, "You're the average of the five people you spend the most time with." We spend a lot of the money investing in others because we want to transform real estate agents' lives so they can be the heroes for their own families and friends. We are not out of the woods yet. However, thanks to our mentors and our expanded team (family), we are well on our way to seeing the forest through the trees.

No matter what you do, or how much you have, you're still going to have tough days. When you stumble or fall flat on your back, get back up, and light your fire so that you can be the best version of you. One hour a day of being free to just dream and write down your goals and passions brings your vision closer to being tangible. Working backward from your goal will require creating incremental daily steps, being strong and disciplined, and plotting your course, knowing you will have to pivot and thinking things through is the surest way to reach your most desired goals. Be aware of your ego, as it is a fickle thing — when you do great, it is your biggest champion and when you stumble, it will be your biggest critic. Surround yourself with the right people and your ego will follow their lead. With a great team you will do more, be more, and accomplish more. My fire is stoked every time I help someone live their life, because I know what it's like to live a life that isn't yours. You will not need to feel the pain of jumping out of a moving car when you plan the path that YOU choose to live your life.

IGNITE ACTION STEPS

Don't let life happen to you. Think through your next move. You cannot control what happens to you, however, you do have 100 percent control over your reaction and your next choice.

Get yourself a great coach. Mentors and coaches have a vision for you and your team. They have a way of sharing the vision and painting the picture so you believe it. Leading your team and drafting behind your mentors are the fastest ways to reach your goals. To this day, I am thankful for all my coaches.

Create your vision in great detail, down to the faucets in your house, the color of the stitching in your car seats, and what you will do when you are at your favorite vacation spots. The same is true for your business achievements, will your profits be 20 percent or 35 percent, what type of teammates do you want to attract, who will be your best clients, what kind of leader will you be, and who will you draft behind? Leave nothing to chance and surround yourself with people who believe in you and your vision. You could be alone for a long time so make sure your vision is what you really want. Marriages and partnerships do not work unless you have shared your vision down to the very last detail and the other people around you support and believe in it.

Get back up every time you stumble. Many times on your journey you will stumble or be put flat on your back.This is a good time to Acknowledge you need to pivot, Accept that you need to make changes, and Act in a way that solves the problem. All setbacks, big or small, are momentary when you get back on your feet.

Parnell Quinn – United States of America
Designated Managing Broker for eXp Commercial Colorado
Founder: Executive Team Lead for The Simple Life.
www.TheSimpleLifeColorado.com

IGNITE THE ENTREPRENEUR

NADIA LA RUSSA

Nadia La Russa

"Power is a test of character; and shines a light on those with true integrity."

The state of the world in 2020 brought me to the depths of loneliness as an entrepreneur. I learned that the person who must care the most about my business has to be me. As an entrepreneur, I saw I needed to be the one who has the most invested, the most belief, and the most to lose. From there, it is my responsibility to foster relationships that enhance my business in a healthy way. It is my hope that in my story you will see you cannot make your life's path incumbent on something or someone else. No matter where you are investing your time and effort, I wish for you to empower yourself.

Integrity is Everything

Even though it was many years ago, and I've had many hard experiences since, November 24, 2011 remains one of the most pivotal days of my life. Looking back, I realize now what a mess I was in, but at the time I was the proverbial frog in boiling water. It was the beginning of my 14th year as an entrepreneur, and my small business bookkeeping firm was in big trouble. I had found myself in the crossfire between the two shareholders of my biggest client, and I was facing a very uncertain future.

The day started out as any other. I woke up and headed in to work. Jaye, my longtime assistant, was already at her desk. She and I had deeply intertwined our lives; not only were we coworkers, we were best friends. We bonded immediately when she came to work with my company five years earlier, and during that time we traveled the world together, held each other as our respective marriages ended, supported each other as new relationships began, and we had even persevered hand in hand through major illness.

At that point in time, it never occurred to me that I would walk through life without her. When I envisioned my future company, she was an integral part of it. When I envisioned my future life, she was a pillar. Her natural presence, contagious laughter, and unwavering loyalty were embedded in my soul, and to imagine life and work without her was like trying to imagine an alternate universe. She had this way of being able to read my mind, and I felt that she deeply understood me as a person. It was one of the rare friendships that I would have described as *unconditional*.

I had never kept anything from her, until that day. On this particular morning, she did not know that turmoil was brewing with this client and that my company was in dire straits. It was not like me to keep a secret like this from her — or to keep anything from her — but in my mind I was perfectly justified in doing so. I wanted to protect her from the fear and anxiety of what our future could look like, and I knew I'd do whatever it took for her and me to come out of this stronger, together.

I greeted her smiling face and we exchanged a warm embrace. We spent a few moments catching each other up on the evening we had before, and I sipped my warm coffee as I sat at my desk and opened my emails. Alone in my office, I could continue to process and plan my next steps for the firm, and consider what the future client load would look like. I knew there would have to be downsizing and layoffs, but I also knew I could find a way that Jaye and I could come through together. I was processing the idea of a simpler work life, a smaller office, and fewer clients that we could service differently.

At 9:29 AM, the email came. It was from Jaye. She had hit send from the other side of the wall, only a few feet from where I sat.

Dear Nadia,

This is a tough letter to write, but it's been something I've needed to do for quite a while. I'm formally resigning from my position with your firm effective immediately. It's been more obvious recently that our work ethics and morals in business are very different and I can no longer go on supporting your businesses. This pains me as I've put so much work, effort, and love into the firm over the last five years. I've learned so much and connected with so many people and will never regret that.

I know this will hurt you, but that is not my intent. My only intent is to live a life full of love and joy, and in this current situation it's getting tough to do that.

This no longer motivates me and I feel like I'm not being true to myself or you by staying here any longer.

Again, I don't regret the years I've worked for you or have any hard feelings, but do feel like it's time for me to move forward in my life and career.

Jaye

I placed my coffee cup on my desk and realized I was shaking. I read the email again. I read it a third time. The words, in plain English, were not hard to understand, but I didn't understand them. Nothing about the email made any sense. Resigning? Immediately? Ethics and morals? What was all this about?

I slowly rose from my chair and went to the doorway of my office. From here, I was in front of her desk, where she sat facing me, her shoulders slumped and her eyes full of tears.

"Jaye?" I asked softly. "What's going on?"

Over the next hour, we talked, but I sensed a great distance between us. I realized in the conversation that she had been planning her departure for quite a while. I also realized she wasn't leaving the job, she was leaving me. My mind spun through five years of laughter, travel, memories, and connection while my heart burned with sorrow. In a blur I collected her cell phone and laptop and processed her final paycheck. I watched her leave and get into her car and drive away. And then I cried.

It wasn't long before I was flung back into reality — the contention between the shareholders of my largest client. With a long sigh, I turned my attention back to that debacle. They were deeply entrenched in what was brewing as a major issue. One of them felt entitled to a larger salary and had instructed me to process his payment. What I hadn't realized was, he didn't inform his business partner. Once the partner found out, and also found out that I had processed the payment, he became suspicious of me. As a result, he hired a finance consultant, George, who had sent me a list of documents for review. Numb from the morning's bombshell, I set about responding to emails when the second pivotal message of the day arrived. Once again, it was from Jaye.

Nadia,

After much thought and prayer I have officially accepted a job offer. I wanted to let you know about it, because it will cause a conflict of interest. George has offered me a position to work under him, and I feel that I cannot refuse such a great opportunity.

The reasons in my resignation letter are all the reasons I need to leave, and this was the best of two offers this week.

I want you to know that despite the conflict of interest, I will always speak highly of you and the firm and will always consider you a friend.

Sincerely,
Jaye

I froze, paralyzed with the sting of intense betrayal. Once again, I reread the email three times. As if in slow-motion, my brain connected what had been happening right under my nose over the previous weeks. George, the new finance consultant for my largest client, had been recruiting Jaye to work for them knowing full well they were planning to fire me and my firm. At the same time, Jaye had been entertaining their offer, while working for me. In less than two hours I had lost my best friend, my most important employee, and my largest client.

Even though I didn't want it to, time passed on its own. As Christmas approached, I felt more and more despondent. I stopped eating, didn't celebrate through the holidays, and would often wake up in the middle of the night, my chest tight with anxiety. I withdrew from social connections, stopped speaking to friends, and cried in bed each night. My sense of trust had evaporated, and I couldn't see a way out of the looming financial hardship that was barreling my way. I very quickly burned through my savings and was wondering how I was going to make ends meet.

But most of all, I was so lonely. Despite being supported by my husband, being showered in love from my children, and having so many people in my life that cared for me, I felt as though I lived on a different planet. Communication became impossible, and no matter how well-intentioned the people around me were, not one of them knew me the way Jaye had.

I knew I needed a major change in all areas of my life, but I didn't know where to start. Thankfully, that start came to me, at the bottom of a bottle of red wine.

"You know," I said to my husband Brent, one evening just after Valentine's Day, "we could do something really crazy. We could sell this house, move to our apartment, and work from the main floor of that building." We owned a building downtown that had two apartments on the upper floor and office space on the main floor. It was a wild plan, but my wine haze was not making my outlook on life any happier, and the effects of the alcohol were pushing the words that had been rolling around in my head out of my mouth.

He laughed. "Really now! And then what?"

"Well," I replied, trying to get the figures to add up, "it would free up about $5,000 a month in cash flow. If we put that into our savings, we could build our own house in less than 10 years." I could see the look of confusion and intrigue in his face, but his stance on the idea remained neutral. We went to bed, and I fell asleep, praying I would sleep through the night and be spared dreams filled with memories of Jaye.

When I woke up in the morning, Brent was already awake. He was lying in bed next to me, his hands clasped behind his head. "If you're right," he said, "I'd like us to run the numbers."

By noon that day, the numbers had practically run themselves. We talked through the various steps: evicting the current tenants, moving into one of the apartments, putting the house up for sale, renovating the unit beside ours to put a door between them, then relocating the office to the main floor. We budgeted out everything — from lease cancellation fees, to movers, to setting up the new office. At the end of the day, according to our calculations, we would be starting our house build a mere five years later, with relatively no debt. All of a sudden, what seemed like a crazy idea, became a no-brainer.

I got to work, and for the first time in months, I started to feel like myself again. I started to envision what the new version of my business would look like. All of a sudden, I could see myself running the firm and being more successful than ever before. It was in this moment that I realized the company was mine to grow and nurture, and that I was the one who had to care the most. I was the one who had the most to lose. What occurred to me then was that I could finally see a positive future without Jaye, rather than the negative future I had been envisioning.

By September, the plan we put in place was living itself out. Life became easy and relaxed again. I still thought about Jaye every single day, but I started to realize I was missing the idea of her, not actually missing *her*. I knew that she had not passed the test of loyalty; and from my perspective, she put her integrity into question long before she had submitted her resignation. I thought of the friend she had been. I wondered how her life had played out since she had left. I wondered if she ever thought of me, of the memories we had, and if she missed me.

I had learned through my various connections that the company she left me for had closed up; the partnership had dissolved and one of the owners had passed away. I knew they had ended their partnership in an expensive legal dispute and that she was now out of a job. She was experiencing the same level of stress that I had the previous fall. In the meantime, I streamlined my business processes, realigned the services I provided to clients, and started working with a therapist to talk about learning to trust again. Despite this, I didn't feel justified or righteous knowing what she was going through. I just felt sadness. I wondered if she was lonely. I remembered the darkness that had enveloped me the year before, and the pang in my stomach was one of deep sorrow. Despite everything that had happened, I knew I still loved and cared for her.

Now, nearly 10 years later, I can look at my life and see November 24, 2011 as a good day. I had given power to someone who wasn't worthy of it, but my choice to reclaim that power and guide my own steps without her made all the good that followed possible. I became smarter as an entrepreneur and person through the loss I endured. I have made sure I am never again in a position to be taken advantage of; by clients or by staff. I set myself up for success, no longer letting my success ride on someone else's shoulders. My firm is doing incredibly well, the staff member I hired to replace Jaye is still with me today; and he embodies the level of loyalty that I require. The experience brought me new clarity and closeness with my husband; my greatest ally, my biggest supporter, and my *true* best friend. We built our house, a gorgeous ranch estate that is a shining gem in our city.

There are days it still causes me so much pain to remember, but I know now that without those awful moments, I couldn't have stepped into the success I have now. By being pushed into what I had never imagined, I did more than I could have ever dreamed.

Ignite Action Steps

As an entrepreneur, we know that our businesses are like our children. Just like no one will love our children as much or in the same way we do, no one will love our businesses the same way or as much as we do.

1. Do a thorough review of your business. Is it dependent upon one key employee or one client? If so, this is a fragile spot. Seek to rectify that by

cross-training employees, marketing to a wider client base, or expanding to a point you are comfortable.

2. Make sure you have contracts in place to prevent solicitation of your key clients, and make sure you have contracts in place with your clients so they don't recruit your key staff.

3. Know your business well. This doesn't mean that you have to run every aspect of the company, but you and you alone are responsible for it. It's up to you to be on top of growth, reducing expenses, and putting in and implementing systems and operations. Remember that trusting it to anyone else is not the same.

4. Hire for attitude, train for skill. When hiring, try to get to know the character of the person as well as their skill level. Most technical abilities can be taught, but the true test is one of character — would your employees ever leave to work for your largest client? One is not of true character if opportunity controls one's loyalty.

5. Don't be afraid to fire clients — especially if they are unethical or in legal and partnership disputes. It's easy to get caught in the crossfire, but remember, your business depends on you to make the best decisions.

Nadia La Russa – Canada
Serial Entrepreneur
www.nadialarussa.com

IGNITE THE ENTREPRENEUR

DR. MARTA OCKULY

Dr. Marta Ockuly

"Life is not just what happens to us — it is what we imagine and create."

I wrote this story to offer you hope and a road map for visualizing and actualizing your most meaningful dream. Trust your inner knowing and leap! There is nowhere to fall but into the arms of grace. The world needs what you were born to do. It begins when you imagine a possibility and give yourself J.O.Y. (Just One Yes)!

Awakening Creativity With Joy Is My Business

I believe we are here to spark change in the world using our human super-powers of imagination, intuition, creativity, curiosity, intention, and expression. By connecting those actions with joy, we can access flow and the high levels of energy needed to fully awaken our creative potential to become agents of positive change.

Creativity has been central in my life and work since I was 18. It continues as my passion, purpose, and driving force. I dropped out of the corporate world and my high-profile advertising position at age 39 to imagine my first 'brick-and-mortar' business into being. It took four years to manifest, but the day I saw *Angel House* I felt filled with gratitude for following my inner knowing step-by-step.

This story begins with a short conversation I had with a friend while we were walking in the park. She mentioned a workshop for 'Emerging Entrepreneurs' she'd be attending the next day and asked if I wanted to join her. I said yes.

That J.O.Y. step led to manifesting my biggest entrepreneurial dream. I arrived at the conference feeling like something big was unfolding. My intuition did not steer me wrong.

The best part of the workshop for me was the deep guided visualization process. I felt the power of my imagination being amplified. I was ready for the freedom of charting my own course and claiming my right to be authentically me. I closed my eyes and tuned out everything but the facilitator's soothing voice. He told us, "Begin to see and feel your dream revealed... What is it?... Where is it?... What helps you know you belong there? What do you notice that sparks your imagination and inner knowing? What will be a 'sign' you found the right place? Now open your eyes, select a large sheet of newsprint paper, a pencil or pen, and begin drawing every detail you recall from this visualization. Please maintain complete silence."

I drew a big 3-story house that looked to be from the 1920s. Then I drew a half-circle driveway. The house was beside a small rose garden with a white picket fence. The driveway began to curve to the right and I drew a three-car garage with a carriage house apartment above it. There was a gazebo with a big swing sitting on a huge base carved out of stone. Next, I drew a parking area big enough for about six cars. Straight ahead, I sketched white pasture fencing and a huge red barn. The driveway curved toward the front of the barn facing the street. There I drew stairs that seemed to lead up to offices on the second level of the barn. In my imagination, I flew like a bird across the yard. The property felt enchanted, as if fairies lived there. There was a meandering brook leading to a small bridge, and just beyond, I drew a stairway going up about 10 or 12 feet to a ridge. From the top of the stairs, I could hear the rush of a waterfall flowing down into a river far below. The facilitator gave us a five-minute warning to finish. I held up my drawing to take it all in. It felt complete.

Next, we were instructed to fold our drawing small enough to fit inside of a book — *without looking at it again until our 'dream' manifested.* This step seemed odd to me. As an avid vision board creator, I knew vision boards were usually placed where they can be seen every day. In the case of *this* vision drawing, I followed this facilitator's directions explicitly. When I got home I slipped my folded drawing into a book. Truth be told, every detail of it was also etched into my mind.

Four years later, as I drove to a meeting, the voice of my intuition spoke to me from the back seat of my car. *An absolute first in my lifetime!* It said, "You're looking for Angel House... write this down." Shocked, I pulled off the road and parked so I could safely take notes. The next 'words' were, "Find a Homes Book." Dispensers of these monthly magazines with local real estate listings were all around town. I found one and retrieved the single magazine it was holding. As I flipped through the pages nothing caught my attention until I reached the center spread. The headline said 'For the Person with a Mystical Vision… This six-bedroom, four bath country manor features a six-stall horse barn, and backs to the MetroParks.' Looking at the photo, I knew it was my vision, come to life. I called the number and left a message. The agent quickly called back and let me know there was an open house the very next day.

I woke early — excited to see the property. Driving to the address, I saw it backed up to the park where my children and I often hiked. Turning into the driveway and seeing the house — I felt I was coming home. Nothing could have prepared me for that moment — literally witnessing the drawing I made four years before, revealed. I felt chills. How could this be happening? In every way it seemed as if my visualization had truly come to life.

I walked over to the front door of the house. An angelic-looking woman opened the door and introduced herself as Robin, the current owner. Her energy was radiant. I told her about my dream of opening a nature-based spiritual center named Angel House, and how I was led to her property by my imagination and intuition.

She responded in a matter-of-fact way, "This property is destined to be a center and you are the one meant to have it." I had no idea how this could happen, but instead of saying that, my intuition prompted me to say, "I am open to this possibility. If it is meant to be, I have no doubt it will work out perfectly." At that point Robin knowingly handed me the keys and affirmed God would take care of the details. I had no words!

Robin invited me into the house for a tour. I shared the visions I was having as I entered each room. I was 'seeing' new décor and antique pieces. She asked if I had these items, and I told her, "No, this is just what I'm seeing through my imagination."

The house was wonderful. I could see plenty of room for my mother, my children, and me, as well as beautiful spaces for classes, workshops, and gatherings. It even had a library I could fill with my books. From there, we went outside and Robin led me up the ridge. She pointed out the fairy garden along the way. We crossed the small bridge, climbed the stairs, and walked toward the water. At the 'edge' of the property, about 30 feet away, there was a small waterfall running into the Rocky River below. The water was so clear I could see fish swimming by. Walking up the trail from there felt like walking through an enchanted forest. When we returned to the house I was overflowing with excitement. I wanted my mom and children to see this property and share their feelings about moving there. I thanked Robin and told her I would be back with my family, then drove home, excited to tell them about it.

When I got home, I happily shared with my mom and kids that I might have just found our new home. The first question my kids asked was, "Is there a rock big enough for us to skate on?" When I looked at them confused, they reminded me of the story I shared with them after returning from a retreat a few years prior. On my last day there, I took a hike and rested on a huge rock for a bit before heading back. When I stood up and expressed gratitude for the resting place, I heard, "You will know your next home when you see a rock like this that is wide enough to roller skate on."

The next morning my family and I set out for Angel House. Just as I slowed down to turn into the driveway my children called out, "There it is, that's the rock!" It was positioned perfectly at the front edge of the property, a few feet from the enchanted area. After I parked, the kids ran to explore the rock. I took the moment to share my concerns with my mom. I asked her, "What if I buy this place and something happens that I can't afford to fix? Or what if I can't keep up with the costs of maintaining a large property and end up losing it?" My mom instantly soothed my soul when she replied, "This is your dream. How could you NOT do it?" Reassured, I took the leap. We moved in three months later.

Word of my center opening spread quickly. Teachers started arriving from around the world to facilitate classes and workshops. We had fire walks, international Sufi dance retreats, primordial sound meditation courses, hospice volunteer training, along with tai chi, belly dancing, ordination workshops, drum circles, and so much more. I taught, "Tuning Into Your Passion and Purpose with Joy" and facilitated *Artist's Way* study groups. The more I taught, the more I thought about returning to school to research connections between creative action and joy attraction.

Teaching and mentoring people interested in their creative potential was my joy. That seed was planted decades before when I worked in the advertising field. Peers often asked me how they could develop their own passion, purpose, creative confidence, and imagination. There were no programs doing that work back then, but at Angel House, I was able to fulfil that mission.

Seven years after arriving, I felt an inner knowing that it was time to pass Angel House to the next owner. My first open house was featured in full color on the front page of the Sunday real estate section of the *Cleveland Plain*

Dealer. Cars lined the street and hundreds of visitors came to see the property, but at the end of the day, no one expressed interest. One week later, a woman knocked on my door and asked, "Is this Angel House?" I told her it was, and she shared that her deceased husband came to her in a dream and told her to find Angel House and buy it. She was also a therapist and wanted to keep Angel House as a center for creative change. It was magical.

By this time, my mom had remarried and moved to live with her new husband. My children had both graduated from high school and were setting off in different directions to make their own dreams real. The ocean was calling me and I relocated to the gulf side of Florida near Siesta Key Beach in Sarasota. I was 51 and ready for fun. I found a sweet house less than five miles from the beach, took up Latin dancing, and most importantly I discovered the Eckerd College Program for Experienced Learners (PEL). It offered adults like me a way to complete our unfinished Bachelor's degrees. My first elective course was 'Creative Process.' I envisioned the version of it I would teach. That's when I added, *'earn a graduate degree'* to my list of dreams.

Things were going great until I developed a terrible sore throat seven months later. Three months after that, I was in the hospital diagnosed with advanced stage AML leukemia and a deadly form of flesh-eating pneumonia. Uninsured, my nurses helped me get social security disability at the bedside so the hospital could get paid. I had to file bankruptcy and learned I could not earn a salary until after I reached retirement age, so I shifted my focus to higher education. My story shows lack of health, income, advancing age, or limited resources are no match for someone with a big dream.

At Eckerd, I completed my BA in Human Development and Counseling with High Honors. I stayed in Sarasota for three more years for outpatient treatments. In 2010, I got the 'all clear' to begin studies to earn my Master's of Science degree in Teaching for Creativity from the International Center for Studies in Creativity (ICSC) at Buffalo State in New York. On my first day as a student in that program, I found the classroom and took a seat. When the professor arrived, he walked to the front of the room, looked around, and asked, "What is the definition of creativity?"

You could hear a pin drop. When no one responded he said, "Creativity is novelty and usefulness." The words, "You've got to be kidding" flew out of my mouth. The professor smiled and said, "This is the scholarly definition of creativity, but you can define it any way you like." I was shocked! My whole identity was tied to creativity and I knew what it was and what it wasn't. The word 'define' literally means, "to describe the nature, scope, or meaning of something." The terms 'novelty and usefulness' did none of those things. Worse — they implied creativity lived in a product to be evaluated, rather than a process people engaged in. I started to feel ill. I closed my eyes and took a long calming breath. As I began to relax, my inner voice said, "What if your mission is to bring a new definition of human creativity into the world?" Boom!!! I went from being upset to bursting with energy. **My passion for this 'new mission' changed the trajectory of my life!**

I graduated with my Master's from ICSC and returned to Florida to teach my new course, "Creative Process: Awakening Creativity for Personal and Professional Growth" at Eckerd for the next seven years. At the same time, I began my doctoral program at Saybrook University under the mentorship of Dr. Ruth Richards who brought the concept of 'everyday creativity' into the world. I also completed a two-year certification in Person-Centered Expressive Arts with Dr. Natalie Rogers, daughter of humanistic psychologist Dr. Carl Rogers. Nine years after my Ignite Moment in Buffalo, I passed my doctoral defense and became Dr. Marta. During those years, I collected data from my own lived experience of creativity, filling 25 hard-bound, 200-page journals with 5,000 pages of data; successfully fulfilling my mission of bringing a new, dynamic, descriptive, imagination-informed *human* definition of personal creativity into the world! The 'cherry on top' of this monumental achievement was Marci Segal (fellow ICSC alumna and founder of *World Creativity & Innovation Day*) requesting permission to use my new definition in association with the now official United Nations observance day celebrated annually around the world on April 21st. I said yes with joy!

The definition of creativity I brought into the world is shown below, surrounded by words from my 500-word lexicon of terms associated with human creativity.

I am now an international speaker, author, coach, catalyst and future-focused positive creativity influencer. As CEO (Chief Encouragement Officer) of *Creative Potential Institute,* I custom design creativity training programs for organizations, leaders, educators, and individuals. In addition to awakening creativity, the Creative Potential Institute acts as a think tank focused on coaching, teaching, and developing programs to awaken creative potential, stretching imagination and future thinking competencies. The objective is to build creative confidence and competence globally. Even though I reimagined how to define personal human creativity moving forward in the 21st century, I understand there is no be all, end all definition. It is one perspective. Use it. Challenge it. Adapt it. Play with it. Try it on for size. Improve it!

If you feel disconnected from your creativity and are ready to awaken your creative confidence, and personal potential with J.O.Y. (Just One Yes), please know that no talent or IQ score can take the place of practice, persistence, or the lived experience of risking and failing. All creativity begins with personal creativity. Start where you are and expect dead ends along the way. Let what fills you with energy guide you. Joy arrives in the process of overcoming obstacles. What's the dream your inner entrepreneur wants you to pursue? Imagine it. Draw it out. Give yourself just one yes and take baby steps. Replace 'no' with 'go' and do it! Need help? Reach out to me.

IGNITE ACTION STEPS

Start a joy mandala practice. Give yourself a few minutes every morning to shift your mood, productivity, and energy for the day by focusing on what brings you joy. We are living in times when shifting top-of-the-mind awareness from worry to optimism can offer tremendous benefits. Be open to acting on opportunities to spark joy throughout the day as well. Doing this practice for 30 days can be positively transformative! See the resources section at the end of the book for a link to download my Activate Joy Power handout. Enjoy the process!

Dr. Marta Davidovich Ockuly – United States of America
Humanistic Psychologist Specializing in Awakening Human Creativity
drmartaockuly@gmail.com
www.linkedin.com/in/martadavidovichockuly/

IGNITE THE ENTREPRENEUR

CLINTON E. DAY

Clinton E. Day, MBA

"Build value and the world will reward you beyond measure."

I want to Ignite your desire to become an entrepreneur so that you may live a life of personal and financial freedom. Only entrepreneurship allows a person to build their own business, create value, and control their destiny. May you be excited and know that as long as you trust the lean startup method, you will succeed. All you need to add is desire. My wish is you become a successful entrepreneur, make lots of money, and help change lives.

Entrepreneurship, Oh What a Ride!

Ever since I can remember, I have been around entrepreneurial thinking. I was fortunate to grow up in the home of a self-made entrepreneur. My father was a successful insurance broker in San Francisco who practiced and preached entrepreneurship. He, Curtis Day, moved from Montana to California with his newly divorced mother at age 14 with one suitcase. His circumstances forced him to be a risk-taker, create new opportunities, and work to support both he and my grandmother. Growing up, I was exposed to self-reliance and creating my own future. I saw first-hand the price of success — friends who were all clients, long hours of work, and little time for leisure. Dad's words ring clearly in my mind, "If you are not self-employed, you are a complete failure!" I did not want to fail.

The entrepreneurial mindset is a set of attitudes, behaviors, and skills that enable people to see opportunities others do not. They think creatively, solve problems, and become comfortable with risk — it was a mindset that consumed my life.

My dad was my mentor, and it was only natural that I attend the University California Berkeley, his alma mater, across the San Francisco Bay where I majored in business. Because it was a land-grant university, every male was required to take ROTC, (Reserve Officers Training). About the time I graduated, the U.S. began military assistance to Vietnam, and I was deployed. It was 'in-country' that I learned leadership, which I would eventually come to see as an essential part of entrepreneurship. That often involved me being sure of my own instincts and taking risks.

My first lesson came one particular night in Saigon where I was the signal group duty officer. I received an urgent call to report immediately to the army headquarters. They had a flash message from Commander in Chief Pacific requiring a reply. I was a lowly Lieutenant, and the officer on duty was a full Colonel. I realized right away it was a test or trial message. The Colonel was extremely doubtful, and it was top secret; he threatened me if I was wrong, and, standing my ground, I was shaking in my boots. As the jeep drove back to my quarters, I knew my army days were over if the Colonel, who acted on my advice, had erred. By the grace of God, I had been correct (and did not receive the court martial implied). My everyday duties in Vietnam molded me into a problem solver. That's what you do as an anti-fragile entrepreneur.

A lot of entrepreneurship is synchronicity and serendipity. Upon return from Vietnam, I was assigned to the Presidio of San Francisco. This posting was a stroke of good fortune for it was there I met my soul mate and future wife Donna. Fresh home from a combat setting, it was a struggle to take the ordinary moments of stateside life seriously. The post commander was hosting a Christmas party, and I had asked my executive officer to attend in my place as I had no great desire to be there. Later that evening, thinking better of that bad decision, I turned my car around at the famous Golden Gate Bridge vista and headed to the party. There, across the room, I spotted the most amazing woman. She was an army Lieutenant and physical therapist (PT) in the medical service, and I was instantly smitten. It was not a glancing blow by Cupid's arrow, but a direct hit which changed the course of my life.

We married, discharged from the army, and joined the civilian ranks working in the city. There, employed at a large hospital and insurance brokerage, semi-existing in long commutes and unfulfilled by our jobs, we felt hemmed in. We were working downtown, and I disliked the trip into the city. And Donna hated that I hated commuting. The bus would arrive, steamed over from everyone's breath, filled with bored and tired people sleeping, reading newspapers, and breathing each other's air. By the time I got through an elevator starter, dozens of coworkers, and reached my desk, I was exhausted.

There had been a series of killings in San Francisco. Donna worked in the UCSF teaching hospital. Her best friend was taking classes at night, in a bad neighborhood, rife with gang activity. She was pulling into the school at the gate when a thug jumped in front of her, pulled out a gun, and killed her. Donna and I were completely shaken by the event. It sapped both of us. We knew in that moment that something had to change. We couldn't keep living this life. And we resolved to design our own world. We decided to become entrepreneurs.

Just like that, completely impetuously, we made the decision, and it was an 'aha' moment for us both. The next day, we stayed home, brainstormed goals, made a list of criteria, and visited a library for research. The only location meeting all yardsticks was Jacksonville, Florida, which I had never visited, and my wife only once. It had large healthcare and insurance industries, and we each wanted to be self-employed in those fields. Florida law said an insurance agent had to work for another broker before licensing. In the interim I was looking for a niche product to match a target market.

Moving to a strange city across the country was a bold experiment. We were a bit idealistic and heavy into goal-setting. When we first met, we had both been reading *Think and Grow Rich* by Napoleon Hill. His book said, "Whatever the mind of man can conceive and believe, it can achieve," and we wanted to give it a shot. We checked into a low-budget motel, handwrote resumes, and went cold calling. I had a letter of introduction to a surety producer, and Donna went to work for a self-employed PT to learn that side of physical therapy. I served the required year working for a large insurance broker when synchronicity again came to the rescue!

The south had many Electric Member Cooperatives or 'EMCs' established during the New Deal to provide electricity to rural America. I was chosen to train as the rep for a national rural electric insurance program. One competitor came into clear focus. My boss heard of an impossible bond (surety for construction projects) issued by an agent across town by a small company called... Cotton States (CS). Then, a month later I could not 'close' (an order for insurance) at a rural electric in Georgia. The competition was again Cotton States, the same regional company based in Atlanta. My curiosity was piqued, and I thought of Abraham Lincoln's quote, *"I will prepare and some day my chance will come."*

The final bolt came in Orlando at a license course where classmates were gossiping about a new company to Florida... Cotton States! *This time bells rang and lights flashed, and I knew this was my opportunity* to take a risk and become self-employed. Everything in my body said act on the synchronicity, and two weeks later I drove straight to the Cotton States home office applying to become an agent. The risk was they only appointed 'captive,' not independent, agents; meaning I would not own the policies until vested. It turned out to be one worth taking because premiums were highly competitive. I was able to 'write' large accounts including the school bus fleet over time. With this step, I launched the first of my insurance agencies. Little did I know that it was a formula I would go on to repeat, thus becoming a serial entrepreneur.

Synchronicity did not end there. I had only been in business nine months when the largest agency in Jacksonville wanted to buy our fledgling business. Many competitors had tried to represent Cotton States, but could not. I soon learned that if your business has a stream of income, it can be sold as an asset. Anything generating revenue can be sold to another going concern who then assumes the revenue stream. This was *another 'aha' moment* that Ignited awareness in us. Eventually, as we grew into Atlanta, we did sell our book of accounts. My wife and I took serious note, filing this 'harvest' option away as a business model that might be used again. And we *did* use it again — twice!

Some of the hardest challenges from daily operations taught unforgettable lessons. One day I was overwhelmed with incoming tasks, one after another. Determined to gain control I shut down my office, drove to a library, and scanned time management books. Upon return, I put several tips into immediate use. One in particular was a major practice, which once mastered, tripled my productivity. It was to make a list of things to do and number them in order of priority. Although I made a daily list, nothing got better. In desperation, I resolved to doggedly completing the first priority before going to the next. Overnight, this determination *Ignited my success*! I became a big, bad work machine.

One of my target markets in Jacksonville was auto dealers. I distinctly remember one owned by a prominent family quoted on a handwritten proposal who gave me the go-ahead to bind coverage. Leaving his dealership, I was banging my steering wheel and screaming at the top of my lungs; I had broken into the city's elite and written my first auto dealer! While most agencies used an accrual method to book commissions, we used cash, and, as a consequence, were undercounting. One Saturday we were totaling cash from the first six months and when finished, I had doubled my prior *annual* salary. Two things happened. We headed straight for a disco club to celebrate, and I bought the first video tape recorder in the city (for an outrageous $2,000). There is a thrill to building something from nothing. I cannot think of anything as exciting as the ecstasy of closing a big account, calculating its commission, and knowing you have improved a customer's insurance. Little since has been quite as exhilarating as that feeling of accomplishment.

As soon as we could afford for Donna to join the agency, we did so. She was a wonderful marketing asset with a charming personality, who had been doing the agency bookkeeping from the start, and to those duties, we added her knowledge of health insurance. As our business grew in Jacksonville, I began to worry over the direct contract which gave Cotton States ownership of my book. Keeping eyes and ears open, I learned an independent agency in Tallahassee who represented CS had another type of contract. By the time I arrived in Atlanta, the Agency Director had prepared an independent contract having learned of my discontent. This change was a 'Wahoo!' big moment which meant we owned our policies and could sell our business.

As clients expanded into Atlanta and we spent more time traveling there, it made sense to relocate. One larger Jacksonville agency agreed to buy our book of accounts, but I made a rookie mistake allowing them to visit the CS home office without me. Upon return, they requested a meeting to inform us the terms had changed. They had authorization to represent CS, knew I had a deadline, and unilaterally lowered the price. I was furious! It was against all ethics and business practices, and I told them they could go to hell and stormed out (Donna was horrified at my profanity). I spent the weekend racking my brain for a creative solution; as an entrepreneur, you always are using creativity to solve difficult challenges. I called the only other Florida commercial CS agent, and asked if he would *say* he wanted to buy my agency. To my relief, he agreed not only to say so, but insisted if the deal fell through, he *would* buy it! Upon learning there was another offer, the original buyers hurried to close the deal based on the original terms. We were more than relieved to lock in a guaranteed price.

Our second venture, an independent agency in Atlanta, was harder to get going. It was a time of high inflation and property casualty companies priced risks low to gain cash flow and make money investing their 'float.' While we tried to find a market as competitive as Cotton States, we were in their home state and a different market. What kept us going was a promise of a large marine policy on coal shipments down the Mississippi River. As I worked on a manuscript marine contract, Donna went back to her roots in health insurance. Because premiums for health were constantly rising, businesses welcomed quotes and needed help. Combining her charm with a methodical comparison of all possible quotes, she started to close group accounts. We had been within weeks of shutting down when her efforts began to hit pay dirt. At the same time, the marine policy we had relied on fizzled out. I too returned to my roots, and fortunately a handful of auto dealers, rural utilities, and service contractors began to 'close.' Trenton Insurance became our largest venture yet.

The biggest challenge was yet to come. Building Trenton in a soft market was stressful to say the least. Slowly over time, I was physically slowing down. It took a dozen cups of strong coffee to get my engine going. A physical showed I was anemic, but the doctor could not find a cause. On a trip to California, while in the air flying from Los Angeles to San Francisco, a pituitary tumor broke through my sphenoid bone and spewed blood. *With a bang, life took a dramatic turn.* For three weeks we waited to learn the tumor was benign, we reset values and decided to sell again — to "slow down and smell the roses."

It was a clear sign from God that stress is a dangerous thing, and change was necessary. I had surgery and took a year off, spending time at a health camp in Utah. The lesson learned was that entrepreneurs must intentionally balance life and work. I was lucky for many reasons — transsphenoidal surgery using a microscope to the pituitary was only 15 years old, a new Parkinson medicine suppressed my out-of-balance hormone, and I knew a Tampa broker who needed a property-casualty office in Atlanta.

After that year, we opened a third and final agency, and it was deliberately much simpler... one company, one product, and partly wholesale. For the first time, we were able to help others by building it for hand over to close friends positioned as principals. Returning to Florida in the winters, I went into teaching as an encore career, first teaching risk management then financial planning. I struggled to find my groove until I realized entrepreneurship raises all boats — and was my true passion!

Once I found my purpose, I went back to school to earn an MBA and certificates in entrepreneurship, started entrepreneurship at the State College of Florida, wrote the official entrepreneurship Bar Chart, and initiated the Current in Entrepreneurship blog. Now, I help others combat the perfect storm of job loss from a Gig Economy, artificial intelligence automation, and COVID-19 unemployment. Nothing is a better solution than starting your own business using the evidenced-based lean startup process developed by Silicon Valley to validate an idea or concept before scaling. The fire Ignited by my passion for entrepreneurship is still burning brightly. Lean startup is the secret sauce that will Ignite everyone with an entrepreneurial mindset. Only entrepreneurship allows a person to build their own business, create value, and control their destiny.

If you have sufficient desire to really, really want your own business then take action! Action cures fear so do it now! Entrepreneurial thought in action creates start-ups and leads to successful businesses. In all my years of business, 45 to be exact, I want to share that it is a wonderful journey. Entrepreneurship is living a few years of your life like most people won't, so that you can spend the rest of your life like most people can't.

IGNITE ACTION STEPS

If you are ready to live your dream, become an entrepreneur, and gain personal and financial freedom, here are the action steps to take:

- Develop the critical mindset by reading *The Entrepreneurial Mindset* by Kyle Garman.
- Choose an idea you are passionate about that fills a need. It can be a hobby, interest, or past work, but have an emotional investment.
- Learn Steve Blank's lean startup method, and master its 'business model canvas' and implement 'customer development tools.'
- Find a mentor among instructors or a SBDC (small business development center). Most colleges or universities have an entrepreneurship program in your country.

Clinton E. Day, MBA – United States of America
MBA, CRPC, CPCU, Author, Entrepreneurship Educator
https://clintoneday.com

IGNITE THE ENTREPRENEUR

CHRISTOPHER DE GEER, DC, MS

CHRISTOPHER DE GEER, DC, MS

"Orchestrate an extraordinary life by scheduling the adventures and variety your soul craves."

You deserve to live a remarkable life — one that you may not be giving yourself permission to envision. Entrepreneurship grants you the ability to live life on your terms. I challenge you to identify and rewrite the limitations you have tolerated for yourself that have kept you from introducing excitement into your current experience.

SCHEDULING THE LIFE YOU DREAM OF

My grandfather was a Renaissance man: a charismatic and respected dentist who vacationed with nobel laureates, honed his craft, and served as a philanthropist for those less fortunate in his community. One of my prized possessions is a hand-carved wooden bear statue passed on to me, which was given to him by a famous artist in appreciation for his quality service. He orchestrated a well-rounded life that inspired my personal journey. He sailed a classic 40-foot monohull, made violins by hand, and built our summer home in northern Sweden, which set the stage for some of my favorite childhood memories. He was the love of my grandmother's life and his sense of adventure kept him active through his 85 years of living.

While he has now passed away, his legacy lives on as I reminisce about his qualities. There's a sense of pride in carrying on the traits of his that I admire the most. His life has served as a personal inspiration and now begs me to ask the question: How will I be remembered? How will I live a life that is balanced with professional success, excitement, love, and adventure?

Growing up in Stockholm, Sweden, exposed me early on to variety and culture. My family traveled back and forth between the United States and Europe, and I was grateful for the diversity I was exposed to and the close friends I made across the globe throughout the years.

Determined to combat my high school shyness, I set myself on a path of living the empowered self I wanted to become. I went away to college in Missouri and became a collegiate athlete. I welcomed diversity and was hungry to expand my horizons. I joined a fraternity and took on a telemarketing job. College represented an era where I had little resistance to jumping into new experiences. It was an environment where I was surrounded by friends who reflected this same eagerness to transform the mundane into memorable experiences. That openness to variety included spontaneous trips to the coastline, high-energy get togethers, and even a few racy co-ed lingerie parties that bonded me and my closest friends; a handful of us still get together on a regular basis, no matter where we've landed in the world.

The end of my university studies was celebrated with a thrilling solo free fall skydive. After college, my enthusiasm for the unknown landed me a job in international business as I moved across the Atlantic again. I later went on to work for a high-end fitness center and thanks to my success in this role, I was offered a management position thousands of miles away in Phoenix, Arizona. The prospect of a new adventure was appealing so I immediately packed my home into boxes and was ready to make the move.

Everything was happening so fast, and I stopped for a moment to reflect on my long-term goals. Some self-reflection led me to decline that opportunity. Instead, exhibiting the entrepreneur that I was but didn't yet know I was, I made the riskier but calculated choice of enrolling in grad school versus taking the job that offered more security and immediate gratification. Having a passion for health and human connection, I pivoted into the healthcare field, just like my father and grandfather had.

For the next four years, I was part of an accelerated chiropractic doctoral program while at the same time funding my journey as a personal trainer in the mornings, evenings, and weekends — that was the most stressful period of my life. It was a never-ending sprint to meet the gym's sales quotas while keeping my grades above average. With trimesters filled with 10 or more challenging classes at once, the material alone would cause anxiety. It felt like being in the middle of a stampede — underperforming at work or school would be the equivalent of tripping and getting trampled over.

The collective consciousness at the university was filled with scarcity and stress. A significant number of students had failed a class or two amid the trying exams, holding them behind a semester. Most were also graduating $150,000 to $200,000 USD in debt. The uncertainty around how to pay this back that plagued the student population became the perfect leverage used by pricey practice management groups and coaching services to offer hope. I distanced myself from this palpable negativity and instead focused on expanding upon the years of personal growth I had previously invested in.

Four years later, I came out on the other end as a graduate. Ultimately, the latter half of my 20s was sacrificed in order to earn master's and doctorate degrees.

Graduation led me straight to a crossroads in my life: work for someone else or start my own practice? I imagined what my grandfather did at this stage of his life. He eventually built a successful business, but did he first debate these same choices? I believed in my own potential. Settling for a role as an overworked, underpaid employee contradicted the image of the life I wanted. Just like skydiving out of that Cessna, I decided to take a leap. I chose to work for myself and began a new stage in my life as an entrepreneur. That role entailed trading the security of an immediate paycheck for the potential greater freedom of living on my terms. Yet that decision did not come without a price.

My first years in practice felt like pushing a boulder up a hill. I worked a side job on the weekend to make ends meet and continued to train clients in a gym. I committed to bringing a quality experience to the patients I had. I invested tens of thousands of dollars in coaching to bring more value in the hope of creating raving fans.

Shortly into my career, I bought a colleague's practice and realized I had opened Pandora's box with a whole new level of challenges with business ownership. Lease negotiations, architectural build-outs, hiring staff, and legal battles with my business partner occupied my time, redirected my focus, and sapped my energy.

In the midst of that bumpy experience, I was involved in not one but two head-on car collisions within a year of each other. My right ear had to be reattached and a lengthy rehab process ensued. For months, I was hesitant to step into a car or approach intersections, and I was constantly on high alert, which spilled over to me becoming short-tempered and abrasive in my personal interactions.

I was frustrated and agitated that my life was not evolving the way I had hoped. Comparison, an evil and defeating mechanism, led to uncertainty and insecurity. I constantly felt I wasn't measuring up to what other successful people were doing. For years, I doubted myself and felt like quitting. I wasn't seeking sympathy; rather, I wanted to be unnoticed for my perceived failures. Overcoming my own self-judgment became a significant challenge.

Despite these external and internal setbacks, there was a whisper of optimism and hopefulness in my psyche that things *would* change. I refused to throw in the towel. At least not yet.

As the years were passing by, I had distanced myself from the adventure my soul craved. I had allowed my need for excitement and variety take a back seat to my redundant habits for too long. The quality of my life suffered as this imbalanced lifestyle did not meet my personal needs. Removing myself from sources of joy made me feel anything but extraordinary. I determined it was high time to reclaim my outlet for adventure. I deserved better! I immediately quit my weekend job and demanded more freedom to experience excitement and variety.

First came the decision to reclaim the adventurous aspect of my personality. I shifted my attention to this new commitment and I began budgeting toward a travel fund. I began saying "yes" sincerely to opportunities. I researched travel options and credit card rewards with the giddiness of a kid at Christmas. The zest for travel was so high that I could have started my own travel agency. Just like my grandfather, I had an affinity for sailing. My brother shared this dream and we scheduled an adventure right away, booking tickets to Miami. Before we knew it, we were sailing the Florida Keys.

A mental shift to appreciate and create variety *right where I was* allowed me to rely less on my external environment in order to feel more satisfied. I became a member of the art museum, found eclectic restaurants, discovered nature paths, joined a sand volleyball league, and started salsa dancing and drawing again.

Two years into this commitment, the excitement really took off! The opportunity presented itself to charter a 48-foot catamaran for a family trip to the British Virgin Islands. We discovered the Baths at Virgin Gorda. We took scooters across Anegada Island and spotted a flock of hundreds of flamingos. Two friendly wild dolphins approached me underwater as I was diving off a remote island near Jost Van Dyke. I scheduled two additional scuba vacations and a trip back home to Stockholm, ending the year with more trips than I had ever taken annually in my life.

Year three started off by celebrating Carnival in Rio de Janeiro, hang gliding by day and dancing samba by night. Giant parade floats detailed with vibrant colors and moving pieces rolled through downtown's Sambadrome, some even equipped with their own waterfalls! This was the kind of experience I was dreaming of: contributing to the energy of the biggest party in the world.

Later that year, we ventured on a family trip to the beautiful waterfalls and coffee bars of Portland, Oregon. In late July, we thought of no better way to celebrate shark week than to scuba dive with sharks in the Bahamas. My mother was along for the experience and surprised me with her underwater courage. In the early fall, we dropped by London on the way to Stockholm for a week of pubs, tea time, theater, and incredible cuisine. We topped it off by winter scuba diving at the Blue Hole in Belize. That year, I was able to create memories in five international countries by going on 12 trips.

For me, freedom is all about having the option to create experiences for myself and those I care about. I've now been able to cross off bucket-list items like going to Oktoberfest in Germany, drifting next to alligators in the Everglades, surfing the Gold Coast of Australia, and bungee jumping in New Zealand.

I have surrounded myself with mentors and peers committed to expanding themselves. These connections all bring unique perspectives that help me think differently and stimulate growth. This has been invaluable to my personal and professional life by shedding light on areas of opportunity I couldn't access from my own perspective.

Initially, I felt the need to justify the abundance of flavorful experiences I allowed myself to have. However, the more I filled my own cup, the better I was able to bring value to those around me, whether in the form of joy, enthusiasm, or inspiration. Prioritizing adventure fuels immense joy and love that is so important for me to share with my family, friends, and clients.

Making the commitment to prioritize and schedule excitement, adventure, and travel has changed my life. It has helped me look for variety every day, which has benefitted me personally and professionally. The eagerness and enthusiasm I feel on a regular basis has drawn me to opportunities and introductions I may not have been receptive of by living in a state of redundancy.

I managed to successfully turn my imbalanced, burned-out business owner experience around into an eclectic, almost fantasy-like lifestyle. Now on a well-balanced path of variety and helping those around me, I feel my grandfather would be proud of the life I've chosen for myself. Unbeknownst to him, he planted the seed of inspiration to love fearlessly and live boldly. My goal now is to serve as an inspiration for those around me to create the extraordinary life they deserve.

Freedom doesn't have to be five big vacations per year. Entrepreneurship allows you to create the balance in your schedule with the experiences that fuel *you* best. Decide which desires you want to fill your life with and commit to scheduling them. Be uncompromising in setting timelines and deadlines for your bucket-list items.

As a business owner and entrepreneur, you are able to choose your experiences based on what you value. Ask yourself, what memories do you want to share with the most important people in your life? For instance, if you want to go to Europe, research the sights you want to see and the food you want to taste. If you want to scuba dive, seek out your local dive shop and meet a new network of friends who share that same passion. The hunger for your dreams will drive you to find the necessary resources to carry out your journey. Fuel those passions and foster those ideas. Give yourself the green light and Ignite the entrepreneurial adventurer in you. You deserve that!

Ignite Action Steps

First, tackle your headspace. Convince yourself you deserve all the success you're striving for. With the amount of joy you start to consistently welcome into your experience, you will be able to spread this to those around you. Give yourself permission to dream up the lifestyle that excites you.

Then, take a step back and assess your life. Honestly acknowledge what you are tolerating and what is holding you back. Until you get fed up with how things are going, there is a big chance that nothing will change. Ask yourself if you are happy with the trajectory your life is taking. Where do you want to be in the future? What vision inspires you?

Acknowledge your limiting beliefs, which are merely your ego's way of keeping you safe. These are the thoughts that poke holes in your plan with worst-case scenarios and doubts as you venture outside of your safe, non-challenging comfort zone. If nothing changes, then there's no risk or additional danger. But if you're desiring something more for your life, *nothing changing* is what's really to fear.

Next, it's time to get focused on creating the right conditions to invite success into your life. Dedicate yourself with daily meditation and create reminders of the life you want for yourself. There's a difference between *understanding* what you have learned and *applying* it. Until you act on the lessons within business or personal growth, none of it matters. Avoid analysis paralysis and get dirty.

It's not going to be perfect to begin with, and that's certainly okay. *An extraordinary life is orchestrated by doing what your soul craves.*

Christopher De Geer, DC, MS – United States of America & Sweden
Clinic Owner, University Educator, Consultant
DeGeerHealth.com

IGNITE THE ENTREPRENEUR

TARA LEHMAN

TARA LEHMAN

"Life is like standing at the ice cream counter, only
you can choose your favorite flavor."

**Countless entrepreneurs believe business success is only attained via finan-
cial clout and a string of qualifications. Entrepreneurial success and client
acquisitions come in as many flavors as ice cream, so explore your opportunities with the same enthusiasm as you would sampling at the ice cream
counter! As you read, I ask you to put any fear-based thoughts aside and
instead, challenge yourself to explore what an *Ice Cream Moment* looks
like to you. It is within these moments that we earn the delightful currency
of human connection.**

MY ICE CREAM MOMENT

How dare he!

Like millions of people, I was spending part of my day scrolling through
Facebook™, and on that particular day I stopped when I saw an acquaintance
of mine, a business coach, had just posted his latest daily inspiration. Deciding
to read closer in case it was something I needed to hear, this is what I read:

"If you aren't making a million dollars, you don't
have a business. You have a hobby."

Maybe this shouldn't have pissed me off since it happened years ago, but it did because it put a label on success and a business owner's happiness. He certainly wasn't making that amount of money his first year, so the comment was very discouraging to me as a budding entrepreneur. As someone who had experienced various adventures as an entrepreneur, I knew it took time and patience to build up to that. His words were not very inspiring.

Reading this made me question if my business idea was good enough and that if I couldn't earn a million bucks, I may as well pack it all in. It was the most unsupportive comment I'd ever heard a business coach make. What right did he have to discourage me from thinking my passions weren't worthy enough to turn into a business? I was so offended, (and clearly still am), that I hit the 'BLOCK' button because I didn't need anyone pushing their definition of success on me.

If your business goal is to simply earn enough to hit up the shopping mall guilt-free or travel to your dream destination and you achieve that in a way that makes you happy, then congratulations — you have a successful business! Becoming a millionaire is not why I became an entrepreneur.

His comment conjured up a memory though. The memory of an entrepreneur I admire calling me a 'serial entrepreneur' and how my back went up because it sounded like a bad thing. Did it mean I come across as someone who gives up easily? Or, on the flip side, did it mean I happily take risks and know when it's time to move on? So, I consulted Google™ (because whatever Google says must be true, right?) and here are six common traits of serial entrepreneurs:

- *Good Time Management*
- *Ability to Set Concrete Goals*
- *Strong Discipline*
- *Unwavering Optimism*
- *Creativity and Innovation*
- *Strong and Stable Leadership*

These are qualities of any entrepreneur, serial or not! So, I'm okay with people labeling me any kind of entrepreneur they wish. I don't have all those traits running on high 24/7. However, the two aces in my back pocket that permeate everything I do are what I'm known for: unwavering optimism and creativity.

Then came 'Snowmageddon.'

January 2020 marked the worst snowstorm in over a century on the beautiful island of Newfoundland and Labrador on the eastern coast of Canada. The Canadian military was flying in relief workers to shovel us out of a week-long state of emergency due to the 76 centimeters of snow and winds of 130 kilometers per hour that pummeled our town. The only way out of my yard was rolling down the snowbank, the roads were nonexistent, and everything came to a standstill. Months earlier I had considered going to California at this exact same time for the launch of my first book, *Ignite Your Health and Wellness*, a place where I'd be dancing in a bright, flowery sundress instead of waddling around in my puffy white and purple snowsuit, but there was no point whining about that now.

My city, St. John's, Newfoundland, had, in just one evening, been swallowed up by snow of such proportions that even if you did manage to dig your way out of the house, you still wouldn't have been able to locate your car. Weather reporters from across the country flew in ahead of the storm since it was likely a once-in-a-career experience to report about and they were right. Winds threatened to blow them over while they captured images of people snowboarding on downtown streets and snowshoeing to check on friends and family who were stuck in their homes.

Those unfortunate enough to be working when the storm hit were left sleeping in their offices until someone could rescue them. Facebook posts from people looking for ways to get food and medicine were multiplying because many simply couldn't get past their driveway. Curfews were put in place to ensure roads were free to be plowed, and admittedly, there was one time I didn't follow this rule and found myself driving the wrong way down a one-way street in the dark of night to avoid the snowplows. With me was a friend, a well-known government official, who had to duck down in the back seat so she didn't risk anyone seeing her playing rebel with me (that would have been social media chaos).

There was sooooo much snow the government had to grant the island permission to dump the snow into the only place left to put it: the North Atlantic ocean. The sequestering was like being grounded by your parents for something you didn't do and not knowing when you would be free, with Mother Nature being the unreasonable parent. Brick-and-mortar stores were losing thousands by the day since they couldn't safely open and the only entrepreneurs making money off of 'Snowmageddon' were snow plowers.

Two months later, Covid-19 forced me back inside.

Being *grounded* a second time served as my reminder that the waves of uncertainty entrepreneurs can face make creativity and the ability to work from home a comfort. This extra time indoors provided the opportunity to reflect on the various entrepreneurial journeys I had taken over the years, what was going well, what needed to change, and how a pandemic was going to get in my way. I had all kinds of time on my hands to get honest with my business future.

I signed up for more online courses than I had time to attend, which taught me what I liked and didn't like about online presentations. As an event coordinator (my largest entrepreneurial passion), I set my sights on coaching people on how to plan and host their own online events. The in-person event industry was crashing and at the very least I had to try something new. All other business ideas were shovelled to the side in a snowbank and my first step was becoming a Certified Virtual Event Coordinator (there didn't appear to be too many of them out there). I started hosting weekly online concerts. That paid me in warm fuzzy feelings. It had less to do with making money as it did with supporting the musicians who had nowhere to perform, and it brought pleasure to those desperate for something to do; including myself. Those concerts, combined with what people already knew of me as an event coordinator, led to receiving requests from individuals and companies to teach their staff how to use Zoom™ and structure productive virtual events. Sure, we can all log into an event, but it's quite another to know how to present properly and network effectively. Not even two months into the pandemic, the journey of coaching people as their kids and pets 'screen-bombed' had begun.

That was how I discovered my 'Ice Cream Moment'.

An Ice Cream Moment is when you've pegged who your ideal client is. The person who has the problem that you can solve. The moment you see your potential client curled up on the kitchen floor spooning ice cream into their mouth because it's more comforting than thinking about what's weighing them down. It's when you seize the opportunity to sit next to them on the floor, tell your story as you gently take the ice cream away. I truly believe sharing your personal story is key to this picture. Years ago, I helped coach Dale Carnegie™ classes and I'll never forget learning that we should never speak about something we haven't earned the right to. It makes all the difference as to whether or not we manage to gain the clients' trust whether it's one-on-one or a virtual audience of 1,000 people. I'm blown away by how many times I've been hired to work on big projects for which more experienced staff could have been hired, but I can still remember the day — even where I was standing in fact — when

I realized it was because I'm good at building relationships and by default, people's trust. That's all people need to know. That they can trust you.

My Ice Cream Moment came when I was asked to present for an organization that I had always wanted to speak for. One hundred entrepreneurs tuned in, thirsty for the knowledge of how to host virtual events, and it became glaringly clear that these were the ones with the problem I could solve. It was humbling because so many of these people were pillars in the business community. These were people slowly realizing that unless they got on the virtual event bandwagon, it no longer mattered how well-known they are and how much money they earned. They weren't trusting that a virtual environment could provide the kind of value their audience needed and they definitely didn't believe they had what it took to host one. Those who had competitors hosting virtual events, well, that was a whole other level of panic to cut through. However, like so many businesses, they could no longer afford to have staff and the pressure to earn enough to simply get by fell to them. That added to the stress of finding the time to plan a virtual experience they didn't understand. It was all too much. Connection grew when I shared with them how I felt about the unknowing circumstances and that allowed them to immediately relate to me. Uncertainty was the common thread we all had, and to an extent still do. Once I achieved that connection and was able to help them see that anyone in the world with a computer and internet connection could be their audience and therefore open new doors. I was golden or so I thought.

Until I had to pivot again!

What we thought was just going to be a few months lingered through all of 2020. People had Zoom™ fatigue, me included. Calls to train people trickled off since most everyone had been forced to learn it by then and live music venues were reopening. Although it was disappointing to see that stream of income decline, I could simultaneously be proud of everything I had learned so quickly during a time of necessity in order to help myself and others. I had to acknowledge that the rise of Covid-19 was affecting the way I wished to experience entrepreneurship.

It was then that I reminded myself that energy = money. I asked myself how much energy I wanted to continue putting toward trying to rise to the top in what was, and still is, one of the hardest hit industries; event planning. As soon as I got honest, the veil fell to the side and I saw that entrepreneurship, for at least the time being, could no longer be a full-time adventure for me.

And, while once upon a time I would have considered that state of mind a sign of failure, these days I'm 100 percent confident that it's not. In truth, failure would have been not taking the time to ask myself the hard questions. So, I decided that with 10-plus years in the event industry under my belt, there are enough people that know who I am, and what I do, that they'll find me if they need me. That left time for me to embark on a whole new adventure.

As soon as I acknowledged what this new version of entrepreneurship looked like for me, an unexpected opportunity fell in my lap. In the past I may have undersold myself but things were different now. I knew more than ever what I could achieve since I didn't allow myself to sit around moaning and groaning about how Covid was wrecking things. So, at the time of writing this, I'm now the Executive Director for a Chamber of Commerce, and that may not have happened if I didn't have 10-plus years of entrepreneurial experience. It also may not have happened if I wasn't a serial entrepreneur because it's those combined experiences that have allowed me to understand the full entrepreneurial journey. It feels fantastic to embark on this opportunity at a time where business owners need help more than ever. The exciting Ice Cream Moment in this scenario is that I am reassuring entrepreneurs that they aren't alone in their struggles. Showing them that as a collective, we achieve success far more easily together than when we try to do things alone. I enjoy being just a phone call or email away for anything they need. It's the best of both worlds: I get to witness entrepreneurship at its finest while having the security that comes along with a stable income and having the privilege to work from home.

Here's the truth though. When I made the decision to not make entrepreneurship a full-time end goal, it felt like writing in this book, *Ignite The Entrepreneur,* made me a bit of an imposter. It made forging ahead with my story difficult because after all, who am I to write about entrepreneurship if I'm not tackling it full-time? But, then I remembered how that business coach's comment made me feel and I now know that not all entrepreneurs are the same. Entrepreneurship can look a *million* different ways. Being in business is an art, and most businesses are designed to help others, which I get to do every day. I am in the center of entrepreneurship because I support other entrepreneurs in doing what they love.

Happiness is the *real* success. Happiness is knowing what flavor of ice cream you choose. Right here, right now, I'm happy. That's worth all the dollars to me.

Go after *your* entrepreneurial adventures. Follow your ambitions and surround yourself with the people who are willing to shovel you out during the storms.

Determine what success means to you and explore your opportunities with the same joy and glee as you would while ordering from the ice cream counter.

Ignite Action Steps

- Decide what financial success means to you and you only.
- Visualize the extra people tuning into your event if you make it virtual instead of in-person only. Let the excitement of that propel you forward because staying in a fear-based mindset affects your ability to make the most of the opportunities these people bring you.
- Identify the six common entrepreneurial traits you already have that are making you successful and be proud of that!
- Choose one of the six common entrepreneurial traits that you would like to become better at and start making it happen. This could be by reading books, listening to podcasts, hiring a business coach, and/or anything else that suits your learning style.
- Envision what your own *Ice Cream Moment* will look and feel like. To achieve this, you must first ensure you know who your ideal client is and, ideally, have a personal story to tell that they can relate to.

Tara Lehman – Canada
Owner, Get Eventive
www.geteventive.com

IGNITE THE ENTREPRENEUR

JASON BAUCH

Jason Bauch

*"If you're going to do something, make sure you
follow through and dominate."*

**I feel that my story is unique and will catch your attention by showing
you that, through persistence and tenacity, you will always succeed. Look
for the opportunities in life. If you get knocked down — get up. If you
consistently get up, you can't lose. By being present in the moment, listening to my intuition, and following my instincts and saying "Yes" to the
opportunities that arise, I have found that success starts to fall into place.**

Trans Ams Don't Need a Back Seat

It happened so fast…

Steam was bellowing out of the radiator of my vehicle. Time seemed to
stop as I started to get my bearings and I took in what had just happened. As
I looked around, I was puzzled how I managed to put the truck in a ditch
between two trees but somehow not hit them. Someone knocked on the door
so I rolled down the window. They asked if I was alright. It's a funny question
to ask someone who just hit a Ford™ F150 head on at 45 miles per hour, only
to end up parked in a ditch between two trees.

As the medics pulled up, I realized that I was going to take my first ambulance
ride. It's not as fun as I thought it would be. I was strapped to the gurney and
probably still in some sort of shock. I remember it being an odd feeling lying
down in a moving vehicle and I was surrounded by a lot of equipment. I never

got the sensation that we were moving fast. It was more of a side to side rocking motion. The paramedics were very calm and joked around with me a little.

My job was driving and that day I did my best to avoid a head-on collision; ending up in the ditch. The hospital did a few tests and released me the same day. Later, they found more serious injuries. I was put on workmen's compensations for the freight company I worked for, living at home with my Mom, and the doctors didn't want me driving, so my world got really small. I had the internet, but it wasn't like it is today and I was bored with nothing to do.

People would often ask, "How are you doing?" Things weren't all that great, so I would give honest answers. I noticed that people started to distance themselves from me. This is what forced me to have two huge revelations.

First, I was miserable to be around. Second, people don't really want to know how you are doing, at least not to the extent I was sharing. I was a huge emotional drag on the people who knew me and had to find a way to turn things around.

I did this through a series of small wins that would eventually result in massive progress. This was no small challenge. I had been off work for six months. Workers' compensation stopped paying my bills three months after my accident, and I was broke. It took me a total of two years of physical therapy to figure out my new normal.

First and foremost, I had to return to work! I started back in a light duty position right after New Year's. The first thing they did was send me for a drug test. That began a pattern of how the company would handle me moving forward, as though my painkillers would become their way to get rid of me. I needed to get used to getting back to the working world and rehabilitate. Coming back to work was like being released back into the wild. Your world gets big again. Some things had changed, but I was welcomed back by my coworkers with open arms. I was just happy to be getting a paycheck again.

I was on light duty, so bouncing around in a truck was out of the question. That meant I was brought into the office where I learned to be a dispatcher. When the company continued to give me tasks that I was not allowed to do, I knew I was being set up for failure so they could get rid of me. I was lucky enough to have made some new friends at the job and they saw how I was being treated. One friend encouraged me to take an interview with a company he was moving to so I figured it couldn't hurt. I got the job and also received a substantial pay raise. They were so happy to fill the role that they even bumped my yearly salary another $1,500. It was a much healthier place to work, but that company had a lot of management issues and I hadn't done my homework.

That experience taught me a valuable lesson. Make sure you are working at the company headquarters. You will be able to make effective change as well as get noticed by people who can advance your career. I lasted about a year before I got fired. The loss was devastating and it took years of reflection before I could admit to myself that they did the right thing by firing my ass. I needed to do some growing up and wasn't ready to become a leader.

I spent the next two months regrouping and trying to figure out what my next move would be. It was a Saturday afternoon when my friend Tony and I decided to go to the local guitar store. Our excursion set in motion a series of events that would alter my future forever. I would get my life on track and formulate the first steps that would become the foundation for my empire.

Tony and I jumped in his Mustang™ and I instantly knew he didn't like his car. You can always tell when someone hates their car. It looked like a rolling ashtray and had trash everywhere. We hung out at the guitar shop for about 45 minutes before Tony started talking about wanting to buy a new Corvette™. The shop was located next to a Pontiac™ dealership and they had two beautiful blue Ram Air Trans Ams™ — one automatic and one in a six-speed. I knew this because I have been a huge Trans Am fan since I was a kid, and with so much free time to kill, I had visited the dealership earlier in the week. I told Tony about the car and we headed next door so he could take a look.

He instantly fell in love with the six-speed so we talked to the salesman who grabbed the keys so we could go on a test drive. Tony drove, the salesman sat in the passenger seat, and I crammed myself into the notoriously small back seat (they are really just there for insurance purposes). Tony started to ask basic questions regarding the car's performance features, but it was clear that the salesman didn't know his product and was talking out of his ass. We were both getting frustrated with this guy, so I jumped in and answered some of the questions that Tony had.

We got back to the dealership and Tony was satisfied with the car so he started working on the finance papers. It was at that time that a light went off in my head: "First, you need a job; and second, you love the Trans Am. Most importantly though, this place clearly doesn't require any experience."

I asked the salesman to introduce me to his boss. A couple of minutes went by and his boss appeared. I introduced myself and asked for a job. I watched the guy look down at my ripped jeans and back up at my Metallica™ shirt. After sizing me up, he smiled dismissively and asked, "Why should I hire you?"

I smiled back at him and boldly said, "Well, if you're willing to hire this guy, who knows nothing about cars, then you will love what I can bring to the table."

He took a step back, let out a little laugh, and said, "Tell you what Jason, come back tomorrow at 2 PM dressed for an interview, and we can talk."

I came back the next day at 1:45 PM wearing a suit and tie, because if you're not 15 minutes early, then you are late. The interview went just as it should for someone who has zero professional training but makes up with it in drive and positive attitude. The boss liked me but said he wanted to think about it and would call me. I gave him 48 hours to call me back and then it was time to dazzle him with my persistent follow-up skills. What did I have to lose? I was like a dog with a bone and this was my best and only lead. I started a campaign to call him three times a day. I refused to leave a message. If I was told the boss was busy, I would just call back later.

My tenacity paid off and I started the following Monday. That is when I discovered that I was working in a shark tank and needed an edge... so I got fast. The moment someone walked through the door, I would greet them with a warm smile, shake their hand, and ask them how I could help. This didn't earn me any friends and actually created a new problem; I had lost any allies at the dealership. The boss saw how hungry I was, but he also saw that I didn't know how to take the customer through the sales process. He pulled ALL of the salespeople into his office and had a closed-door meeting while I was left to greet whoever wandered onto the showroom floor. He then proceeded to light up everyone in his office and asked how the new guy was running laps around his people. This did me no favors and put a target on my back. Thankfully, the boss saw my blind spots were product knowledge and sales structure, so once I closed my first customer, he invested time and training into me.

After watching all his sales videos and learning everything I could about the different vehicles and their features, he sent me and another junior sales guy to an automotive sales school, ironically located on Trans Am Drive. It was every bit as good as I expected, and I walked away armed with an understanding of the sales process and some basic strategies. That combined with my relentless pursuit of success allowed me to meet the next person who would change the course of my life.

A young lady named Suzie walked in looking for a very specific Grand Am. I didn't see anything in our inventory, so I checked with my boss who advised me that we had just taken delivery of this exact car and it hadn't hit the system yet. I came back to my office and delivered the good news. Suzie was ecstatic and quickly agreed to our deal. We chatted while she filled out her credit application and I discovered that her dad was an executive at Ford and was very upset with her choice in vehicles. I looked everything over and noticed that she came from the same air freight company that I had hired to deliver loads for me at the previous job. We laughed at how small of a world it was, then Suzie asked if I was interested in getting back into transportation. I paused for a second, leaned back in my chair, and considered what she had said.

That was the first time in my life that I actually had career options. I realized that as much fun as I was having at selling cars, I really couldn't see myself doing it forever. I gave her my card and asked her to call me tomorrow to discuss the potential job. As she drove off in her new car, I realized that something big had just happened but I had no idea how big it would be.

I set up an interview with the company she worked at. It was beginning to gain market share in the industry and it was the world headquarters, so that box was checked! I showed up 15 minutes early, as I customarily do, and was taken back for a preliminary interview. I must have nailed that because she called in the manager of their Perishable Department. We talked a little and then he did something that I would later find out he did often in interviews: he tried to talk me out of the job to gauge my sincerity, even going so far as to tell me that I didn't *want* the job. I flat-out said I did, and that I knew that I would be an asset to this company.

Looking back, I now know my speech didn't get me the job; it was my networking that got me the interview. It turns out that Suzie was very close with the owners of the company and had told them the story about how I had gone the extra mile to get her the little black Grand Am sitting in the parking lot. That was enough for them.

Starting that new job opened so many doors. I met a great friend and mentor, Michael Cohan, who helped me grow into the person I am today. Through him I met Christie, the woman for whom I would move to Texas and later marry. Over the next decade, I continued seizing opportunities as they came up. I worked for one company that ultimately dissolved, but that allowed me to eventually accept the role of President for a company I helped build.

I have since started my own company with my good friend Bryan Couch and taken on the role of President and CEO of 360 Freight Solutions. I also launched an online course called Brokerz Edge that teaches people how to be a freight broker using successful strategies I have developed over the last 24 years of being in the transportation industry; the only industry where a person with a high school education can make a six-figure income. I knew that if I applied myself and focused I could turn my life around from a guy that was one paycheck away from living in his car, to a guy that could command a multi-million dollar business.

Who is Jason Bauch now? I am a President and CEO, a founder and an owner. I am a husband, I am a father, I am a son, I am a brother, and I am a friend to countless people. I am a mentor and a student. And I am someone who built all I have on a high school education and a refusal to stay down. I dropped out of community college after my first semester and it was the best thing I ever did. This is how I have earned myself a place in the life I have today. I was able to beat enormous odds. I went from being both physically and financially broken to realizing that I had a responsibility to turn my mess around and build some kind of future.

Every time I got knocked down, I jumped back up, smiled, and laughed. As with any fight, I knew as long as I kept getting up I would eventually win. I got out of my comfort zone and became trainable. I maintained who I was and networked my ass off to make sure that I made the most out of all the opportunities I came across. I stopped looking for an excuse and started to control the controllable. The most important thing I did for myself was take responsibility for ME. Even if it wasn't always the easiest way, I did things my way, and that has made all the difference.

As long as you stick to who you are, making and owning your choices, you can stay in the driver's seat for the rest of your life. By standing on the sidelines and not doing what you are good at, you are losing money. It's your moral obligation to serve both yourself and your family by pursuing your entrepreneurial dreams and talents. There is never a right time to do it, you just have to go all in; build, create, and figure out the details as you go. You can plan all you want, there is never a perfect time. Learn to expect the unexpected and expect to face challenges along the way. When people want what you have, it means you are doing something right. Be all in, be committed, and DOMINATE!

Ignite Action Steps

I am 45 years old as I am writing this. The advice I would give a 22-year-old version of me would be, "Jason do this." It's powerful to think bigger than where you are at right now. Try these few action steps as they give you a framework and awaken the entrepreneur in you.

Hold to your values. Make sure that you are the best person you can be. The whole world isn't against you. Trust your own instincts. Believe in yourself and don't let money change you.

Learn how to manage your money. Never spend more than you make. Budget yourself so that you can increase and build your company. When you can, create a reserve for the unexpected and just because you are making the money doesn't mean you need to spend it.

When people let you down, don't take it personally. Not everyone can run at your level, or even think like you, so be humble about it and move on from the things you can't change.

Make sure you ask better questions and then listen to the answers. People always say that the thing you don't know is the thing you should know. You have got to learn how to ask better questions. One of my mentors always says, "The quality of your questions determines the quality of your results."

Jason Bauch – United States of America
Founder of Brokerz Edge and 360 Freight Solutions
www.brokerzedge.com
www.360freightsolutiosn.com
🔲 Jason Bauch
🔲 @jasonpbauch
🔲 @jasonbauch
🔲 Jason Bauch

IGNITE THE ENTREPRENEUR

ANA-MARIA
TURDEAN

ANA-MARIA TURDEAN

"I feel bold, as I am the torch lighting the way through the darkness."

I want to inspire you to use your artistry and talents for designing beautiful, sustainable products and contributing to the future of humanity. No matter where you are in your creative journey, you can leave a beautiful mark with your art, whether it is photography, painting, drawing, sculpture, or digital art. I encourage you to share your work with people from all over the world so that your gifts and greatness can be enjoyed.

SHARING YOUR ARTISTRY WITH THE WORLD

I have always been a creative person. I remember spending many hours as a child painting or drawing different things like houses, flowers, and sunny skies on any piece of paper I could find, much to the exasperation of my parents and sister. What I enjoyed drawing most were horses. I used hundreds of pages of A4 paper drawing horse figures with extremely long legs in the beginning, like in Dali's *The Temptation of Saint Anthony* and *Don Quixote* masterpieces. Gradually my technique improved to the point that my horses looked real. Colors and imagination played an important part in my art. I was always using bright hues and beautiful tones, usually with tempera paint, watercolors, or oil crayons. I found inspiration in the stories I heard, in fairytales, in the images on my TV screen, and in the beautiful places I was visiting.

The first art museum I visited was The National Museum of Art of Romania, in Bucharest, at the age of 14. I remember the day I stepped through the elegant corridors of the royal palace that hosts the museum — it was like entering a fairytale. I was enchanted by the beauty of the engravings of Albrecht Durer and other golden age masters, and by the paintings by European artists such as David, Picasso, Rubens, Rembrandt, and many others. I liked the vivid colors and details of the Romanian artworks that hung on the beautiful pink walls of the palace. I also enjoyed the textures of sculptures by Constantin Brâncuși and Dimitrie Paciurea. It was an absolute joy to watch a group of children laugh while listening to the museum guide's stories and jump with enthusiasm to answer her questions.

This experience was so profound that I made sure the first thing I did before going on a trip abroad was check the name and location of the art museums in the area. I am blessed to have visited many beautiful museums across Europe. The ones I enjoyed the most are the Louvre Museum in France, the National Museum of Art of Romania, the Van Gogh Museum in the Netherlands, the Mucha Museum in the Czech Republic, the Stanislaw Wyspianski Museum in Poland, the Dalí Theatre-Museum in Spain, and the Musée National d'Histoire et d'Art in Luxembourg. Standing in the middle of a museum, surrounded by masterpieces, made me feel entranced. I had the feeling of traveling back in time to the lands depicted in the drawings or paintings. Gustav Moreau's *Jupiter and Semele*, one of my favorite paintings, depicts the scene in which Semele, a mortal woman, sees her lover, Jupiter, in all his divine splendor. It was too much for her and she died by lightning. The painting, considered Moreau's testament, is extremely beautiful. All the characters, costumes, and columns are depicted with intricate detail and brilliant color.

I stopped drawing and painting in high school as I could not find inspiration anymore. When I was in the last year of secondary school, I went with a col-league to an art exam at a school for aspiring artists. We were asked to sketch still life. A few days later, I found out that I passed the test, and I could attend classes meant to prepare me for the admission exam to art school. Unfortunately, I became seriously ill with trichinosis and was hospitalized for several weeks. After coming home from the hospital, I had to focus on learning what I missed at regular school. I thought my chance to pursue my passion had come to an end.

Having missed my window to enter art school, I instead shifted my focus to attending an economics high school. This led me to a career in accounting; stable and financially rewarding. Still, as I began working as an accountant in the corporate world, I always had a sense that I was missing something. I felt like every day was just passing by without anything special. I had a certain restlessness which I could not name.

What I did know was that I loved posting creative photos on social media, but I had no idea that this could be a full-time occupation.

After three years of working in my monotonous accounting job, I received an email from an executive of the online photo design tool called VIDA, who somehow saw my drawings on Facebook™. She asked if I was interested in collaborating with them. I opened a free account on the platform, but when I explored it further, I decided not to take her up on the offer. I doubted that I could create something valuable after not painting and drawing for many years.

That opportunity stayed stuck in my mind and tugged at my creative desires. I kept up my museum visits to simulate my mind, but inside, I was bored. Two years after receiving the email from VIDA, I was blessed to attend Mindvalley University in Tallinn, Estonia. There I had the chance to meet amazing individuals working in different disciplines, including in the creative sector.

One of the people I met there was Yoram Baltinester, a public speaker, author, and coach. During our later conversations on Facebook, after we had both returned to our homes, I told him that I missed doing something creative. He advised me to practice my talents for two hours every day.

The first thing I did was create a video to find potential renters for my place in Poland. I took a few photos of my room and the common area of the flat with my phone. Then I edited the images and added them to a video editing app. I built a slideshow with the photos and inserted one of the songs from the app. Once the video was completed, I shared it on Facebook, hoping it would convince people to rent my room. Loads of enthusiastic individuals contacted me to come and see the space.

At that moment I realized that I had spent half a day doing creative work and enjoyed every second of it. The time had gone by so quickly, and I was extremely happy. I was sparked by that moment to pursue my dream of sharing my creativity once again with the world.

A job opportunity came up in Romania, so I left Poland and started working for a start-up company that promoted dresses and accessories for special occasions. The first step was to renovate a flat that we planned to use as an office. I was traveling back and forth from my parents' home and the flat; a one-hour drive I would share with the other workers. It was a tiring process as I was waking up at 5 AM every day and running back and forth to perform different tasks, but I was happy that I was learning new things and being of service.

The job allowed me a lot of free time when I was not traveling. I used this spare time to post content on their social media pages and work on the business' website. At the same time, I started searching old boxes, storage areas, and my parents' basement for my precious childhood drawings until I finally realized where my drawings were — in my parents' countryside home.

When I finally found them, I was both happy and grateful. They reminded me of my childhood and how much I loved to create art. I gathered them together with old photos, scanned them, and applied them to the templates on the VIDA platform, gradually creating beautiful collections of sustainable clothes, scarves, accessories, and home decorations. Additionally, I used my phone to take photos of the dresses featured at the company I was working for that emphasized the delicate beadwork and colorful fabrics. I was ecstatic with the beauty of the final product that resulted from my collaboration, and I had a lot of fun while creating it. I started to see how it was possible to turn my art into a business and become an entrepreneur. My heart was filled with happiness.

Unfortunately, we did not receive the necessary approvals from the neighbors to run the company in the flat we renovated. I was really upset that we could not move things forward after all that effort. I started searching for a job, as I needed a source of income to pay my bills. I got into customer service, but my mind was still on art and I kept creating new items to sell on my own.

The first collection I created was called THE EYE, inspired by a pastel drawing I made when I was approximately 14 or 15 years old. I brought this drawing to life using the *hachure* technique, putting line upon line with colorful oil crayons. From there I kept designing, gathering influence from everything from old paintings to brand new photos taken with my smartphone. I gradually got familiar with the VIDA platform and started spending less and less time designing on social media. I was excited to watch my designs travel the world in the digital space. It felt like I had launched a rocket and it was speeding around the planet.

Unfortunately, my excitement quickly vanished: February yielded zero sales, March zero sales, April zero sales, May zero sales. "What is going on?" I asked myself. "Why am I not selling anything despite posting on social media every day?" To find answers to these questions, I started following the activity of influencers. I noticed that they were using hashtags on all their social media posts and I knew I had to replicate this. I started posting photos of my designs with hashtags. I had my first sale almost immediately: *Multicolored Jewels Statement Clutch.* I created the collection using a photo of the beads on an elegant evening dress. I was thrilled to see that the products I loved to create, initially for fun, were now being appreciated by many others. I was eager to find a way to turn my passion into a thriving business.

I spent the following months learning digital marketing from free events and tutorials. I even joined Facebook groups for entrepreneurs, where I was sharing vouchers for my VIDA designs. I was able to make a few sales every month without spending money on paid ads, but I knew that I could do much better.

A year later, I left Romania and moved to Prague, Czech Republic to find an investor and expand my business. The flight was okay, but once I got off the plane, I encountered problem after problem, each consuming precious hours of my days. From opening a bank account to finding accommodation and commuting, everything was a challenge. Just when I thought things were tough, the world changed dramatically. The coronavirus pandemic left me jobless in Prague. I knew that it would be harder than usual to find a job as now part of my effort had to be redirected to prevent getting the virus: disinfecting hands and the products I was purchasing, cleaning the room, the clothes, and the common space of the flat more often than usual. To survive those difficult times, I kept my body healthy with internet dance classes, but I still needed to find a creative outlet. I made videos using photos from my VIDA collections and in time they were shared across social media, making people aware of my art even though this was not resulting in sales.

For the first time in 21 years, I started drawing again using crayons I bought from the supermarket. Once the drawing was completed, I took a few photos, chose the best one, and transformed it into wearable art on the VIDA platform. I AM ENOUGH, LUCKY, QUESTION, and LOVE are collections I made during lockdown. I was extremely happy to have time for this wonderful activity. I took photos on my way to the supermarket, during short walks, and while attending a flower exhibition in Prague, which led to my SPRING, DANDELION, and IRIS collections. Since VIDA factories were temporarily closed, I knew that all I could do was to create products and content to raise awareness of my work while selling affiliate products to make ends meet.

I used the time spent indoors to draw future sustainable clothing and accessories with older photos from my beautiful travels. I discovered Canva software during lockdown and started creating colorful patterns, which I applied to designs and social media to make my accounts more appealing. To expand my marketing knowledge, I participated in an online competition called The Airship Customer Engagement Quiz. I was in first place until I got hungry and could not focus anymore. I earned the second prize but had fun and learned a lot. I felt encouraged. Despite difficulties generated by the coronavirus, this was proof that I was on the right path.

My next step was to join the Entrepreneurship World Cup Czech Republic with the goal of finding an investor for my upcoming business: ANA'S MAGIC

WORLD. I prepared the business plan to pitch to investors and attended meetings regularly. However, due to coronavirus, the deadlines were postponed several times, and with no updates from local organizers, this led to great uncertainty. I applied and interviewed for hundreds of jobs while searching for an office for the upcoming business, taking steps to organize a fashion presentation, finding rental cost details, and searching for partners.

As I could not find a job until the end of spring, I sadly had to move back to Romania. Struggling with the difficult job search, the inability to sell VIDA designs, and conflicts with the competition made me feel tired, unmotivated, and upset; but I did not want to quit.

With the little energy I had left, I decided to go back to what I loved and start designing again. I switched from drawing to creating patterns in Canva and applying them on products such as protective masks. Then, just when I considered prematurely ending my entrepreneurial journey, I sold my first SATURN protective mask. Suddenly I started selling an item or more almost every day. I could not believe my eyes. It felt surreal. The sales continued through to the autumn, despite me crashing from exhaustion and being offline for a couple of days. Once I could barely move my fingers, I took some days off to recharge by exercising, going for walks in nature, and meeting with friends.

My next move was to Sweden when I received an offer for the position of Social Media Marketing Specialist. Though I spent less time posting designs as I adapted to my new job and environment, I still took a lot of photos of the stunning beauty of Sweden. I made two collections inspired by this natural beauty: ERROR AT NOON and SUNRISE IN SWEDEN.

Even though my business did not take off as quickly as I expected, I have never lost my passion for my artistry or the vision for my company. I am committed to continue creating beautiful clothes and sharing my talents with the world. I have learned that if you do the work you love, sooner or later you will find your success. Monetization happens when you stick to it and don't let the *little* things or the *big* things stop you. I now know that it is possible to earn a living doing artistic work. I want all artists to know that life is beautiful, colorful, and magical when you follow what's in your heart.

I hope that this inspires you to continue your creative journey. I feel blessed to be able to do the work I love, and now I want to share what I have learned with other creative individuals, wherever they may be on their journey. I plan to organize free webinars and workshops and join business plan competitions this year, so that I can move things forward with ANA'S MAGIC WORLD and impact future generations.

I encourage you to find ways to share your art, post your creations, and show your talents on social media and in as many unique ways as possible. Be yourself, find your signature look, and make sure that clients know your influential fingerprint. You have the ability to inspire others, and despite any world 'challenges' or personal 'hardships' you can make things happen. Your creations will make the world more beautiful for all of us.

IGNITE ACTION STEPS

1. Gather old photos, either in digital or paper versions. You can look for them in old photo albums or on devices/CDs where you stored them. Gather old drawings and paintings and scan them. Use the vintage, dated vibe to inspire you in new ways.

2. Find an online platform that allows you to harness your creative passion.

3. Create social media accounts for your designs. Add your photos and mention that you are a designer in your profiles. Add appealing covers on the platforms. Be unique!

4. Research what hashtags are relevant to your designs. I recommend using #hashtags that are often used, relevant, popular, and follow the trends.

Ana-Maria Turdean – Romania
Designer and artist ambassador at VIDA & Co.
https://shopvida.com/collections/ana-mariaturdean
⊙ amturdeen

IGNITE THE ENTREPRENEUR

ALLISON
LEWIS

A<small>LLISON</small> L<small>EWIS</small>

"Sitting in your fears is submitting to others' delight, while standing up and conquering them lets you live the life you dream."

Throughout my own journey I have encountered and conquered many fears, and my hope for you in reading my story is that you will find your voice and become fearless in your own personal and professional journey. In order to do this, you have to be visible, and then you will soon see that your drive and excitement will increase your exposure, amplify your ambition, and excite your mindset.

B<small>ECOMING</small> F<small>EARLESS</small>

As I close the door to my mid-size SUV and drive away from my office in a small rural town, I feel the weight lifting off me. Each day I leave behind this country setting to drive home toward the city, elated because I know I am driving to the life I want — the life of a blogger, influencer, and entrepreneur who uses their presence and audience for good, and not shying away from sharing all I have to offer because of fear.

When I started as an influencer seven years ago, I was very apprehensive about what the people closest to me would think. Mostly due to fear or the fact that many of us are taught from a young age that when we grow up, we should get a job working for someone else. The confidence and conviction surrounding this leads us to believe that veering away from this norm into the unknown can cause stress and financial hardship.

I don't know about you, but at such a young age I was not equipped with the skills to understand this, or to process what I was afraid of in many cases. In fact, it is usually up to us as adults to figure that out on our own, but as we grow, we soon realize that the sense of fear is inevitable, especially for those seeking success through entrepreneurship — me included! If I would have caved and submitted to those fears of 'self-doubt,' having to be 'perfect,' or 'falling in line,' I would not now, nor ever be, on top of my game. That uneasiness and those unsubstantiated fears almost put an end to what has been the best decision of my life.

For the longest time I did not stray from the norm. I know, boring! It was due to that nagging voice we all have in our head that creates doubt and tells us we should do what is 'normal.' On one side, there is this moral sense of conforming to society's expectations — finish school, go to college, find a career working for others, get married, and have a family. On the other side, there is this curiosity that whispers, "What if I deviate from the norm? What will happen then?"

As children I am sure we can all remember being taught to do one thing and not another because you do not want to be perceived as being 'different.' We carry this fear with us throughout our life and we can either find the motivation to become fearless or to succumb to those fears and always think, 'what if?'

I am not 100 percent sure when I grasped the concept that you don't need to be a rule follower ALL the time, but I do remember when I first heard the phrase "conforming to society's expectations." It was freshman year of college in my English 101 class. At that moment it felt like a light bulb went on. I remember thinking: "Huh… I don't have to do what everyone expects me to do, or tells me to do." I know that sounds obvious to many, but I guess that it just didn't come as easy to me. It wasn't that I was controlled by anyone. It was more that I already had preconceived notions of how things should be or that others already envisioned me to be a certain way, so I had to deliver on that.

It's crazy the pressure we put on ourselves sometimes trying to keep everyone else happy by not living our own truths. Maybe I should have gotten the hint sooner when another one of my college professors in my Women's Studies class gave me the book, *Lies My Teacher Told Me*, but that's a story for another day. When you step back and actually think about it, life really isn't what it is presented to be. If we take a close and honest look, we soon realize we can choose the life we want to create. And the worry that is holding us back from exploring what we want out of life should be validation enough to see what is waiting on the other side.

As we grow and learn from a young age, we tend to pick up traits and characteristics of our family, outside influences, and our overall surroundings. Like it or not, these traits are what shape us into the adults that we become. But it takes only one instance, one experience, for you to realize that you are living life on someone else's terms. A single moment can spark that 'what if' and bring out that small sense of rebel... hiding in the back that tells us not to conform.

My sense of fear arrived at a young age. I grew up in a pretty traditional family. Dad, Mom, two brothers, and myself. My parents came from a small town in eastern Kentucky. Many of us know the story, humble beginnings and wanted their children to have more than they did. That set the precedent, especially for me, being the only girl. Although it was never said, there were expectations (or maybe more like expectations I put on myself) not to disappoint, which fell right into our family's societal norms.

For most of my youth and young adult life I did not color outside those lines, which as you can guess was because of internal fear. The thought of upsetting others was terrifying to me as a child, so I set out to be a 'good little girl' that does everything right. I was scared to mess up or fail. Looking back now, as a kid I put myself in a warped sense of reality. "Do good, and everything will fall into place." I wish that were true, but I soon realized it wasn't.

There are themes that run throughout many of our lives: '*do what is right*' and '*don't stray from the norm*' or there will be consequences. Those fears often dictate the choices we make. It is up to us to change those themes.

After graduating from college, I started working for the University of Kentucky College of Agriculture, Food, and Environment: Cooperative Extension Service, as a Family and Consumer Science Extension Agent. Despite its long title, this was a great job that checked all the boxes of society's recommendations of how life should go. I was literally just going through the motions: go to work, come home, watch my murder mysteries, and head to bed. Get up, rinse, repeat.

One day I realized that I was almost 30 and had not lived up to the *other* expectations that were in the handbook of 'Life According to Everyone Else.' No kids, no husband, and nothing that really motivated or challenged me. I was not happy, maybe even a little bit depressed, as I was searching for something more and wondering why a steady job wasn't doing it for me.

By my tenth year in my university job, I was growing less interested in wondering and more determined to find something more. I was looking to fill my cup with something that gave a sense of happiness, purpose, and impact in the world beyond my small town so I spent some time racking my brain trying

284 / Allison Lewis

to figure it all out. For the longest time I didn't even give a thought to myself creating my own opportunity to fill that need.

Until, one day a spark just Ignited in me that said, "What if?!"

I had always followed social media influencers and thought that it was pretty cool that they got paid to recommend products and travel, but for the first year or two I never thought of myself doing this. But then... one day that voice hiding in the back reminded me that it was ok to be a rebel and create the life that you desire.

I still had fears and overwhelming doubt about actually becoming an influencer and blogger. I was so unsure what others would think that I started a whole new Instagram™ page to be an influencer, but I did not tell anyone. I mean, in hindsight, who was I actually influencing if I could not tell anybody about it? In one sense this could be because I did not want to hear any naysayers and in another sense it could be out of the fear of failure. I went on like this for a while trying to build that social media profile, not telling anyone that was close to me.

Until one day a friend asked me a random question.

We were going to a college basketball game. As we pulled up in the parking lot, I felt excited seeing all the fans ready to cheer on their teams. We were playing our rivals so I knew it would be a rowdy bunch, but nonetheless good banter, beer, and basketball. We departed the car and headed to the arena with the other fans in the brisk cold air. There was a sea of red and blue. I proudly wore red, and she wore blue as we chatted the short distance; mostly about what was going on with work and people we know.

It was silent for a minute then she asked me something that caught me off guard, "Do you have two Instagrams?" I hesitated, nervous that I might say the wrong thing or that I might have been found out. I hadn't told anyone about my second page out of fear and that nagging voice that said, "People won't understand... you should just work the job you went to school for.... blah, blah, blah."

Facing this question at that moment, it was obvious I had no option but to shyly say, "Yes." I started telling her what I was doing and how I wanted to build up my social media and my brand as a blogger and influencer to help others by suggesting products, other brands, and places that fill a need in their life. To my surprise, she thought it was an excellent idea and that I would be great at doing it. This led me to think, "What was I so afraid of again?"

That was a turning point in my life and my entrepreneurial career. At that moment I realized that fear was holding me back and if I ever wanted to be an entrepreneur or make an impact in the world, I had to set aside my fears and go for it. I felt relieved; that I could breathe and finally stop holding back. As I rode the high of this new confidence, I got excited to dive right in and tell other people about it. I went from feeling like I had to hide to WANTING to be more visible.

After that moment, I was hit with a rush of memories as I was reminded of the many times I had let fear get in the way of living life and being successful at doing the things I loved. For instance, in high school when I really wanted to try out for field hockey, but talked myself out of it because it wasn't something that my friends did...(see following the norm). Or after college when I didn't apply for jobs out of state because I didn't want to be in another city all by myself.

I learned then and there that if we continue through our whole life like this, we will soon regret all the missed opportunities, and eventually wonder how different our life could have been if we would have taken a leap of faith.

I personally do not want to look back and regret not doing something because of fear, so I now face it head-on and ask myself, "Why am I afraid?" I also surround myself with like-minded people to push me forward and bounce ideas off of, and make it a priority to attend networking events. What has also been a game changer for me is writing down my goals, so I can visually see them. Don't get me wrong, I still ask and welcome advice from others, but now I do not let anyone's thoughts allow me to be trapped by fear or cloud my judgment when it comes to my life or my business.

When I actually opened up and let people in on what I was doing is when my business and entrepreneur journey took off. I was actually *showing* my ability to influence people, not hiding it. I had to be visible. I had to 'put myself out there,' not knowing the reaction I would get. If I would have stayed stuck in that same bubble because of fear, I am sure I would not have become this successful.

Realizing those fears and not continuing to succumb to them has taken me on a journey I never thought possible. It is this drive that prompted me to start another business, which helps others monetize their social media and be more visual on social platforms.

Recently I was featured in an article in Forbes™ magazine. It was titled *Fear: Killer of Success*, and in it I spoke about how to put systems in place to conquer your fears. This would not have been possible if I was paralyzed by my own unfounded fears or still listening to that voice inside my head telling me not to jump in and start my business. Being featured in a national publication showed me how far I had come and motivated me to continue my dreams.

Along the way I have learned that self-success is a hard goal to come by when you are focused on pleasing others. The more I realized this, the more it pushed me to explore my own thoughts and feelings of why I did not take the step sooner. I learned that fear was inevitable, but how I dealt with those fears was what mattered. I confront them head-on and work to remove any barriers that stand in my way.

Honestly, to be successful you have to have fears, it is what makes you resilient, but it is what systems you have in place to conquer those fears that actually elevates you toward real fulfillment.

Today, I help others do what I did. I show entrepreneurs how to amplify their following and monetize their social media. I give them the courage to step beyond their fears, (which we all have) and cultivate their digital lifestyle. This allows them to create the life they desire by being their authentic selves. I get to work with the most amazing influencers, big and small, to make sure that their voice is heard and they never have to be afraid to go after their dreams.

When consuming yourself with doubt, stop and think about what are the factors contributing to this. Look at the reasons and decide if they are truly relevant. If anything is holding you back, assess the causes. Then search to find your inner *why* around taking the leap into entrepreneurship. You will soon see that your drive and excitement will outweigh fear, self-doubt, and the thoughts of others. If you have gifts and talents, share them because you will never know if that skill is what will start your entrepreneurial journey and create the success you are looking for. Be brave and trust your ideas. Let your own opinion influence you!

IGNITE ACTION STEPS

It is time to take action in your own journey and become fearless.

Six Steps to Become Fearless

1. Say, "What if?" to those nagging pains in life and those goals that you have been hanging on to and have done nothing with. Write these down so you can actually see them: What if I invest in this business? What if I quit my job to start that business I always wanted? Once you do that, reread them to decide if you should conquer that goal.

2. Write down all the societal norms you have been living by that you have been beating yourself up about, even when they do not exactly fit your lifestyle. Compare and contrast how different your life would be if you chose to live by them or not live by them. Do these norms fit your life now with the person you want to be?

3. When consuming yourself with doubt, stop and think *why*, as well as assess the reason you are taking the leap into entrepreneurship.

4. Set systems in place to conquer your fears. Surround yourself with people who motivate you to accomplish your goals. Find a mentor that can guide you on your entrepreneurial journey.

5. Network. Go to events and conferences that are centered around your business or have like-minded people.

6. Finally, take the leap of faith! You will never feel the exhilaration until you go for it.

Allison Lewis – United States of America
Blogger, Social Media Influencer, Social Media Manager & Coach,
Podcaster
www.absolutelyalli.com
@absolutely_alli & @absolutely__social

IGNITE THE ENTREPRENEUR

ANAY PATEL

ANAY PATEL

"The entrepreneurial spirit is one which embraces every-thing about the journey with passion."

My wish is for you to understand that the journey to becoming an entre-preneur is full of highs and lows. Don't be afraid to let go of failures and step into the next iteration of your life with resilience and trust in yourself.

ENJOY THE PROCESS

I can still vividly remember the day my first incorporation certification arrived at my house. I held the envelope in my hands, my palms sweating with anticipation. It was the most memorable feeling of excitement. I was young; it was during my high school years, and I had started a gaming company with a friend. It was the first taste of my dream of owning a business. I actually began two ventures. The first was a gaming company with a schoolmate where we decided to incorporate the company before anything else. Our goal was to create content on YouTube and receive money from advertisements. At the time, we were so sure this would be an easy way to generate passive income. However, we didn't take into account the effort needed to promote the videos or the constant editing and uploading of the footage, which is ultimately why this project didn't get any traction.

The second endeavor I embarked on was creating music, and I called this company "Gridlock Studios." I even went as far as printing fridge magnets for the brand, thinking I could stick them on fridges at all my friends' and family's houses. I would make instrumental songs and other sounds using Garageband. Starting projects like this allowed me to create brands, which became a key piece for me in my early years. Being able to create brands or ideas out of nothing energised me. I've always enjoyed the process of building things that never existed in the world before, and it has led me inevitably to building my own company.

Once I got to college, I had the opportunity to work as an intern for a start-up company in Shoreditch, London. It was my first experience in a real team dynamic and I remember struggling at the beginning to find the balance between having fun within the work environment and getting stuff done. During my time there, I learned critical skills that I have developed and find useful to this day; however, I didn't know their importance at the time. One of those skills was networking; the ability to mingle with strangers and build a relationship within a short period. Since my first networking event, I have been to hundreds more. The initial feeling of uneasiness still sometimes resides; however, throughout the years, I've learned to get into flow faster.

The next essential skill was public speaking. I was fortunate to have the opportunity to give a speech to a group of investors and business associates. I'm able to recall talking to the crowd, standing there, facing an audience of 60 people, my palms sweating. I kept looking down at my cue cards to make sure I knew what I was saying, not realizing I was talking more to the ground than the audience. It wasn't the best talk I've ever done but people were supportive with words of encouragement and provided some helpful feedback. This skill has served me well ever since.

The last essential skill, and perhaps the most important one, was learning the basics of programming, which opened my eyes to understanding code and led me to understand a different world. Websites always fascinated me, how these creations would come to life on our screens. Once I had the opportunity to learn more, I had to dive deeper into the mechanics of how these things truly worked. Gratefully, the lead developer for the start-up was happy to teach me the basics of HTML and CSS — the core programming elements of any website. Then we moved on to learning more dynamic languages like PHP and Javascript. One of the first assignments he gave me was to duplicate the BBC Homepage, which seemed impossible at the time. I spent hours at my desk, frustrated with the minute details that needed to be duplicated on the website, not knowing how to achieve it. However, through determination, I was able to reach my goal.

Once the internship was over, I used those newfound skills in my first attempt at becoming a freelancer and building websites for others. I approached all my friends and family, asking them if they needed a website or knew somebody that did. Sure enough, a family member helped me find my first client: a beauty shop that needed help advertising. When it came down to pricing, I was ambitious in the amount I asked for, but they happily agreed and just like that, my web design business was launched.

At the time, I was also working part-time in Sports Direct on a zero contract making £5 an hour. Through my freelancing, I was going to make more money in a shorter time. When I realized this, the first thought that was in my mind was, "Why should I let someone else determine my value?" It was one of the most critical moments in my early life when the knowledge that I wanted to own a business made me excited for all the possibilities that lay ahead for me.

In the summer break between finishing high school and starting university, I was invited to join a new start-up by the founder of where I originally did my internship. This time, I was going to be part of the core team. I was excited by the opportunity and eagerly agreed to join them. Their idea was a new type of social networking app, centered around trending topics. A couple of people from where I had interned moved into this new start-up with me, so I had a sense that we would work well together. However, the project quickly hit rough water only a couple of weeks after I started with the company. It was a situation that arose out of the blue and deeply impacted me. My loyalty to the company and my integrity were tested. I knew that I had to put my personal values above the opportunity of building a business, knowing that other opportunities would come my way. This event fundamentally made me choose to leave the organization as my trust was broken. This was the first time I was involved in team politics and thoroughly didn't enjoy it.

Once I began the first year of university, I moved from London to Hertfordshire. To my disappointment, there wasn't a big start-up culture at the university. I found myself quickly bored with the curriculum and what the university had to offer. Soon after, I found myself deep in programming once again. I built a website called Launch-A-Preneur, a platform that highlighted young entrepreneurs to bring awareness to their companies. The project started with nothing, but over a few months, a couple of thousand people visited the website monthly.

At the start of my second year, I moved into a very entrepreneurial sharedhouse. It was clear from the beginning that the people I was living with knew where they wanted to go and were very focused on their goals. It was great to be able to talk more about business and objectives with this group on a daily basis.

When the academic year had begun, I had set a goal to buy a car. That year, I was doing a great deal of visualizing. I kept imagining myself sitting in a secondhand car, what it looked like, how it would drive, the feeling I would have. I was working three different types of jobs to attain my goal. The first was in the clothing department at Morrisons, the next at the Royal Mail, and lastly, I was doing web development projects on the side, which made up most of my income. Thanks to that web development, I hit my target around a year later, purchasing a brand new car from the showroom, which was even more than I had imagined possible. Looking back, I wonder why I had worked so hard in three different jobs and not solely focused on my web development. I know the answer, fear — the fear of the unknown. It conditioned me to think that I needed a stable income and this stunted my entrepreneurial growth.

In my final year of university, I was very pleased with my achievements but knew that I had so much more to offer. My computer science degree wasn't of much interest to me by then and I didn't want to wait a whole year to graduate before starting my dreams. So, I decided to register for a web development company while at university. It was a very exciting time. Early on, I remember I spent a lot of time focused on designing the first website, creating a bespoke design, incorporating awesome technology, and making it SEO friendly. I was able to incorporate all the lessons from the previous years.

My time after graduating from university was fascinating, but also one of the scariest times. I felt a lot of pressure as I knew, my family wasn't 100 percent supportive of my choice. They always asked me, "When are you getting a real job?" causing me to have some doubts about my choices. Was I making the right decision? My family valued the more traditional way of getting a career — something that I have always felt opposed to. It's taken years for my family to accept the path I have chosen.

During those early stages, there was so much that needed to be done. I remember when I was going to network early in the morning. Most of the time, I would be the youngest person in the room which felt slightly intimidating. On a few occasions, when I would introduce myself to people, I could tell that they weren't very interested in what I had to say purely based on my age. I was never really affected, and thought the opposite; it was great that I was the youngest in the room. Though I was trying to attend two to three events per week, the feeling of nervousness, which was similar when I gave my speech in my internship, was always in my system. Even years later, the feeling I have is still there. However, I now understand that nervousness and excitement are caused by the same chemicals in our body and I've learned to manage their effects.

My first year in business full-time was an overall great experience, and I learned so much that I continue to build on throughout my career. One of my biggest struggles was learning to manage my time efficiently. Moving straight out of university to a full-time business, I was learning many new things that I didn't know existed, like different forms of networking, the importance of coaches for your business, PR tactics, and much more. After a few months, I was building a small client base of people. I decided to get a co-working space in central London in Chancery Lane.

Moving to a dedicated space for work was transformational. During lunchtimes, I was grateful that I lived a short walk from a local food market. Every lunch, I would walk down the busy market, full of working professionals, and was fascinated by the amount of variety that was available. All the different types of smells from each cuisine. All so close to where I was working, it was fantastic. The office space by its very existence provided a concrete focus point for all of my entrepreneurial attention. Working at home had become mundane and working in the office was incredibly inspiring. Each day, as I started the commute to the office, my mind would move away from distracting thoughts and step into a space centered 100 percent on the task at hand. I started to feel within myself that I had a proper job. That not only was I an entrepreneur but I was a *successful* entrepreneur and business owner. Being in the office brought me a lot of energy. And while London commuting was never a highlight, it was great to give me dedicated time to listen to a podcast or audiobook to help me grow my business and expand my mind.

Once I got more settled into the new work environment, I was finding the environment itself to be a smarter investment. I met with people in my office and didn't have to waste time traveling back and forth from my house. It saved a lot of time, which I could better use on the company. Though I had a much more productive work environment, there were still lessons to be learned. I was still struggling to create a steady stream of clients, so there was always uncertainty about how I will find clients for each month. It was time for a new chapter: one where I had business partners.

I remember the first interaction we had at my local coffee shop. It was exciting and energizing! I knew from the very first interaction I had with my two new partners that there was something different and we could have a great collaboration. We quickly saw that we had aligned visions and interests, which soon led to co-creating an educational website based on the concept "Integral Theory." After a few weeks, the potential we saw in forming a partnership was electric, so we agreed to work together on further projects. We then signed our

294 / ANAY PATEL

first major client, a mobile start-up company. Things were changing and for the better! And we were charging higher prices than I would normally have considered.

During that time, my partners helped me become a better designer, develop new skills in programming, and understand my weaknesses as an entrepreneur. We were very intentional about making sure we were all the right fit before we committed to something. We did many types of team-building exercises, which proved to bring the team together. I felt like I was beginning to become a real entrepreneur.

One of my partners was highly skilled at programming and the other was right in the sweet spot between programming and business development, giving complementing skills to the whole team. I put a lot of trust into this partnership, thinking about all the projects we would be able to accomplish, and knowing we were working toward a similar mission and vision.

However, a few months went by and though we had work coming in, there was some tension building between me and one of my partners. During this time, the agreement was that we were going to set up a company after our trial period, or join my existing agency with shares. Even though we did much work trying to understand the best way we could work together, when we wanted to make concrete legal agreements, things started to fragment to a point where it was unclear if this was the right route for me. At the time, I just wanted to build a team and scale my business, but I realize now the importance of agreements before the relationship begins. It was sad to see that despite working together for months, there were still critical issues arising, and I was frustrated by it.

One afternoon in the office, I was wasting time browsing the internet and came across a YouTube video advertising an event in Bali. The theme of the event was "Envision Your Future." I was intrigued. Images of people listening to speakers, learning hard, and playing hard in the evening afterward flickered across my monitor. The people with their focus, intensity, and team spirit resonated with me so much, especially as I was in a place of confusion and uncertainty about my next steps. I remember that at the time this event cost over $5,000, which was a lot of money for me. However, I knew it was where I needed to be. I took a leap of faith and took out a loan to help pay for the ticket and hotel so that I would be able to have a fully immersive experience.

Time went by quickly and before I knew it, I was packing to go on this adventure to Bali, where I didn't know anyone or barely anything about this event. I was really trusting my intuition. Once I arrived at the hotel, I was so nervous. While I was networking, surrounded by high-level people, I began comparing them to me and I felt like I had imposter syndrome. But I wasn't an imposter. This thought was a mistake. Over time, I realized my reason for being there, which was my mindset and the curiosity I had. Connecting with people's truest self and finding out their passions was so energizing for me. By the end of the four days in Bali, I realized the event had given me a new paradigm of how I was able to do business and build authentic relationships.

Once I came back from Bali, I put that paradigm into use within two months. I decided to step away from my partners. I only wanted to work with clients who inspired me, and that made me learn and grow as I was working with their brand. I decided to build a marketing agency that would work with more conscious companies that were doing good for our planet, to help amplify their mission. Now, I'm in full alignment, in love with my clients, and enjoying every minute of the journey that I am on.

As you embark on your journey of being an entrepreneur, understand that there are always going to be trials and tribulations, but the most important lesson is to move forward and learn from each moment. Understand that each setback is an opportunity for growth. Don't be married to your mistakes. Lean on your network, draw on the wisdom of your peers, and trust in the process. The most valuable move you might make is to step away from what isn't working and embrace a new and better future.

IGNITE ACTION STEPS

Learn the science of asking great questions. If you have the ability to ask a question that provokes a different thought, then you have the ability to open up someone's mind to a new possibility. Know when to ask open-ended questions. Go a bit deeper by saying, "And then...?"

Seek out mentors to help guide you through different situations in your life. Leverage their knowledge and experience to get a different perspective on your situation.

Anay Patel – United Kingdom
Founder
www.anaypatel.com

IGNITE THE ENTREPRENEUR

YAMILCA RODRIGUEZ

Yamilca Rodriguez

*"It's never too late to reinvent your future,
recreate your life, or reignite your dreams."*

My intention is for you to understand that there will be things that happened in your life where you could have taken a step back or shut down completely. But, because of the strength that you may not think you had (but that you surely do!), you persevered and moved forward. Even if things didn't go exactly the way you imagined, don't give up. Sometimes we aren't at the right junction, it's not the perfect time, or we have not yet made the right connection; that just means we are in conception mode and it requires change, transformation, and hard work to get the idea, project, or business to the moment of its birth. Everyone has it in them to tap into their strength, throw themselves into what is necessary, and collaborate with others to foster change — *real change!*

Dreamers Can Achieve Dreams

In my mind's eye, I always see airports as being filled with people getting onto planes as they step into an entirely new life, but I never thought I would be one of them. I had traveled a lot as a child with my family, but I never imagined I would be flying on my own. Yet, there I was, 27 years old, standing in the airport just outside my home town of Caracas, Venezuela, feeling nervous and excited at the same time about starting a new life… all by myself.

I had no idea there would be obstacles and tests that I would have to pass to have the life I envisioned for myself. I was like one of those computer games where you have to get through all the dropping bricks, jump from one bridge to the other, and avoid the shots from above just to get from one place to the next.

The first time I left Venezuela was when my dad was offered a scholarship to take his entire family to sunny San Diego, California to do his PhD. I was 8 years old and did not speak any English at the time. My only word was "hello." I wanted to make friends and got committed to learning the language. Within three months I was speaking fluently enough to communicate with other children in my neighborhood. We loved San Diego. The weather was magical! The beaches too with the perfect amount of wind, sea, and surf. There was always so much for all of us to do. We lived in San Diego for six years before going back to Venezuela, not to Caracas, the city of my birth, but instead moving to Cumana. Cumana was *hot*. And *humid*. Like being in a constant sauna. And it was a totally different culture from San Diego. In San Diego, I felt like I was free to be myself, but in Cumana, it felt like I had to follow *rules*. Don't wear shorts, decent girls don't wear shorts! Don't just wander about with your friends! That's not what decent ladies do! Though the beaches in Cumana were amazing, it was definitely not the carefree lifestyle of San Diego that I'd grown to love.

The second time I left my country to live somewhere else was because of a student admission pamphlet. The pamphlet was from an American university and what caught my eye was the industrial design program. I had acquired a three-year technical degree in industrial design in Venezuela, but this pamphlet ignited the feeling of so much more. It was a 'university degree' in the profession that most interested me, in the country that I had so loved as a child.

I had a dream to go to the United States and study in one of the countries that really fostered and perpetuated industrial design. I wanted my dream so badly. I would pray everyday, calling on the spirit of my aunt, an educator, who had passed away and was so determined that I should have the best education. She always took care of me and our family and I felt I needed to connect with her vision for me. I knew that she, in spirit, would help me make it happen. I recognized that my path was not going to be easy, but if I persevered, I would be able to achieve my soul's desire and make my aunt proud. I began to move forward as if it was *going* to happen.

I was nervous and excited for the new adventure ahead of me and the opportunity to go to a great school. My Uncle Nestor, who was also my godfather, made arrangements to take me to the airport the day of my departure. He was very eager because he wanted to introduce me to a client of his — he drove executives from the airport into the city and all of the family thought his job was very cool. He drove fancy cars, was always well-dressed, and owned expensive cologne. At the time, he was the young single uncle and we loved hanging out with him and his hip friends. I was the oldest of all my cousins, spoke two languages, and had graduated with honors from high school. Uncle Nestor was very proud of me.

The day we drove to the airport was a beautiful sunny day (like most days in South America). My uncle was driving one of his favorite clients, that he had known for years, and I was joining them so he could introduce me. I was waiting for him at the front door of my aunt's house in the suburbs. When Uncle Nestor got out of the car, dressed in his suit and tie and smelling of oak and jasmine, I smiled. As we shared the ride I noticed his client was older, in his 50s, a bit overweight with balding gray hair, and wearing a gray suit. As we headed to the airport, he struck up a conversation in English. He wanted to know where I was going to live, and I responded, "In Cincinnati."

Upon arrival at the airport, the man got out of the car first and walked around to my window. I thought he was going to open my door, but he didn't. Instead, he stood there with his hand on the door handle and looked down at me through the open window. He squinted in my direction, his lips twisting into a half smile, and very nonchalantly yet ignorantly said: "You are a Hispanic woman and you will never be successful in the Buckeye State." I just looked at him in disbelief and said nothing.

My uncle said farewell to his client and got back in the car and we headed to a different area of the airport. I didn't have the heart to tell him that his beloved client told me I would never succeed in the conservative Buckeye State. I didn't want to ruin my uncle's view of his longtime customer. Uncle Nestor left me at the gate with a kiss and a hug, wishing me the best and saying that I could do anything I put my heart into, and that he was proud of what I was doing. In one way, I felt like it was going to be difficult to immerse myself in a culture where people thought of Hispanic women as simply maids and housekeepers. The other side of me knew that my goal was to go to the university, and I believed, no matter what, that I was smart enough to do that.

When the plane took off, I washed away the worried feelings and thought to myself, I have the talent and the perseverance. I was going to a country where I knew no one and I was not yet officially accepted into the university. Instead, I was determined to make it happen — this was my dream and no one was going to take it away from me. I knew it would be challenging, but I felt confident about the chances to not only survive but to thrive! Despite what my uncle's client had said to me, I knew it wasn't true.

When I arrived in Cincinnati, I wasn't sure how I was going to make my dream of going to the university happen. I got up the next day, bought a newspaper, and looked for a job and ways to make my vision come to fruition. Three months later, I started at a community college, and six months after that, I interviewed at the University of Cincinnati and was accepted to the industrial design program. I was elated! That's when I knew the impossible was possible. I saw that I could be more and was not just a dreamer but someone who could manifest her dreams. Statements like that man's, on the other side of the window, just inspired me to go all in to show him, and those like him, that they are wrong. Dreams *can* come true, if you believe and trust in your convictions.

Someone told me once that not everyone had my gift to share with the world. And that if I had this gift, I needed to do whatever it took to use it for good and help others on their journey, as so many people did for me. Being the oldest of four taught me to be empathetic toward others and that anything is possible if you do whatever it takes.

Studies show that there are four main characteristics of being the oldest child; responsible, bossy, winning at all costs, and success. I was not a stranger to hard work or responsibility; and yes, I was always the responsible one. The one that was on time with homework and meetings. I always felt commitments were things that you had to do and not a choice. This was just the way I was. I was called 'bossy' by my siblings, but I thought of it as decisive, knowing what I wanted. I was always the person who took action and led the way through my childhood and adult life. Winning at all costs, I loved winning, and I was uber-competitive. I wanted to be the best in class, gymnastics, and at home. Success, I wanted to be successful in life. I didn't feel the pressure from my parents; I felt the pressure to succeed, and it came from within me.

That pressure didn't let up just because I was in my dream program in the US. If anything, that made it more significant. I remember wanting to be one of the top three students to win the thesis prize at my university. I did all my homework and studied what other people did, and I knew what kind of projects won the thesis prize, so the thing to do was to go all in. To believe I could do it. To make it happen. I knew that anything was possible if I really wanted it!

I was the only Hispanic woman, in the class of mostly males, to achieve second place. It was an accomplishment that I never thought possible, and it felt terrific. It was incredible to beat the guys and take home the thousand-dollar prize. Deep inside, I felt accomplished, and I proved to myself that I could do anything I set my mind to.

I graduated magna cum laude from the University of Cincinnati. During college, co-ops opened doors for me into the world of design and branding. After college, I freelanced for a few months, and soon after, I landed my job at one of the biggest brand companies in the world, Procter & Gamble™. As I walked through those open doors, I felt like a helium balloon, lighter than air. I called my mom to tell her how much I loved her and that her daughter had made it through college and got the best job ever!

Soon after I took the job, I was at a quarterly business meeting, and one of the speakers was a Hispanic woman, president of one of the divisions. She wore a black pencil skirt and a white blouse with puff sleeves. She had her long hair pulled back in a bun. She looked stunning. As I watched her speak to hundreds of people about the state of the business, I thought, "Wow! It's possible!" That woman, Hispanic like me, powerful in her femininity, was a leader in one of the world's most prestigious companies and showed that my dream was achievable.

When I left, 13 years later, I left for love. We got married and moved to a new city so we could be together. During my time in Cincinnati, I had been promoted twice and completed my MBA. I had forced my way through the glass ceiling, and I was ready to do something completely different. In a city labeled with racial issues and segregation, I worked for an agency whose culture was draining and on the verge of harassment. I didn't want to work for anyone else anymore, so I decided to start my own branding business. It was the beginning of my venture into the entrepreneur life.

My expertise at Procter & Gamble was creating ideal client avatars and predicting their desires to develop future products and experiences that people loved. I had traveled the world working on billion-dollar brands delivering customer experiences. That allowed me to develop my own branding methodology to help entrepreneurs understand their brand personality, define their ideal client, and make unforgettable experiences for their ideal client. I focused on the customer's psychology and created a model that would be easy for people to apply; *The Archetype Method.*

I spent 12 months creating content and practically working for free. The business was not going anywhere. I thought of going back to a nine-to-five job. I started to network and made connections. I joined a few non-profits and even became the president of one of them. All of this helped me understand that relationships and networking were the keys to a successful business, and I became the queen of networking. I made it my mission to connect to a fault. I was always on the go in networking meetings, balancing my time on the road with actual work productivity. I launched a Kickstarter campaign and received $10,000 to start my business.

It took me years to understand the difference between working in a company and being the boss; I'm still working on that today. As entrepreneurs, we have a vision for where we see ourselves, and we continuously strive to grow. There are days when I want to quit, when I question if I'm on the right path, when I feel like I'm not moving forward, but I know that serving my clients and focusing on my values will bring happiness and the feeling of accomplishment my heart desires.

I've been on Forbes™, TEDx™, and other local magazines. I feel that there is still so much work to be done to help others achieve their dreams. There are times when the path is foggy, and it isn't easy to see the end. That is what keeps me committed to helping female entrepreneurs achieve their dreams. I'm still on that journey myself, and I think I will be on it for a long time, and that is completely fine with me. Each accomplishment builds on top of the others, and that is what keeps me going.

To keep my mission alive I do many rituals that create love and abundance in my everyday life. The more I tap into my intuition, the more I can feel the lightness in my heart and follow my desires. I play with imagery visualizations of my future self and what kind of impact I want to have. I sense the right connections, the right moments, and know that anything is possible and that I can be feminine and lead with confidence. I always keep my family in my thoughts. My uncle still writes to me on Instagram™ and says how amazing I am. I see the connections I make as gifts — the gift of love and compassion for all individuals in this world.

I never thought of myself as being able to manifest my soul's desires until my friends said, "Well, you wanted this, and you got it!" That made me see that every time I put my mind to something, it happens. Life is magical and shows us all different opportunities and exciting paths to follow. It is up to us to decide which one we want to take to make our dreams come true. Your dreams are just waiting for you. Take action and choose which path you'll take. You have to make a decision on what you want; don't let anyone else's opinions stop you.

Ignite Action Steps

My five steps to love and abundance.

1. I begin my day with a 20-minute *active* exercise routine, sometimes HITT, dance, Pilates, or yoga, and I make sure to change it up.

2. My meditation: I sit and put on my theta healing music for meditation. I start with scanning my body from the top of my head to the bottom of my feet, relaxing each area. I imagine letting go of any toxins that I need to release and see them wash away to the bottom of the earth. I imagine a ball of energy at the center of the earth, and I bring the energy from the bottom of my feet to the top of my head, filling every cell and organ. I then start to count down from 20 to one. I imagine myself on a beach listening to the waves; free and cared for. I imagine myself in a lush, forest; safe and relaxed. I imagine myself in my dream home; peaceful and comforted. I then imagine a movie screen. On the right side of the screen I see my current life, in the middle what I can do, and on the far left what is possible. I see my goal. Then I take a deep breath in, open my eyes, and stretch.

3. I take an Epsom salt bath with two cups of Epsom Salts.

4. I write my affirmations in my journal.

5. As I drink a cup of tea, I write the one thing I need to accomplish today!

Yamilca Rodriguez – United States of America
Co-Founder of the Archetype Method
www.archetypemethod.com

IGNITE THE ENTREPRENEUR

COSTINEL
PASAT

Costinel Pasat

"You don't have to have all the knowledge to start something and succeed."

It is my hope that you will realize any dream can become a reality if you have the courage to pursue it. You don't have to have all the knowledge to start a business and succeed, but you do have to be loyal to customers and dedicated to them. Give them the best version of yourself. Know that if you provide them with a positive experience, you will have repeat business and loyal customers that will always refer you to their family and friends. People do business with people who share an honest part of themselves.

Speaking the Customer's Language

I was born and raised in the Transylvania region of Romania, mostly known as Dracula's land. My hometown, Poiana Brasov, is a ski resort situated in the Carpathian mountains. It's a magic place, the best place to be and be raised. The fresh, cool air was the only air conditioning we needed, and our childhood was spent playing outdoors in nearby forests, identifying wild plants and mushrooms and keeping an eye out for bears, wolves, lynxes, and other animals. We were safe, although we were separated from much of the outside world. Tourists and their new technology were fascinating to us, and even simple things like pencils with erasers or shiny sneakers made us say, "Wow!"

The four seasons in our town were equally beautiful, from the snow covered trees in winter to the purple saffron covered valleys in spring. However, the winter was the most popular season. Our town, located at 3336 feet, was a perfect location for skiing and holiday gatherings. I remember big amounts of snow in front of my house. As kids, we were barely able to walk in the snow, but it was so fun. The image that comes into my mind is of a happy childhood. After the snow melted, one can enjoy a jewel of green landscapes. A person can find and take advantage of many trails to hike. Poiana Brasov is also close to Bran Castle and Peles Castle, famous for their medieval architecture.

Where I grew up was a wonderland, mostly for the tourists, but for me as a kid I had to go to school as well. In my early teens I would spend my days studying automobile mechanics, and at night (mostly on the weekends), I was a disc jockey at one of the hotel bars which turned into a disco club after 10 PM. I combined pleasure with business. I was earning some money and I was also enjoying it. I felt proud because I did not need to ask my mom for an allowance.

My dad chased the American dream. He wanted to escape the limitations that came from the dictatorship in Romania. He wanted something better for himself and for his family. I remember how my dad was always hustling. He had the entrepreneurial mindset: working long hours and trying to build multiple businesses. However, there were so many obstacles from the local government.

One day, my father got an invitation from a friend to visit the USA. He did not think twice when the opportunity was presented to him. One can say that his prayers were listened to and answered. He emigrated to the USA with a tourist visa when I was 12. At the time I did not know why he had to leave. I became the father figure to my siblings and had to grow up fast. I had to be a good example for my brother and sister which brought us very close. I could not afford to get in trouble, as many of my peers did.

My dad decided to leave us enough money so we could survive until he was able to support us financially again. He had spent a lot on the airplane ticket and arrived stateside with 50 dollars in his pocket. He stayed in New York for five months and then moved to Florida. In the Sunshine State, he did an apprenticeship in the roofing industry and finally he got his license.

Six years after leaving Romania, he managed to bring his family to the USA.

We had traveled over 6,000 miles from Romania for almost two days to reach my father. We arrived in Miami, in the late afternoon on a very sunny and beautiful Sunday. It was March 2, 1997, around 3 PM. My very first dose of my new reality started when we landed at the airport. I realized that this is *it* — from now on I had no more friends or people that I could count on. Even 'the love of my life' was back in Romania. I was heartbroken, homesick, and I barely spoke any English.

Somehow we had managed to pass through the airport immigation desk despite the language barrier. I could not even explain to the officer that my dad was waiting for us outside. Finally, we made it to our new home an hour later. My dad had just purchased a house where we all could live together after six years of being separated. It was a really nice place and it had a pool. We hadn't seen too many houses in Romania with a pool, so for us it was unbelievable.

My second dose of reality was the climate. It was so humid. I remember I was not even able to breathe normally. It took me at least two to three months to get used to the hot, sticky, balmy weather.

The first couple of days in my new country consisted of my dad taking us all over the place to register our stay in the USA. He got my siblings into the school system. On the other hand, I was not able to go to high school. At 18, I was "too old" for them. Of course, my dad wanted me to go to school because he did not want me to do the hard labor of working on roofs. "You either go to school, or you come work with me in the roofing industry," he said. He wanted more for me than breaking my back on physical work. He tried to get me into an ESOL school, but they weren't very effective in advancing my education. "What other work can I do without speaking a word of English?" I thought.

A week after I arrived in this new country, I started working for my dad as a laborer in the roofing industry. Climbing the ladder over 50 times that day was exhausting. I'd never been so dehydrated. I'd come from -4 degrees Fahrenheit in Romania to 70 degrees in Miami. Over the next few weeks, I analyzed myself, asking what was it I really wanted. I realized that I was a handy man eager to help others, and as an ambitious person I dreamed of one day having something grand and luxurious of my own.

The first four years living in America were the hardest ones for me because I saw how difficult it was to earn a living. My parents were constant inspirations for me. My mom had a tough job with raising three children. She was trying her best. Once she arrived in the United States, she needed to find ways to learn English. Additionally, she had to earn a living and ended up securing a housekeeping job at a hotel in the Hollywood Beach area. With dedication and determination, she was soon running the housekeeping department. My words to describe her are 'go-getter.' After she had hit a ceiling where there were no more opportunities to grow, she took a position at the Hard Rock Stadium in Miami, managing the housekeeping department for events that ran anywhere from 2,000 to over 75,000 people.

Only after going through the battle of establishing our residency were we able to really think about the other things that were important to our happiness. For me, it was the chance to see the love of my life again. I finally went back to Europe just to see if the spark was still there one might say. It all started as a platonic relationship. With many phone calls and hundreds of letters back and forth, our relationship was still strong. In 2005, after eight years of not seeing each other, we reunited during the winter holidays.

We had spent two weeks together. We felt like no time had passed between us. I was so inspired and in love that in the following years I traveled back and forth many times. I remember one year having 12 travel stamps in my passport. At that time, she was living in Spain. Just like many others, her family relocated outside Romania in search of better life opportunities.

In 2008, just before the market crash, we got married and purchased a business in Zaragoza, Spain. It was a coffee bar called El Capricho. I had zero experience in the hospitality industry. My 'girl' had previously worked in the industry, but never owned or managed a business before. However, she was determined to be successful. After the business was acquired, a light 'face-lift' was done with refurbished furniture and blinds and a fresh coat of paint. She had a big grand opening under new management. It was received very well among the local clientele. Meanwhile, I was still in the States, cheering her on and amazed by her success.

A few months later I was able to join her in Spain. Once again I was in the same shoes I'd worn in 1997. I had to learn a new language, culture, and business model. However, my affinity for business and perseverance helped me to persevere. I learned to speak Spanish in less than six months. Additionally, it took a lot of hours and sweat to learn and accommodate the new business. We both worked hard, however, we never stepped back from our dream. We stayed consistent, we showed up, and we opened and closed at the same time every day whether we had clients or not.

We can laugh now looking back, but some early mornings I was the first client to pay for a good cappuccino in our *own* business. As a culture, Spaniards have the custom to drink more than one coffee in a day. The first one is usually in a coffee bar near their house. It was a little struggle for us to become that first morning coffee for our clients, since we were new management and also immigrants.

As a sidenote, the business had previously changed hands five times. The previous owners were not consistent and the clients were fed up with irregular operating hours. Soon though, the word spread among the neighbors of our customer-friendly attitude and support of other local businesses and we finally got our coffee bar rolling. We grew fast and became popular. Our clients were bringing their families to lunch and dinner as well. We even increased our hours of operation. The location was perfect for kids to play safely while their parents enjoyed a break on the refreshing terrace. We were always doing research, trying to improve our customer experience. We knew we had made it when we finally got to have a few days off while the business was still operating without our physical presence.

Yet, as most good businessmen might agree, the best time to sell is when the business is prosperous. After all, nothing stays forever, so when we got an attractive cash offer to sell the business, we saw the opportunity and did not hesitate. Soon after the business was sold, my wife and I relocated to the USA. I continued to work in the roofing industry. My wife wanted something better, so she started taking English classes. First, she got her Associate of Arts, followed by a Bachelor of Science in Medical Sonography.

On the night of July 7, 2014, my wife blessed me with a beautiful baby boy. My inspiration and dedication changed when I became a dad. I knew that by becoming a parent one's priorities change. But little did I know that the change would be so huge, or come in such a drastic way. In the same week as my son's birth, the family business was catastrophically affected when people we trusted betrayed us. I felt like a train had run me over, and knocked my breath and my sense of purpose out of me. But then, looking at the innocent little boy in my arms, I knew what mattered most was what had changed. Despite the devastating hit to my family business, I forgot everything else around me as I saw the new journey I would take. I remembered what I had: not just my family, but my knowledge, my skills, and my determination that would make it possible for me to move forward. I took some time away from the business and immersed myself in every moment with my new baby and wife. I could see now the answer to the question I often asked myself about my own parents. Why would someone go through so much pain and suffering and start over with nothing?

It's because you do everything you can for your family.

I cannot express in words my gratitude toward my father for the sacrifices he made 30 years ago. I inherited his values and many of his strengths, especially his ambitious character, and I relied on these when I needed to decide on how to move forward in my business. I felt it was my duty to make the Pasat name a legacy, achieve success, and help others succeed also.

I was already very knowledgeable and very good at finding the water issues on a roof. But after lots of reflection and research, I decided to improve myself and my skills even more. I took the opportunity to get a Photovoltaic (PV) Certification. I am now certified to install energy-saving PV solar panels on the roof for my new and old clients. The decision I made was great because it provides my clients another service. When customers were asking about this product, we were among the few roofing companies that offered it. It was also a great time to start specializing in solar power. At the time, the government was offering a 30 percent tax incentive for those who qualified.

As a company, we are driven by the people that we get to help. The roofing industry is very competitive and large. Some or most people out there will do the job only to get a check. There are few pioneers left in this business who try to innovate; who try to make things better for the industry and the homeowners. Nowadays, as a homeowner you have to understand the roofing industry pretty well in order to find out what is best for your house. I found it sad that in our industry customers weren't being presented with all the options. I vowed that our company would be different, still keeping the same vision of the pioneers in the industry.

I continued to find inspiration and change in all kinds of places, seeking more improvement in my life. I stopped watching TV and started exercising more. I also started listening to audiobooks. I got some paper books from Napoleon Hill, Grant Cardone, and John Maxwell. Just by doing this small shift in my life, my attitude and my banking account changed. Clients were pouring into my business from different places, some even calling from an old paper telephone book. The universe was blessing us.

I always want to provide excellent service to my customers and provide a smooth experience in the project process. Nobody is perfect, however because I know to keep an eye out, I can resolve any small issues before they become big. I consistently touched base with every client I work with. Just by doing that 2020 was a year that proved that what we are doing works! We acquired more clients than the year before and had more appreciation for our customers.

Also in 2020, I connected with like-minded business people; even though it was mostly on virtual platforms. Nowadays, 90 percent of our customer base comes from referrals. It says volumes about our company that our customers recommend us to their family, friends, and community. We are humbled, proud, and grateful to have achieved this milestone. I keep working to find ways to give back to the community and have become a better giver and a blessed receiver than I was many years ago. I feel rewarded to know I am living my dream today next to my wife and our two awesome, healthy, and smart boys. I came to this country without the language or knowledge of the business I would ultimately start, but I had the courage to pursue my goals.

No matter what job you are doing or company you are running, being dedicated to your customers is what defines success. Having a passion for excellence and giving the very best experience creates the best success. That means being among those who pursue the dreams that will change things for the better. It is those who chase the entrepreneurial (American) Dream who are truly building *their* dreams and desires.

IGNITE ACTION STEPS

Be courageous — If an immigrant like myself from a very small town in Romania, without knowledge of the English language, can achieve and surpass some of the challenges, you can succeed also.

Be dedicated — Give your customers the best version of yourself and always look for ways to improve your clients' experiences.

Be loyal — Your customers will return that loyalty to you.

Costinel Pasat – United States of America
Entrepreneur, Dad, Roofer.
CEO and Founder of Pasat Roofing & Solar Energy
www.costinelpasat.com

IGNITE THE ENTREPRENEUR

BEN BEARD

Ben Beard

"You can turn your challenges into your greatest opportunities for growth."

My hope is that my story can help you find your own 'one big goal' that you can build around to create the life you have always dreamed of. Unanticipated obstacles changed the course of my life. It is my intention that you will be inspired to turn your biggest challenges into opportunities for your greatest growth.

How I Learned to Seize the Day

Little kids aren't known for having patience, but starting around 6 years old I loved nothing more than sitting on the floor in my bedroom and building for hours. It started with Lincoln Logs™ and LEGO™ toys. I built simple houses, then whole towns, and then went back to building more complicated houses that could be taken apart level by level. With each year, with each build, my designs got more complex and creative. When my parents were shopping for a new house, I collected each of their floor plan books as they tired of them, sitting in my room and poring over them for hours. I tried to replicate full plans like I saw in the books instead of just slapping up walls around the outside of my largest base piece and leaving the interior empty.

The fun in Legos had nothing to do with playing with them. For me it was all about the build. Finding the right pieces, trying to match the colors around the building, and making the whole structure symmetrical was what I loved. I usually built from my imagination instead of from a plan, although I wished I had plans so that I could rebuild some of my favorites again and again.

As I got into high school my knees couldn't take sitting on the bedroom floor, and it got increasingly embarrassing to admit to my friends that I still played with building blocks. Fortunately my high school had technical classes, so I was able to take a cabinet-making class, a general construction class where we built an entire house throughout the school year, and an electrical class, where we wired the homes built by all of the high schools in the school district. I loved these classes because they were hands-on and I could get up and move around while learning.

Outside of school, I had a scout leader who had made a lot of money flipping houses and another who let me help him fix up and sell his rental home. This sealed it for me. I wanted to be a house flipper and make big money to support the rest of my dreams.

I was very financially motivated, so I got a job as early as I could. The one place that would hire me before I turned 16 was a small local water park that let me be on the grounds crew. The next summer I graduated to being a lifeguard at the same park. This was a common job among my friends and siblings. It was a great experience and I loved being out in the sun all summer working on my tan. I dreamed about becoming a 'head guard' before graduating high school.

This is where a process that I refer to as 'Revelation by Seizure' came into my life. I was in the middle of my junior year of high school, preparing for my second summer as a lifeguard. But one day while playing in the sun at a family gathering, I collapsed. I have vague memories of getting dizzy and a white haze fogging my vision. The next thing I knew I was trying to wake up while lying on the grass with faces swirling over me. Then, I was seeing white ceiling tiles pass overhead while being wheeled down the corridor of a hospital.

Eventually I woke up and was told that I had suffered a grand mal seizure — the full shaking on the ground that you think of when you hear the term "seizure." This ultimately meant disaster for a 17-year-old boy. No driving for three months and no lifeguarding that summer. I was devastated and spent several days locked in my room, angry at the world. My confidence was shaken, literally, and self-pity wanted to settle in as I imagined all I couldn't do that summer without the freedom to drive. Thankfully I had amazing parents who helped me to see that I had to overcome this obstacle and find a way to still take advantage of the break from school.

I couldn't be a lifeguard since I was now a safety risk myself. This meant I could go back to the grounds crew or find a new job. Luckily, one of my best friends worked at a plumbing supply shop and was willing to vouch for me. I got the job and learned all about landscape plumbing. I figured out ways to connect different types of piping that weren't designed to go together and had fun troubleshooting irrigation plans to help keep lawns greener. I loved putting the pieces together to solve a customer's problem, and I learned a lot. The seizure had been a blessing.

My desire to solve problems led to a degree in Construction Management at Brigham Young University in Provo, Utah; a course of study that I loved. As I got ready to graduate, I started thinking about my plans for life post university and decided I wanted to join the military. Both of my grandpas had served in the US Army in World War II and I loved books and stories about the war. I really wanted to serve my country and started talking with the university recruiting staff. I was told I could put my degree to use by entering the army as an officer in the Engineering Corps. This excited me and I prepared mentally and physically for the entrance exams.

The weekend before I was scheduled to take the Armed Forces Aptitude Battery exam, I was taking apart a broken fence for my parents. While bent over swinging a hammer, I suddenly felt hazy; my vision turning white. I stood up to take a break and catch my breath, then bent over to keep working. The next thing I knew, I was strapped to a gurney inside of an ambulance with a massive headache and a dislocated jaw. I had suffered my second seizure. Again, no driving and now no chance of joining the military. I was crushed. I lost a lot of self-confidence, and gained a lot of fears about my future.

I had a couple weeks over Christmas break to develop a brighter outlook before I started my final semester of university. Out of the blue, a friend offered to set me up on a blind date with a beautiful woman, Heather, who would soon become my wife. A few days after our first date, I was offered a job. When I told her the company was based in Las Cruces, New Mexico, she asked, "Where is that?" I answered truthfully, "I have no idea." The thought of not having a job lined up before graduation had me rattled, so I didn't want to pass up this opportunity. Heather and I prayed together and we decided that I would take the job.

Moving to New Mexico, without Heather, began with a 900-mile drive with only a printed map for directions and my pet goldfish in his 'mason jar home' strapped in the passenger seat for company. I started work two days later as a Construction Superintendent and instantly took to the job. It was fun to work with subcontractors to build homes as quickly as I could, solving problems and getting to know new people. After training for a month, I was given my own load of 25 homes to build.

That year was amazing. I enjoyed learning about construction in the field instead of from textbooks and lectures. Heather joined me that fall and we found a great little apartment with views that captured the pinks, oranges, and reds of the gorgeous New Mexico sunsets every night. Life was almost perfect. I was taking on more responsibility at work, and was asked to build the company's first model home in El Paso, Texas. That meant I had to commute for about 45 minutes, instead of the 15 minutes I was used to going around town, but I was excited about the challenge of breaking ground in a new city, building new floor plans, and meeting new trades and homeowners.

On the jobsite one day, I leapt over a freshly poured concrete sidewalk. The moment I landed, pain shot from my foot straight to my head. I had landed on a rock and twisted my ankle. I limped up the steep front yard and barely managed to sit against a courtyard wall before passing out. I woke up with several guys yelling at me in Spanish, bending my arms and legs, trying to control the flailing movements of my third seizure. Somehow I was able to recover my senses quickly this time and get back to work almost immediately. But to my horror, I discovered that in New Mexico I would not be allowed to drive for *six* months! For a guy that made his living driving from one subdivision to another (not to mention my 45-minute commute to and from work) this was a nightmare.

I was terrified about how my bosses would handle this situation. Fortunately, they appreciated my knowledge and skills, and were willing to work around my limitations. I asked if I could transition into a job in the office. As long as I only had one place to be at a certain time each day, I could make that happen no matter what. They agreed and offered me a job in the Purchasing and Estimating department.

Thus ended (hopefully) the 'Revelation by Seizure' season in my life. I felt that each time I had experienced a seizure was a turning point, guiding me on a path that I couldn't see until I looked backward. The first moved me out of lifeguarding and into a job where I could learn something and would build my resume for my future career in the construction industry. The second kept me out of the military, allowing me to take a job in the private sector. With the third, I moved out of the field and into the office, which led to a major shift in the direction of my life.

When I started in the office, I knew that I needed a change. I was tired of listening to the radio. I knew every song on the country station and was sick of talk radio. I decided I would listen to podcasts and audiobooks. In fact, if I was going to work in an office, I wanted to learn something about business, so I set a goal to earn the equivalent of a Master's degree in Business Administration (MBA) while sitting at my desk working.

Over the next two years, I listened to thousands of hours of podcasts on business, entrepreneurship, leadership, and self-development. I read over 75 books related to these topics. I was hungry for knowledge and loved consuming so much impactful content. I began to shift my mindset. I started to remember the dreams that I'd had as a young boy about being extremely successful financially, and started to see that I might have more potential than I had recently given myself credit for.

Thankfully Heather was a great companion as I chased all of this personal growth. She supported me each step of the way, taking on challenges and turning them into successes together with me. I focused on my career as she was busy taking care of our home and two kids with a baby on the way. We studied together in the evenings, thinking through and starting several side business concepts over the next few years, though none of them really came to anything. Eventually we realized that I was out of room to grow at my full-time job, so we started to look for a new idea that could be more than just a side hustle. Ultimately we found the right connections and decided to start our own production home building business.

We launched Red Cliff Homes a few months before my 30th birthday. I quit my day job and then spent the next two days calling everyone I knew, including my subcontractors and suppliers, to let them know about my plans. Those were some of the best days of my life as I received so much support and encouragement, along with offers to work with me in my new company. Within two months I had purchased 12 lots and started construction on as many homes. I found a real estate agent to list and sell my homes, and we were off to the races.

During our first year in business we closed 27 homes for just over six million dollars in revenue. We weren't hugely profitable yet, but we were paying ourselves more than I'd made at my day job, and knew that we were building toward something great. We had goals and plans in place to do bigger and better the following year.

By the end of our second year in business, we were getting ready to close 39 homes and had hired several employees. Somehow one Saturday morning I ended up watching a coaching call with Grant Cardone where he was selling a three-month mentorship program. I knew that I needed help growing my business, so I signed up. This turned into a second three-month program, and even more events which I still attend to this day. For me, the *real key to success* happened in the first few weeks of that initial program.

We spent a lot of time talking about goals. As an avid reader for several years, I knew the importance of written goals, but still didn't actually have them for myself. Grant helped me see the need to set goals so large that I could form a lifestyle around them and then figure out a plan to accomplish them. I thought about physical goals (weight loss, muscle gain, etc.) but couldn't get excited about any of those, or think of how to turn them into a lifestyle. I thought of business goals, but also couldn't feel settled on any of them. They either seemed too outrageous or not big enough to excite me. I wasn't sure what to do about this whole goal-setting thing, and almost decided to just lie and say that I had done my homework without actually completing it.

Until one day I had a crazy idea.

I have always loved boats and the water. I competed on my high school swim team and continued to swim non-competitively on and off over the years. I had also gotten into road biking, so I initially thought of setting a goal to do a triathlon. But I hate running, so that was no good. Then, I remembered a wild dream that I'd had as a young swimmer — the ultimate challenge of swimming the English Channel!

Now here was a goal I could get excited about! But more than excitement, I realized that this was the moment that I had found a goal big enough that I could build a new lifestyle. It would take a major pivot, which is just what I needed. In order for me to get ready to swim the English Channel, I would need to spend a lot of time training. New Mexico is landlocked, so I'd have to travel to beaches for training swims, as well as to England once I was ready to take on the Channel. I would need to have my business in a position that I could afford to put the time into training, and have the money required to travel and perform the swim itself. This gave me financial goals as well as a much clearer vision of the future for my health and my business.

Once I had this goal in place, my life started to change. It was so much easier to set goals in other areas of my life because it was all based off of this one plan. I gave myself until 2023 to swim the Channel so that I could get my body, my business, and my finances in shape because I wasn't actively swimming at this time and hadn't for several years.

In the following weeks I got back into the pool to start training. Heather got me a book about a successful Channel swimmer for Christmas that I've now read several times, and I recruited several people to join my support boat crew. Amazingly, this huge goal allowed people around me to follow my example. Heather clarified some of her goals and now wants to compete on TV's *American Ninja Warrior.* We both started making training programs for each of our goals and supporting each other in them.

When COVID hit in the spring of 2020, the pool was closed indefinitely. I took this opportunity to purchase a swim spa that allows me to control my training schedule. To keep things in balance, we also built a ninja warrior training course for Heather in our backyard. We're both fully committed to helping each other reach our inspiring goals.

I still have a lot of work to do, but I can already see myself climbing out of the water onto a French beach, exhausted but thrilled at having reached a massive goal in my life. And from there we'll see what happens next. Future goal ideas include climbing Mount Everest, biking across the USA, or even going to Europe to bike the Tour de France route. No matter what goals I settle on after swimming the English Channel, I know that I'll take on big challenges to turn them into successes. I'll find a big goal around which I can build my life, seizing my next opportunities no matter what it takes.

You can build a life centered around your dreams. Find something that truly inspires you and use that to shape your future. Challenges are actually opportunities to pivot and grow. Find the 'one big thing' that really matters to you and build a life upon that.

IGNITE ACTION STEPS

Let your challenges guide you. My life changed direction dramatically each time I had a seizure. What obstacles in your life could be pointing you in a new and better direction?

Find one big goal and build a life around it. What inspires you? What can you do that is so big that it will make others around you want to chase their own wildest dreams? If your goal isn't that big, it will be hard to build a life around it. Think lifestyle change, not a quick fix.

Ben Beard – United States of America
President, Red Cliff Homes
www.redcliffhomes.com
 benbeardofficial
 redcliffhomes
 benbeardofficial
 redcliffhomesnm

IGNITE ᴛʜᴇ ENTREPRENEUR

KULBIR MUTI

KULBIR MUTI

"Those patient, slow, and steady will be the ultimate victors."

My personal intention is for the reader to be inspired by my story of perseverance, and to never give up, constantly growing and pushing forward in creating the life they desire. Education helps, yes, so does training, and learning skills, but, most importantly, it's the intangible traits — hard work, confidence, dedication, persistence, and not giving up that will help you succeed in the end.

THE DAY I REFUSED... AND TRANSFORMED EVERYTHING

I come from a family of seven. My mother and father, though both born in Pakistan, decided to immigrate to Punjab, India, to seek opportunity. For a Punjabi family in the 1960s and 70s, born into poverty, materialism or becoming wealthy wasn't what was necessary; survival was of the utmost importance.

I have been working since I was 5 on my family's farm, picking potatoes and other vegetables. I come from a modest background and had to lead the charge for my family. One of five kids, and one of four brothers, I was the youngest, working in the fields, doing agriculture, maintenance, seeding, and growing vegetables — herbs, spices, corn, wheat, and rice. Each Saturday, my whole family would walk the two miles to where we would sell these products to a local vegetable market in the city Subja Mandi. Despite my young age, I also raised cattle to maintain the land. I did most of the labor, giving me the work ethic that would later help me build my future businesses.

I was also attending school. I went to school up to grade four but quit many times, as my father could not afford to pay the fees. I attended, quit; attended, quit; and passing grade five never transpired, so I just kept working. A couple of years later, after a good harvest when there was more money, I started again, and finally passed and made it to grade six. I was behind, so I thought I'd skip classes and do the exam for grade eight. I passed grade eight, moved schools, and did grade 9, 10, 11, in Nakodar, India. Then I went to college, studied up for a bachelor's degree, and quit in my final year as plans to immigrate to Canada started to take shape. I did not finish college.

In 1980 I visited Canada. What an amazing place of opportunity! This was not present back home in Punjab. Things have changed, Punjab is growing, but there was nothing for me there back in the 1980s.

My sister, who had immigrated a few years before, sponsored me to immigrate to Canada, something I will never ever forget. My family was very fortunate, my parents, three brothers, and one sister all moved out of Punjab, looking for opportunities elsewhere, in Canada and the United States. None of us was left behind. This is extremely rare as usually someone is either left behind or chooses to stay. This happened to my wife's brother; he stayed behind, and it's been tough. It's not that we don't love our homeland; we do. But, in the 80s, there just wasn't any opportunity. Lack of opportunity is one issue, another even more profound is lack of societal stability; socially and politically.

After some time spent in Vancouver, Canada, getting settled in, I went back to India. In 1985, I went back to get married. I was the last of my siblings to do so, often hearing from my family and friends about the fact that I was not married. The comments were not positive to say the least. I met my new bride as I was walking down the street, strolling along — it was hot and I was sweating beneath my shirt. I saw this woman, tall and beautiful, and immediately fell in love. I remember thinking, "That's who I want to meet." Dating was not much of a thing at this time, nor was meeting each other before marriage. The first step was to tell the parents and set up a meeting with the families. The next step was to get married. I was finally married! It happened quickly! That was normal. Then it was time to start a family; working, wanting to get back to Canada, enjoying married life, and watching a baby grow in my wife Rani's belly.

Fortunately, I was able to return to Vancouver and only had to wait a few months for Rani and our firstborn Ravi to join us. When I came back and resumed my job in 1986, I was earning $3.63 per hour for several months and this soon grew to 7 dollars, then 8 dollars, and then I reached 10 dollars an hour. But I had other aspirations.

My brother was also working in Vancouver at this time as a janitor. He tried to convince me that I'd be better off working with him, as opposed to venturing off on the entrepreneurial route. He told me that it was risky, and I should take what I can get, support my family, and call it a life. I refused. Having worked since I was young, taking care of my family, finally finishing school, and bringing my family to Canada, I knew deep down that anything was possible with perseverance. Little did I know that not taking my elder brother's advice would turn out to be a key turning point in my life.

Instead, I quit my job as a drywaller and I took out a $200,000 loan to jump-start my business. Deciding to be an entrepreneur was the best decision I ever made for myself and my family. It has provided me with a life I couldn't have imagined. To this day, my brother, although happy for me, does point out that very day when I told him no and ventured off. I don't want to say he is envious, but I know that a part of him wishes that he took a similar path. To be honest, everyone is different, we should all be happy with where we are, and if we're not, we still have time to right the ship.

Making it in Canada required a lot of work. I came with nothing, no money, few items of clothing. Not as bad as you think at the time, but still not enough. I saved almost every penny I had, tucking a few bills into a jar on the kitchen counter for spending money and putting the rest safely in the bank, only spending money on basics, shelter, and food. In my early years, life was all about survival. I had to draw on that early resilience and thriftiness to make sure my family was taken care of. Having stable housing and taking care of my wife, two kids, and parents was of the utmost importance. My wife was a stay-at-home mom and spent her days nurturing and caring for our kids and my parents. Her days were busy with cooking, driving kids to school and sports, and making sure my parents were happy and well cared for. I was working almost 17 hours a day to make ends meet. The long days were grueling and I would come home to family to play with my children and rest, tired, but determined to keep going, motivated to succeed and make a better world for myself and my family. My motivation came from not wanting my kids to go through the struggle that I did when I was growing up in Punjab. I wanted them to have security, to have the opportunity for good schooling, and to know that they are loved. To be honest, no one should have to work endless hours and still worry about whether they will have food on the table or where they will sleep.

I didn't feel I could progress in life working for someone else, so this is why I started my own business. After about 10 years of coming home at the end of the day with my shoes caked with drywall dust, my hands rough from the day's hard labor, and the bulk of my efforts driving someone else's prosperity, I started a real estate development business. Real estate development is where I really grew as a businessman, and I'm so grateful for the opportunity. But real estate was also where I found an outlet for my passion for helping others. Real estate really boomed after the 2008 financial crisis, and we've been on a 10-year bull run since. Vancouver is one of the most amazing places to live due to its nature and scenery, and it's clear to me why people want to move here.

My passion lies in the intricacies of building, managing all the small details to perfection to create the most beautiful homes possible. What separates me from the competition is that I spend my entire day on-site during a build. I do not leave the management of projects in the hands of my tradesmen. They are skilled at their trades and I want to support them to focus on that. Being on-site allows me to check every little detail so that I provide a house that is of great value to its new owner. It's better I find an error than a potential buyer finding it. When a prospective buyer comes through one of our developments, they are usually in awe at the attention to detail. Of course, there will always be buyers out there who absolutely hate your product, or want you to do something a little differently... Only to then write an offer on your place. Oh, that is fun. I'd rather spend on quality, make less, and leave a homeowner happy. That is the ultimate goal. I've heard many buyers come in and complain about other developments, and developers cutting corners. This is not my style.

The 2008 financial crisis was another turning point. We had just finished building a home in a smaller city near Vancouver and the market crashed. The home listed beside us sold for cheaper than market value, as fear and uncertainty spread into the worldwide market. We too had to sell our home for much cheaper and all the hard work went for nothing.

An opportunity of a lifetime came. My son and I decided that we were going to do something different with our real estate business. We decided to move to another city, Burnaby, outside Vancouver, and start to develop multi-family homes, specifically, duplexes. As we entered this new market, we found sellers looking to unload duplex-zoned properties in a very slow market. Sellers were not receiving offers, prices were very negotiable, and we had cash to play with. As a result, we decided to start buying up properties, tearing down the old houses that were on them, and developing duplexes. We found that the city was much easier to work with, making it a much simpler process. We are now 10 years into working in Burnaby and our plan worked. A vision, execution, hard work, and never giving up meant that I was able to take my family and business to greater heights. Prices in Vancouver aren't as favorable anymore for developers, but other opportunities will surely arise in the future. We did miss out on some opportunities, but for the most part, we came out ahead.

You are probably thinking, this man must be educated. Truth be told, only to Grade 5. I learned everything in my field of work, and I am a very practical person. I often joke with my son, "You have the theory, but I have the practical knowledge!" My son is now an entrepreneur himself.

Over the years, I have also helped a lot of my employees start their own construction companies. I'm extremely proud of this feat and am happy to pass along my knowledge to help others succeed in life. Back in 1983, when I first arrived in Canada, my cousin took a chance on me and helped me get to where I am today, and I decided that I would pass this forward. Collectively, we have constructed many projects and helped build our community.

One approach that has worked wonders for me is saving money. You know, in business, there is a concept called the business cycle. I guess it's not so much a concept as a reality. Business cycles feature ups and downs, and some years your business does great, while you may struggle for a year or two here and there. I find that this is what makes and breaks not only people, but businesses. I've always saved money and kept more cash in reserve than your average person and business. During tough times, it's helped me get by and focus on growing and investing when things get better. This is where I've seen people fail beyond the point of recovery. My compassion has led me to bail out many business owners during recessions. It is important to not take on too much debt. Saving during tough times allows a business to invest in cheaper opportunities.

Another piece of advice I can give is be careful when you lend money to others. I experienced unscrupulous behavior by people who never paid me back. I also worked with family and friends and this ruined a few relationships. My advice would be to not work with family or friends, unless you have a written agreement, and are on the same page. My son and I are on the same page. It's worked out well so far. The vision, mission, and alignment is there between us.

If there is something I could have done, it would be to take more care of myself. I don't recommend working long hours, and I need to monitor my health more in older age. Nothing major that I have to deal with, but I do have to monitor my blood pressure, and it is hard on my knees when I run.

Now that I am in my mid 60s, I'm enjoying semi-retirement. I don't believe I will ever fully retire. I just love my craft that much. You simply cannot get me to leave the jobsite. I absolutely love building and hanging out on-site with my tradesman. Choosing to follow my passions through an entrepreneurial path has made my life joyous. I encourage you to find out what you really like to do. Once you know that, consider whether you need to be working for someone else or if you should be pursuing an entrepreneurial journey that will fulfill your every passion. Nowadays my son takes care of most of the day-to-day operations, and I am free to do this just for fun by taking on a couple of projects yearly, most managing from the site. I'm also more of an educator now. Building and construction will always be around and people need a place to make their own and raise a family.

I never gave up. I didn't want my family to go through what I had to. It wasn't an easy life. Working since age five, dropping out of school many times, and working a job that was very stressful on my body. But, once I stepped off the beaten path and became an entrepreneur, I accomplished my goal and provided my family with a good life. My son and daughter are doing well, and my wife and I have more downtime together to watch our favorite shows, garden, and enjoy some amazing food! It is the result of working hard along with loving what I do.

Let my entrepreneurial journey inspire you. I came from nothing... absolutely nothing. A vision to care for my family and give them a better life, a desire to give back to the world, and never giving up have led me to launch a business I love and finding a place of fulfillment that I wish you can all obtain for yourself.

Take time to learn what you love, then take a chance on going after that. Don't let what is easy stop you from aspiring for what you desire. There will always be opportunities, find yours. Look for an emerging market, seek where you can help, be inventive in tough times. Offer what other businesses are not and do it with pride and conviction. Show up each day and don't let others run your business. Be a part of all the processes and include yourself in all the steps. Yes, trust those that know their job, but most of all, trust yourself.

Ignite Action Steps

- Have a passion and work toward something — it'll drive you to succeed.

- Hard work — nothing can beat this. This is a trait that allows you to accomplish anything.

- Dedication to your vision and your craft is key.

- Persistence and NOT giving up. No matter what others are doing, do what you know works for you and your business.

Kulbir Muti – Canada
Real Estate Developer
www.mutiproperties.ca

IGNITE THE ENTREPRENEUR

ANNABEL WILSON

ANNABEL WILSON

"Entrepreneurs are modern magicians, weaving dreams into infinite possibilities where others only see dead ends."

My wish is to inspire you to unleash your inner entrepreneur and become the fully empowered architect of your own life. Being an entrepreneur isn't just about leaving a soulless job and risking everything to pursue your dream. It's having the courage and conviction to take continuous action that's aligned with your purpose; regardless of where the journey takes you. We can all be entrepreneurs, no matter what we do in life!

THE POWER OF PURPOSE

My life began when I threw myself down a mountain. I didn't scream as I felt ligaments and cartilage in both knees tear and pop, nor when the bones in my legs were forced against each other, far past any natural angles. There was only black silence. Tumbling over and over again down hard packed snow and ice, my head kept rolling over my feet; still firmly stuck in the racing skis I had been so proud of mastering only a few days ago. My hands desperately tried to claw into the snow to slow my fall to no avail. Five hundred and 25 vertical feet later, I eventually slid to a stop in a crumpled heap, where the piste tapered flat.

As I hobbled on and off crutches back and forth between the surgeon and team of rehabilitation specialists who painstakingly and painfully rebuilt my torn ligaments, cartilage, and muscles, I began the slow process of physical healing. A lifetime of repressed emotions and trauma bubbled to the surface during this process and pulled my marriage, family, and very being apart.

The summer after my skiing accident, I stood in the burnt, smoking remains of what had once felt like Camelot. How had we arrived at this wreckage? How did something so golden turn so black and rotten? When my 8-year-old daughter had to be pulled away from me, the first time family holidays were divided, we were both crying hysterically. I will never forget her little face, scrunched up in anguish, and small hands pressed against the car window as they drove away.

Engulfed in grief, guilt, and shame at the pain I had inadvertently caused, I resolved then that I would do whatever it took to understand and heal the root causes behind my unhealthy patterns of behavior to become the healthiest version of myself. I would go wherever the path led, for the distorted beliefs and generational trauma to stop with me. I would not pass this onto my innocent, vulnerable children, nor any other being.

As a child of traditional parents who valued academic achievement, financial stability, and unquestioning loyalty above all else, I had been raised to toe the line, repress emotions, intuition, and passion, and to follow rules at all costs. As I became an adult, I slowly changed from being a carefree, wild spirit to someone who believed emotions and vulnerability were signs of weakness. I thought I had to fight for every victory, that it was more important to be perfect and right above all else, and life was a zero-sum game where if one person wins, someone else loses.

Yet the tiniest spark of golden light that was left inside me longed for another way of living. Through all the muddy and constricting layers of programming, buried deeply was a soul that yearned desperately to be free. Free to live a life guided by an open heart, passion, intuition, compassion, and unconditional love and acceptance for all beings. Free to return to my happy-go-lucky essence who loved nothing more than creating elaborate stories and acting them out with my sister and a cast of our favorite stuffed animals, dressing up in outrageous outfits and clowning around to make others laugh. The child who had a ready smile for the world, who spent hours drawing, writing, and dreaming. The child who delighted in any chance to walk and run barefoot, who had an irrepressible curiosity to explore the world and its inhabitants, and who was always the instigator and willing partner in crime for mischief and fun.

Yet slowly that cheeky sprite vanished as I bowed to societal and family pressure. Even though I outwardly maintained my fiercely independent spirit, I unconsciously conformed to socially acceptable measures of success. I accumulated degree after degree, worked for well respected blue chip multi-nationals, married and had two children with a perfect-on-paper man, started lifestyle businesses, socialized only with glamorous, jet-setting friends, and acquired with insatiable hunger the highest material markers of success. With every year that passed, I became increasingly disconnected from my true self, and trapped more tightly in a rigid prison of perfection and 'must-haves.'

Chasing someone else's fleeting idea of joy, grasping at external validators of self-worth that never filled my internal void, I was a hungry ghost whose spirit was crushed into submission under the oppressive weight of a multitude of unfulfilled, abandoned dreams. I felt like I was slowly dying emotionally everyday. By the time my marriage ended, we were acrimoniously battling it out in court with our legal teams under hideous fluorescent lights; love had turned to toxicity.

The day after my tearful first parting from my children, I sat quietly under the glorious Californian sunshine by day and the cosmic light of the Milky Way through the inky darkness of night. I was surrounded by nature's blessings of natural hot springs and pods of humpback whales and dolphins basking in the adjoining coastal waters. I was supported by the accumulated energy of some of the greatest spiritual teachers and decades of wisdom seekers at Esalen in Big Sur. It was in this magical place that I was fortunate enough to attend a week-long workshop with renowned spiritual guide Russ Hudson.

Sitting on threadbare carpets in that classroom, the workshop was the first time since early childhood where I felt safe to lower my protective armor, remove the stifling mask of perfection, and allow my vulnerability to emerge. My heart cracked wide-open, and I connected fully to my true self and Source. It was a state of pure bliss far greater than any substance, person, or materially induced pleasure I had ever previously felt. I stopped seeing the superficial and started seeing people as their essence. Their ages, ethnicity, all external markers fell away and I could only see the divine golden light, beauty, and rawness of their inner child. When I look at pictures of my class at Esalen, our faces, which had started the course closed, wary, and withdrawn from the world, shed years of shielding and fear to emerge with softness, openness, and unconditional acceptance of self and others. The magical, childlike delight and light of awakening in our eyes after the workshop reveal a state of pure connection, undiluted joy, and wonder. It was like a magnificent fiery phoenix had given birth inside all of us.

Under Russ' guidance at Esalen, I understood for the first time that the vulnerability, emotions, passion, and intuition I had been trained to repress and eradicate were the very keys to unlocking my purpose, freedom, peace, and wholeness. I also understood that this issue was universal, that all of us have aspects of ourselves that we repress and block that prevent us from living a joyful, connected, and fulfilling life.

With my awakening, so awakened my purpose. Through my own pain and anguish, and witnessing that of so many others around me, I could no longer ignore my ever-increasing awareness of global disconnection and suffering. I understood with total clarity and conviction that I was here to serve as a channel to uplift and empower humanity. I committed fully to the idea of starting a business that would create a platform, services, and products that enable users to create substantial and sustainable positive change in their lives.

Taking continuous action to stay aligned with my purpose has been a hair-raising journey. In my first foray into private equity, as one of two female managing partners of our *capital-for-purpose* fund, sitting across the table from seasoned, high-powered, all male investment teams managing billions of dollars of assets, I was regularly attacked and overwhelmed by feelings of imposter syndrome before key meetings. My inner critic was in full flow, while my inner child, conditioned by years of scarcity programming, cowered in self-doubt and fear. My inner critic would shout, "Women hold less than two percent of director level positions in finance, how are you remotely qualified to be a managing partner? You've never been in finance much less private equity before, what do you know, why would anyone invest $100M in your fund?" Whereupon my inner child would spiral into a deep pool of despair.

Despite our success in securing an anchor investor, this undercurrent of unworthiness and fear would surge to the surface time and time again. It struck particularly badly the night I was in Nairobi, before I was due to fly out to Rwanda to teach a group of female entrepreneurs how to write a business plan. "Who are you to teach this? You're not qualified! You never even took the New Venture Development course at business school! Your start-up experience doesn't matter! You're a complete fake! These women will have traveled all day for nothing! They deserve better!" shrieked my inner critic, while I curled up in a ball, thousands of miles away from home and anyone I knew. That trip had many this-can-only-happen-in-Africa moments, including an unscheduled stop in another African nation embroiled in an active civil war. The workshop itself was filled with joy and learning, and I came home in extreme gratitude that I was able to give something meaningful to other entrepreneurs.

Through those moments of intense darkness, it took every measure of courage, willpower, and well-being tool I knew to consistently overcome external challenges and heal debilitating limiting beliefs and toxic thoughts. Having a purpose I unconditionally believed in was instrumental to my resilience. Regardless of the maze-like path my life and career took since my awakening, I never wavered from my purpose.

All of those experiences have led to my current *profit-for-purpose* well-being tech start-up, *Living Ashram*. I've ridden the roller coaster of exhilarating highs and rock-bottom lows. There were multiple times when the path became cloudy and unsure, and many dark nights of the soul, coupled with intensely liberating breakthroughs where decades old mental and emotional shackles fell away like harmless shadows.

Across the span of years and modalities, my global journey and recovery process had the additional benefits of increasing my compassion and empathy for others and bolstering my commitment to my purpose. It ultimately enabled me to create the methodology of a fully integrated, root level up, whole human approach to well-being and health. We teach this approach at Living Ashram to this day, through our well-being app, diagnostic assessment, workshops, and courses.

When I created Living Ashram, there was no question we would be anything other than a 360-degree ethical, profit-for-purpose business. We create products and services that empower people to make substantial and sustainable positive change in their lives, while simultaneously uplifting and empowering targets of abuse to live healthy, independent lives. Business can be a powerful source of positive change.

I worked tirelessly as a sole founder; painstakingly assembling an advisory board consisting of a neuroscientist, clinical psychiatrist, psychotherapist, nutritionist, elite sports therapist and trainer, breathwork specialist, and other leading well-being specialists, and the roster of talent across technology, design, and business development we needed to create our products and services. As we were a small, wholly self-funded start-up, I sought out values-aligned strategic partners and experts who weren't purely financially motivated, and was fortunate enough to earn their support. I will be eternally grateful for their gracious generosity.

I poured through extensive learnings from my own healing journey and conducted market research to understand customer pain points and what needs were not being served by existing solutions. I explored how to deliver them in accessible ways to time poor, highly stressed individuals and companies, and worked with the team to create our products and services. The work is never done, it is ever evolving, refining, and growing. We are always pivoting and adjusting to new information and lessons we learn.

Being an entrepreneur has been one of the most hellish and profoundly rewarding experiences in my life, especially while juggling life as a solo parent of two young children. I wouldn't trade the invaluable lessons I've learned for anything in the world. I'm now entering the next stage of growth as an entrepreneur; merging and integrating with a larger, values-aligned health and well-being company.

The last two and a half years brought so many powerful insights. I realized, with increasingly growing awareness, that I could spend the next 10 years building and scaling a company, or I could pivot to focus on the purpose and reason why I started my company in the first place. I also knew that it was crucial to be supported by an incredibly talented, mission-aligned team, and have access to an established and willing customer base who are hungry and ready for positive transformation.

"Traitor! Sellout! You gave up! You never give up! When did you become such a quitter?" my inner critic initially shouted. It took a lot of deep soul searching to reach my decision. Once I did, the choice felt completely aligned and right. I understood that I will always be an entrepreneur wherever I am. I understood that the heart, intention, and purpose of my start-up will continue to exist and flourish wherever I go. When I accepted this truth, the offers and opportunities from mission-aligned companies flowed in. My entrepreneurial journey is far from over, and I am so excited to explore where the next stage will take me.

Awakening to our purpose unleashes the entrepreneur within us all. It enables us to get unstuck, to find infinite possibilities where there initially appeared only to be dead ends. Whether we work in the corporate world, a blue-collar job, are a captain of industry, a stay-at-home parent, run a team of 10,000 or just 1, each of us has the ability to harness the courage of a lion and the power to bring our vision and purpose to life.

We can each take continuous action to bring the entrepreneurial traits of creation, creativity, innovation, collaboration, resilience, agility, willingness to learn, listen, evolve, pivot, and lead, and the relentless drive to get the job done, to whatever we do in life.

What's driving you in life? What's the purpose that gets you out of bed everyday? Even when your world feels like it's falling apart, and success appears to be a million miles away, you have what it takes to pick yourself up and keep trying. When we find and stop fighting our purpose, we discover fulfillment, peace, and total liberation. Dare to pursue your dream, to say yes to yourself, to say yes to your purpose!

IGNITE ACTION STEPS

1. **Find your why: purpose.** Dig deep to really understand what's important to you, set your intentions, and determine what clear actions you can take to realize them.

2. **Do your research.** Do extensive research to see if there's a market for your product or service. Understand the key factors affecting success in your market. (Who buys? When do they buy? What are their budget and priorities? Are there any macro factors that could challenge or support your business?) Understand who the key players are and how you are unique or different (is your USP really a USP, is it easily communicable and understood), and if you can build a scalable, profitable business given all these factors.

3. **Don't do this alone.** Ask for help and support when needed, and never be afraid to release team members, partnerships, and suppliers when they are clearly not serving the business. Hire the best, values-aligned team and advisors you can afford with skills that are complementary to yours, and empower them. Speak to as many people as possible who have walked this road before you (successfully and unsuccessfully as we can learn valuable lessons from both).

4. **Lose the ego.** Take regular step backs to reflect, constantly refine, and pivot whenever required with ZERO ego and complete humility. It's not about being right or wrong, it's about meeting the needs of your market in a viable way. Identify what's working, what's not, and where you need support. Ask yourself, is this the most efficient way of doing this? How can I do this smarter? Who can I collaborate and share with?

5. **Growth mindset:** there's no such thing as failure. Learn from everything. Pivot as often as needed.

6. **Always trust your intuition.** That's your gut, not your mind. It's rarely wrong. Never rush through the process. Remember to have fun and be playful!

Annabel Wilson – United Kingdom
Founder Director, Living Ashram
www.livingashram.com
⟳ @livingashram

IGNITE THE ENTREPRENEUR

MEGHAN
HUTHSTEINER

MEGHAN HUTHSTEINER

"If they don't give you a seat at the table, bring a stool!"

I hope you have the courage to take your own path while being open to different avenues to achieving everything you want to achieve. There is value in even the lowliest of jobs to get you shining bright in your uniqueness and move you to where you want to go. Take action and give faith a fighting chance, knowing you are where you're supposed to be. Being a consumer of knowledge has its advantages, but action is the proper fruit of knowledge. Giving up is never an option. Be fearless!

HATERS ARE JUST CONFUSED CHEERLEADERS

Sitting beneath the oval dining table, imagining the blue carpet was the ocean where I floated by was my favorite thing. From my hiding spot, I'd listen to my mom's closest friends share coffee, tea, and their lives. Their talking was a perfect distraction from my *laissez-faire* floating on my made-up body of water. While they enjoyed the buzz of their good conversation, I went undetected, inserting myself as the main character in their stories and playing out the scenarios in my head. When I would come out from underneath the table for clarification of something I had heard, I was inevitably told to go outside and play. I pleaded to stay because I knew if I learned how the adults did it wrong, when it came my turn to do the same thing, I could put my spin on correcting and skip their failures. I promised not to interrupt again, but I was always sent scurrying outside.

I was so crestfallen at being dismissed by my elders. I didn't get to learn from their conversations and missed them sowing a seed in me. Heading outside, I would aim for the swing my handy dad had made for my sister and I. That swing became my favorite and best thinking spot. That was the birthplace of my song, which I sang out of rhythm and out of tune, "Never Forget the Children." I made a promise to myself as I joylessly pumped my legs: I would be the voice for children… after I learned to use my own.

I was never an academic. I only lasted a few weeks in grade three when my teacher and my mom thought it was best to put me back into the second grade. My ability to read and comprehend what I was reading was wanting. By the time I had completed five out of 50 questions, the rest of my peers would already be lining up for recess. Ultimately, the teacher placed me in the center for Special Ed kids when taking tests, and I was angry. Angry at myself for not being able to think, and angrier at the teachers for accusing me of being stupid. Feeling hurt, I would refuse to answer when they would try to help. I felt patronized and broken, and they only reminded me of that. I was screaming inside, "I'm not dumb!" but I couldn't get out in words what my brain knew: I could do it! Later, my teachers would label me 'daydreamer' — a negative thing in their view. They took the one thing that I thought I had going for myself and dirtied it. Fortunately, I knew that to be successful, I would have to perfect that daydreaming and monetize it or else I truly would be left behind.

'Monkey' was my dad's nickname for me as you couldn't keep me in one spot. Sitting still was a challenge, though if you put a good storyteller in front of me, I could sit and listen for hours to the wisdom and knowledge they offered freely. Life awakened in me. I innately knew that conversations would give me the knowledge and understanding I needed while avoiding traditional schooling. And as these storytellers saw my interest, they would teach me how to do things! As a bonus, I was rewarded with a quarter or sometimes a dollar for projects I completed. I felt the first entrepreneurial fruits of my labor, and how good that feeling felt!

There were a few things I was certain of as a child: I had personality, athleticism, faith in Jesus, fearlessness, and my curiosity for life was insatiable. I also knew that "no" wasn't actually "no," it was just someone telling me I had to do it differently. While I wasn't going to be valedictorian, in spite of being held back, I simply made an oath to myself that I would never, NEVER, give up! There would always be someone better than me, but the way my character is built is unique and whatever life was going to give me, I was committed to this one habit from which I would never waver: *whatever I started, I had to finish*. Giving up was not an option. Once I finished, if I didn't enjoy it after completion, I then moved on. This taught me the difference between pursuing negative, meaningless goals and pursuing goals I wanted to put my full effort into.

When I came of age to join my first recreational sport, I excitedly asked mom to sign me up for cheerleading. No surprise, "Sorry, it's too expensive," she would reply in the middle of vacuuming or doing laundry. She was never a woman to go into debt for anything as that would be sinful. Luxury spending was saved for our family reunion trips and only sparingly dispersed among my five other siblings and I. I often felt like a spy watching my classmates enjoy the perks of being from a family that could afford the extra things. Yet, I was comforted knowing that money wasn't going to always be a struggle. Seeing classmates with new clothes and full lunch boxes buying all the books they wanted at the Scholastic Book Fair™ merely reminded me of the work I had ahead of me.

Cheerleading was where I put my foot down. Missing out in being in a group sport with my peers wasn't going to happen on my watch! "Mom, are you serious! You can't come up with the money to let me do cheerleading?"

My mother always did say that I had the most stubborn personality of all her kids, and my stubborn self saw her refusal to mean it was negotiation time with Mom. "If I can come up with the sign-up fee, will you let me join?" All I needed to do was secure a yes; in my mind, it was a sure thing I was going to make the money. When I got that yes, I started confidently knocking on our neighbors' doors, asking if they were willing to donate their pop bottles. After one week of collecting soda pop bottles, I was only five dollars shy of the sign-up fee. The admissions ladies were impressed that a 9-year-old had worked so hard. Knowing there would be more fees, they said to put the money toward my uniform. I loved the structure of cheerleading and the ability to bring every ounce of me to the sport. Getting the chance to showcase my flips and flexibility in front of an audience was more than satisfying. I had found a place where I could really shine.

A few short years later, my parents' split catapulted me years beyond my birth age. When my mom got a job working at McDonald's™, I became responsible for the house and my three younger sisters. I would come home from sixth grade and make sure the house was clean, my sisters were fed, and that we all had our homework done.

Money certainly became tighter and I would often come home to no electricity, heat, or food. Each setback required a huge amount of creativity — a hands-on life lesson that would serve me well in the years to come. I learned early that these things weren't going to break me. It made me more determined to solve the puzzle of life or beat the game. If I switched my perspective, I could use it to my advantage. I learned how to put on a happy face at school to cover up what was happening at home. This new lifestyle lasted even into my college years. I worked hard and became an NFL™ cheerleader, while still working an eight-to-five job. I would then have cheer practice from 5:15 to 10:30 PM and no one knew I came home to the utilities disconnected and no food. Mom lovingly would boil water in a Crock-Pot™ multiple times and fill the tub so I had a warm bath to clean up in, making sure I didn't get sick from taking cold showers.

By this time, I had earned a bachelor's in Theatre and Dance, a minor in Broadcasting, an associates in Business, and an esthetics license, all in the hope that I'd find my purpose and something would stick. Finding a job I would enjoy in a city I didn't care to be living in was awful and I was having no luck. I was working as a cashier at a nightclub in Las Vegas while studying for my cosmetology license when a new friend offered to introduce me to a guy who owned a body shop. I can only express my mental state as 'defeated.' How could it be possible that I couldn't find something better? I was not going to work for a dishonest, sleazy, greasy auto body shop! My friend assured me it's not an everyday run-of-the-mill auto shop and to just take a look. I dragged my feet to the interview and to my pleasant surprise, it was a high-end auto body shop. The owners, who were married, came across as honest and kind. I saw and felt the love and family-friendly feel they created. I didn't care much for the auto industry, but I loved the feeling they had built there, so I now had a second job and school!

After completing cosmetology school, I started working full-time for the auto shop as a receptionist. During the 2008 financial crash, I watched the owners working frantically to bring work in the door. I would envision me being the one out and about talking to potential business prospects, but when I asked them to let me try, the owners said, "No". They knew that this business would chew me up and spit me out. To them, I had no experience, being a little blonde girl who knew nothing about cars and sales. Well, the one thing I had going for me at this point in my life was that this sweet little face hides my competitive spirit quite well. I watch intently how people interact with one another and I've gotten to learn quite fast the talkers, bullshitters, and the genuine ones. I knew what the customers needed, and given the obvious stereotype that I presented them with, I needed to show people that our body shop was filled with hardworking and honest people who cared very much about every customer who walked through that door. We didn't just offer good body work, we were a triple win: great customer service, exceptional body work, and an unbeatable warranty no other shop would offer.

We were on the brink of closing the doors and declaring bankruptcy when once more I begged the owners to let me give it a shot. It was obvious to me that the most money came from the direct referrals from an owner's auto insurance company. I proposed they let me go to all the agencies and build a one-on-one relationship with them. They said there were too many, so I replied, "Let me start with our best insurance agency!"

I researched over a hundred locations in the area and broke them up, hitting 25-35 agencies a day, three to four times a week. I gave them more than just a pretty smile; I went to the best bakery in Vegas and said I would advertise the bakery by delivering their gourmet brownies to over a couple hundred businesses a month. The bakery saw the value in this and, each go-round, supplied me with 30 boxes of the richest, moistest, most decadent chocolate brownies I've ever had. The bakery loved me for increasing their sales and the insurance agencies loved the brownies. That softened their hearts and welcomed me to share what wonderful service the auto body shop would supply their customers if they would just give us a chance.

The success gave me the boldness to walk into Ferrari™, Lamborghini™, Rolls Royce™, Mercedes™, Lexus™, and BMW™, to mention a few. These dealers would also chose our shop for their overflow of repairs. While I didn't recognize it then, this was my inner entrepreneurial spirit in full swing! It was never my plan to stay in Vegas and with the shop in the black again, I needed to open that 'next door' in my life. At 27, I felt I should already be a veteran struggling actress. If I was going to make it happen in the next couple of years, I needed to move to Los Angeles.

I drove to LA and after a disastrous first attempt at finding a roommate, I walked from apartment to apartment in hope of finding the perfect place to call my own. How could it be that not one apartment complex was answering their doors or returning my calls? Where was I going to sleep that night? The next two days felt like the movie *Groundhog Day* and defeat was setting in. I didn't want to spend another night in my car so I figured I'd head back to Vegas, but before I did, I would complete one dream drive through Beverly Hills … the famous and desirable stamp of success if one could put a return address with the zip code 90210. I drove down the most stunning street that had a canopy of lush trees and stunning structures that only an elite few could call their home, and then I passed the humblest, most adorable brick building on the street. I stopped in the middle of the street just past the building, reversed the car, and called the number on the sign. The manager said, "Come on in, the door's open." The lower apartment was suitable and had great sun lighting up the kitchen. I could already picture the evening meals I would enjoy as I came home from a long day of casting calls. Excitement started to flood through my veins again but a sense of lack of safety slammed that door shut as I pictured intruders breaking through the window and putting me out more than I could afford to catch back up.

The upper studio wasn't as ideal with a brick building blocking any sun, and it was out of my price range. How in anyone's right mind would they pay $1,400 for a studio apartment that didn't even come with a fridge or stove? Tenacious as always, I offered $1,100. She said, "I'll call you back." Oh well, I gave it a try! Later the next day, my phone rang with an offer of $1,125. I knew instantly that life was going to get interesting! Unwilling to give up, I asked if it was possible to get appliances and a parking space. She said she'll call me back. She could get me a stove, but I would have to get a fridge and while the parking space normally goes with the bottom apartment, it hadn't been rented yet therefore I could have it. 90211 works just as well, so here I come!

Next obstacle: again, I needed a job. I leaned on my cosmetology training and attended the international hair show two hours away in Orange County, to network and find a job. I marveled at this one barber who easily made intricate short styles. It was impressive to me because I struggled with short cuts. The determination that had pushed me to be successful with the auto body shop led me to introduce myself in hopes he might give advice on how to study those cuts to be able to leverage myself better and perhaps open my own shop one day. To my surprise, he asked me to interview with him at his salon in Beverly Hills. The very next week, I found myself putting my skills and salesmanship to work just two miles away from my new apartment in the heart of Beverly Hills, and it wasn't long until I was helping run the business.

Mom instilled in me at an early age to *pray over it and believe, and it shall be given unto you.* All my experiences and choices have given me the wisdom to overthrow my forced adopted beliefs of being handicapped and that the learning system had damagingly unjustly deemed me useless to society. I am the one who truly knows my strengths and weaknesses and there was a method to my madness: my mind, body, and spirit knew what was good for me and I innately mapped out areas where I needed to learn and grow. If I couldn't get help in the way I was able to process it, I wouldn't waste anymore time. I went on to the next thing, building a repertoire of tools to fall back on if any other failed. In financial terms, I diversified my portfolio. I am so grateful for each and every lesson learned. Everything has come together as it should be.

As a child, I thought knowledge was a test of who knows more and that my learning disability would hold me back in life. Now, I know that knowledge is a tool that can be earned in many ways, and the question is who can apply it most wisely? When I talk about being an entrepreneur, I don't have all the academic tools that most teachers promise are essential for success. But I do have an entrepreneurial spirit that lives inside me and drives me to take action and to pursue every avenue toward achieving my success. I shine brightly just as I am, and that gives me the strength to go where I need to go.

Many people are beginning to recognize the interconnection of mind, body, and spirit, and the importance of treating the whole person rather than separate body parts; in return adopting a holistic approach for healing. Through the lessons of all my entrepreneurial ventures to this day, I am certain this interconnection brought me to my place and purpose. With thought and care, I enjoy helping others find healing and freedom in all three areas. I hope that my self-awareness, conviction, and practicing what I preach gives my clients firsthand testimony and encouragement that they, too, can have healing when they make clear, concise, conscious actions.

What drove me to be an entrepreneur wasn't the most widely used definition of the end goal: a lucrative business. It is someone who has the heart to create success within the mind, body, and spirit. To challenge the status quo and overcome obstacles when others just see a wall and give up. When you think of entrepreneurs one-dimensionally as people questing after financial success, you often miss the *essence* of entrepreneurship. When you put your heart into it, and truly love entrepreneurship, you'll find endless creativity for it and reinvent yourself as many times as needed until you reach the successful fulfillment of your deeper purpose.

Don't fear using your talents at even the lowliest of jobs. You just might find these jobs uncover a greater talent and drive within you; surprising even yourself with your fearlessness. To be a triumphant entrepreneur is not about reaching a particular financial number. It is in the faith that God created a strength with your weaknesses, uniqueness, creativeness, flexibility, and drive to persist and do something greater than yourself. Prosperity will find you. It could be a single-degree change in your mindset that makes all the difference. Don't ignore your moral compass; it lies in each and every one of us and embodies the uniqueness in us all! Listen to your instincts to draw a deeper understanding of *the what* and *the how* as to *why* you think and feel a certain way.

Giving up won't be an option. To be a part of the conversations at the table… don't be shy; pull up a stool if you have to!

IGNITE ACTION STEPS

- **Delay gratification to be ready for future prosperity.** The best investment is in yourself. Nobody spends money on new skills, knowledge, and new ways to develop themselves and says, "Man, that was a mistake!"
- **Place your focus on the desire to become not what was or what others think you should be, but *what can be*.** This could be the catalyst to many leaps and bounds that will get you closer to feeling peace with each breath being taken.
- **Become hyper aware of the choice of words you use to express your thoughts, feelings, and desires so that they coincide with and express accurately and with ease the depth of your heart.** This will allow your body to execute on autopilot, making it all look effortless.
- **Show up consistently, rain or shine.** You don't have to be perfect each and every time. The mere motion of following through regardless of the struggle will only make it easier to be present and bring more next time, because you already know you can overcome doubt!
- **Don't let doubt sneak in through what seems to be an innocent cop-out.** Saying, "I can do it," is your first step in establishing the program that you're going to 'play full-out' to help you reach your success.
- **Make a fear list and be very precise as to why those are your fears.** When finished, give your list the title '*Future Victories.*'
- **Don't lie.** Even the smallest lie robs you of the joys, experiences, and truths that guide you to your ultimate purpose on Earth.
- **Either you *believe* or you don't.** Pick a side and have the faith to see it through.

Meghan Huthsteiner – United States of America
Holistic Health Practitioner, doTERRA Essential Oil Advocate, Clinical Aesthetic Medical Assistant, three-time International Best-Selling Author, Director of International Business Development at Ignite Publishing
circadianhealth365@gmail.com
@circadianhealth
Meghan Huthsteiner
Meghan Huthsteiner

Allison Lewis

- 7 Steps to Social Media Success: http://bit.ly/absolutelysocial
- Forbes Article: https://www.forbes.com/sites/celinnedacosta/2021/03/28/gabrielle-bernsteinfear-killer-of-success/
- The Business of Blogging & Social Media Influencing Masterclass: https://www.absolutelyalli.com/product/one-on-one-coaching-with-absolutely-alli/

Ashley Baxter

- Ultimate Marketing Guide: https://learn.itsashleybaxter.com/ultimateguide

Brenda Neubauer

- *Secrets of a Millionaire Mind* by Harv T. Ekker
- *The Gifts of Imperfection* by Brene Brown
- *Feel the Fear and Do It Anyway* by Susan Jeffers

Clinton E. Day, MBA

- Check out the *Current in Entrepreneurship* blog at: https://clintone-day.com
- *The Startup Owner's Manual* by S. Blank and B. Dorf
- *Set Your Own Salary* by C. Day
- *Entrepreneurship Quick Study Guide* by C. Day
- *Mindset: The New Psychology of Success* by C. Dweck, Ph.D.
- *The Entrepreneurial Mindset* by K. Garman
- *The End of Jobs* by T. Pearson
- *The Lean Startup* by E. Ries
- Watch this Ted Talk by Bill Roche: https://youtu.be/Ihs4VFZWwn4
- "How to Find Your Passion and Live a More Fulfilling Life" by Leo Babauta: https://www.lifehack.org/articles/featured/how-to-find-your-passion.html
- "The Customer Development Process" by Steve Blank: https://youtu.be/xr2zFXblSRM
- Find mentors among instructors, incubators, or a Small Business

Development Center (SBDC). Most colleges have an entrepreneurship program, and many cities have an SBDC.

Dr. Marta Ockuly

- Download the *New Definition of Creativity Postcard.* Email me at: drmartaockuly@gmail.com for the link.
- Download the *Activate Joy Power* handout with sample joy mandalas at: https://www.joyofquotes.com/joy_power.html
- In 2009, I launched https://www.joyofquotes.com as my gift to the world. It is filled with positive, empowering quotes and coaching on hundreds of topics and invites visitors to 'get inspired and pass it on.'

Jonathan Domsky

- If you would like an invitation to join my monthly free Zoom Wednesday Workshops the third Wednesday of each month, sign up at: www.Untangled-Coaching.com
- If you would like to hear the full version of the Compassion Meditation described in the story, search on YouTube for 'Untangled Coaching Compassion Guided Meditation.'

Judy (J.) Winslow

- Get your own *Being Unforgettable Starter Kit* at: www.Unforgettable-Brands.com
- Landmark Education: https://www.landmarkworldwide.com
- *The Success Principles* by Jack Canfield
- *The Science of Getting Rich* by Wallace D. Wattles

Meg Huthsteiner

- *3 Feet From Gold: Turn Your Obstacles into Opportunities* by Greg S. Reid and Sharon Lechter
- *12 Rules for Life* by Jordan Peterson

Mikko Jarrah

- Check out Vishen Lakhiani's 6-step meditation on Youtube.

Steve Neale

- *Emotional Intelligence Coaching* by Stephen Neale, Lisa Spencer-Arnell, and Liz Wilson
- www.limbicperformancesystem.com

Theresa Alfaro Daytner
- *Man's Search for Meaning* by Viktor E. Frankl
- *Seeds of Greatness* by Denis Waitley

Parnell James Quinn
- *The E-Myth* by Michael E. Gerber, the classic entrepreneurial mistake — all work and no strategy, and no clear vision.

Yamilca Rodriguez
www.archetypemethod.com

PHOTOGRAPHY CREDITS

Allison Lewis - *Jama Finney Photography*
Charles Hai Nguen - *William Kidston*
Judy (J.) Winslow - *Jolanta Bremer*
Theresa Daytner - *Mary Kate McKenna*
Yamilca Rodriguez - *Jama Finney Photography*

Thank you

A tremendous thank you goes to all those on the IGNITE team who have been working tirelessly in the background teaching, editing, supporting, and encouraging the authors. They are some of the most genuine and heart-centered people I know. Their dedication to the vision of IGNITE, along with their integrity and the message they convey, is of the highest caliber possible. They each want you to find your IGNITE moment and flourish. They all believe in you, and that's what makes them so outstanding. Their dream is for your dreams to come true.

Production Team: JB Owen, Dania Zafar, and Peter Giesin

Editing Team: Alex Blake, Andrea Drajewicz, Chloe Holewinski, and Michiko Couchman

Project Leaders: Tanja Powell and Ravi Muti

A special thanks and gratitude to the project leaders for their support behind the scenes and for going 'above and beyond' to make this a wonderful experience. Their dedication made sure that everything ran smoothly and with elegance.

A deep appreciation goes to each and every author who made *Ignite The Entrepreneur* possible — with all your powerful and inspiring stories embracing this idea of being an entrepreneur within each and every one of us.

To all our readers, we thank you for reading and loving our stories; for opening your hearts and minds to the idea of Igniting your own lives. We welcome you to share your story and become a new author in one of our upcoming books. Your message and your Ignite moment may be exactly what someone needs to hear!

Join us on this magical Ignite journey!

WRITE YOUR STORY
IN AN IGN♦TE BOOK!!

THE ROAD TO SHARING YOUR MESSAGE AND BECOMING A BEST-SELLING AUTHOR BEGINS RIGHT HERE.

We make the BEST best-selling authors in just four months!

With over 700 amazing individuals to date writing their stories and sharing their Ignite moments, we are positively impacting the planet and raising the vibration of HUMANITY. Our stories inspire and empower others and we want to add your story to one of our upcoming books!

If you have a story of perseverance, determination, growth, awakening and change... and you've felt the power of your Ignite moment, we'd love to hear from you.

Go to our website, click How To Get Started and share a bit of your Ignite transformation.

We are always looking for motivating stories that will make a difference in someone's life. Our fun, enjoyable, four-month writing process is like no other — and the best thing about Ignite is the community of outstanding, like-minded individuals dedicated to helping others.

JOIN US TO IGNITE A BILLION LIVES WITH A BILLION WORDS.

Apply at: www.igniteyou.life/apply   Find out more at: www.igniteyou.life